KITCHEN & BATH
SUSTAINABLE DESIGN

KITCHEN & BATH SUSTAINABLE DESIGN

Conservation, Materials, Practices

Amanda Davis, NCIDQ

Robin Rigby Fisher, CMKBD, CAPS

WILEY

"It's kind of fun to do the impossible." —Walt Disney

Brandon Cole 1984–2014

Cover image: Left photo [kitchen]: Design by Robin Rigby Fisher, CMKBD, CAPS. Photograph © Dale Lang, NW Architectural Photography
Right photo [bathroom]: Design by Elina Katsioula-Beall, CKD. Photo by Suki Mendencevic
Cover design: Wiley

This book is printed on acid-free paper. ♾

National Kitchen & Bath Association
687 Willow Grove Street
Hackettstown, NJ 07840
Phone: 800-THE-NKBA (800-843-6522)
Fax: 908-852-1695
Website: NKBA.org

For general information about our other products and services, please contact our Customer Care Department within the United States at (800) 762-2974, outside the United States at (317) 572-3993 or fax (317) 572-4002.

Wiley publishes in a variety of print and electronic formats and by print-on-demand. Some material included with standard print versions of this book may not be included in e-books or in print-on-demand. If this book refers to media such as a CD or DVD that is not included in the version you purchased, you may download this material at http://booksupport.wiley.com. For more information about Wiley products, visit www.wiley.com.

Library of Congress Cataloging-in-Publication Data:

Davis, Amanda.
  Kitchen & bath sustainable design : conservation, materials, practices
Robin Rigby Fisher, CMKBD, CAPS.
    pages cm
  Includes bibliographical references and index.
  ISBN 978-1-118-62772-3 (cloth : alk. paper); 978-1-118-62772-3 (ebk.); 978-1-118-95765-3 (ebk.)
  1. Kitchens. 2. Bathrooms. 3. Sustainable design. I. Fisher, Robin Rigby. II. Title. III. Title: Kitchen and bath sustainable design.
  NK2117.K5F475 2014
  747.7'8–dc23
                                                                                    2014012666

978-1-118-62772-3

Printed in the United States of America
10 9 8 7 6 5 4 3 2 1

Sponsors

The National Kitchen & Bath Association recognizes, with gratitude, the following companies whose generous contributions supported the development of this new volume of the NKBA Professional Resource Library.

PLATINUM SPONSORS

WWW.COSENTINO-GROUP.NET

WWW.KOHLER.COM

GOLD SPONSOR

DELTA FAUCET COMPANY

About the National Kitchen & Bath Association

The National Kitchen & Bath Association (NKBA) is the only nonprofit trade association dedicated exclusively to the kitchen and bath industry and is the leading source of information and education for professionals in the field. Fifty years after its inception, the NKBA has a membership of more than 55,000 and is the proud owner of the Kitchen & Bath Industry Show (KBIS).

The NKBA's mission is to enhance member success and excellence, promote professionalism and ethical business practices, and provide leadership and direction for the kitchen and bath industry worldwide.

The NKBA has pioneered innovative industry research, developed effective business management tools, and set groundbreaking design standards for safe, functional, and comfortable kitchens and baths.

Recognized as the kitchen and bath industry's leader in learning and professional development, the NKBA offers professionals of all levels of experience essential reference materials, conferences, virtual learning opportunities, marketing assistance, design competitions, consumer referrals, internships, and opportunities to serve in leadership positions.

The NKBA's internationally recognized certification program provides professionals the opportunity to demonstrate knowledge and excellence as Associate Kitchen & Bath Designer (AKBD), Certified Kitchen Designer (CKD), Certified Bath Designer (CBD), and Certified Master Kitchen & Bath Designer (CMKBD).

For students entering the industry, the NKBA offers Accredited and Supported Programs, which provide NKBA-approved curriculum at more than 60 learning institutions throughout the United States and Canada.

For consumers, the NKBA showcases award-winning designs and provides information on remodeling, green design, safety, and more at NKBA.org. The NKBA Pro Search tool helps consumers locate kitchen and bath professionals in their area.

The NKBA offers membership in 11 different industry segments: dealers, designers, manufacturers and suppliers, multibranch retailers and home centers, decorative plumbing and hardware, manufacturer's representatives, builders and remodelers, installers, fabricators, cabinet shops, and distributors. For more information, visit NKBA.org.

Contents

Preface

PROFESSIONALS AS STUDENTS

When the National Kitchen and Bath Association (NKBA) approached us about coauthoring a new volume for the NKBA Professional Resource Library, we were honored and ecstatic. We had been recommended based on our educational work at Portland Community College and specifically for work that had been done thanks to a grant from the National Science Foundation. Our colleague Denise Roy, who teaches in the Architectural Design and Drafting Department, wrote and secured grant monies for the education of educators who teach in the building arts.

The goal of the grant is to provide opportunities for educators to add or increase concepts of sustainability in their curriculum through activities. Rather than conducting research, educators in architectural design and drafting, interior design, and building construction technology went to work for individuals and organizations as interns. The result has been nothing short of phenomenal. All three departments now have a strong focus on sustainable design, and the students can't get enough of it. This mission to educate professionals continues with LOCATE: Technical Education for High Performance summer sustainability conferences. For one week in June, educators in landscape, construction, architectural design, and interior design converge to learn through activities, tours, and from each other.

The goal for this book is similar: educate for applicability. Write about concepts but also discuss implementation and benefits. A sustainable approach to kitchen and bath design includes touching all parts of a project from construction materials to systems to material choices. A chapter on creating a green office and business approach is included in the book. Sustainable design is about cutting waste and reducing carbon emissions, but it is also about creating more comfortable homes that have reduced operating costs.

Writing this book has been journey. It has been rewarding to stretch ourselves professionally and to put the knowledge that we share each day with our students into a textbook format. We were given the opportunity to write a textbook that we would want our students to use. It is many an educators' dream.

We have enjoyed both attending and presenting at the LOCATE Summer Sustainability Institutes. We have both presented our teaching of green design at the KBIS Educators' Forums over the years. We both feel that we are always, simultaneously learning, practicing, and teaching.

We hope you enjoy this book.

When the last river has been polluted, the last tree cut down, the last fish has been caught, will we realize we cannot eat the money?

—*Native Cree saying*

Amanda writes:

I'd like to acknowledge the support and guidance of Johanna Baars, Publications Specialist at the NKBA. I also want to thank Green Hammer Design Build and C. R. Herro at Meritage Homes. Both companies serve as inspiration for green building. I'd like to thank my family for supporting me through this process.

Robin writes:

Writing a book on sustainable design was a longtime goal of mine and has been challenging and exciting. It could not have been done without the help of many people. I'd like to thank Johanna Baars at the NKBA for her patience and prodding; my teaching partner, Dorothy Payton, for her knowledge and insights; my assistant, Brandon Cole, for his project management and Photoshop skills; Bernhard Masterson for his energy, knowledge, and love of mud; Richard and Anna DeWolf for their insights; Nancy Foster for her vast knowledge of toilets; Rhonda Knoche for her support; Tracey Stephens; Green Depot (Portland, OR); Joel Fraley CKD; Janel Campbell, CKD,CBD; Corey Klassen, CKD, CBD; and Hannah Mizar, illustrator extraordinaire! Last, I want to thank my family for their patience and support during this journey.

Acknowledgments

The NKBA gratefully acknowledges the following peer reviewers for the valuable feedback they provided in their review this book.

Darrill Andries, CKD

Janel Campbell, CKD, CBD

Mark Goldman, AKBD

Sigrid McCandless, CMKBD

Karen Richmond, CMKBD

Teresa Slye, NCIDQ, LEED

Understanding the Need for Sustainable Design

On my first Boy Scout trip, in the mid-1950s, I learned the basic environmental principle that we should leave the campsite as we found it. We were told that the next group of hikers deserved no less and that in fact we should clean the site up if those before us had been careless. I did not as a child understand that the campsite would be global or that the next hikers would include unborn generations.

—John Sitter

Learning Objective 1: Discuss the concept of designing for benefit rather than austerity.

Learning Objective 2: Apply sustainable design concepts to kitchen and bath projects.

Learning Objective 3: Identify the basic needs for applying sustainable practices.

Our world is in dire straits; human impact on the earth is affecting the future of the planet (see Figure 1.1). Consider these facts:

1. The average temperature of the earth has risen by more than 1.4° F over the last century.[1]
2. Oceans are warming and becoming more acidic, ice caps are melting, and sea levels are rising.[2] From 1880 to 2011, the average sea level rise was 0.07 inches per year, but from 1993 to 2011, the sea level rise was between 0.11 and 0.13 inches per year.[3]
3. Emissions of greenhouse gases (carbon dioxide [CO_2], methane, nitrous oxide, and fluorinated gases) have increased due to human activities such as:

   - The burning of fossil fuels.
   - Anaerobic decay of organic waste in landfills due to industry processes and commercial and household chemicals (see Figure 1.2)

Global warming or climate change occurs when the greenhouse gases redirect too much radiation toward the earth. Radiant energy, in the form of heat, comes from the sun. In a most amazing natural cycle, unnecessary (and potentially harmful) radiant energy is sent out of the earth's atmosphere into space. With the exponential increase in the amount of greenhouse gases in the earth's atmosphere over the last 150 years, this process is being interrupted. The gases are trapping the energy as heat (see Figure 1.3).

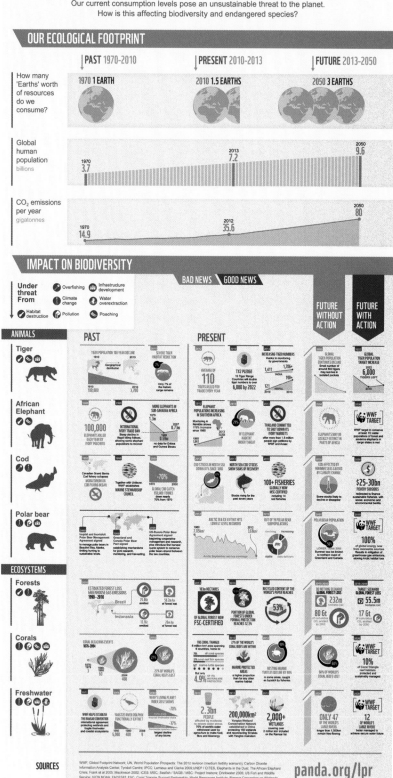

FIGURE 1.1 World Wildlife Fund Living Planet Report © 2014

World Wildlife Fund, www.panda.org

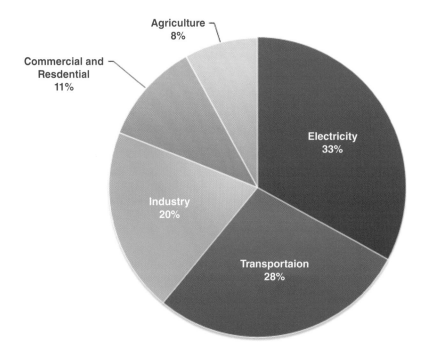

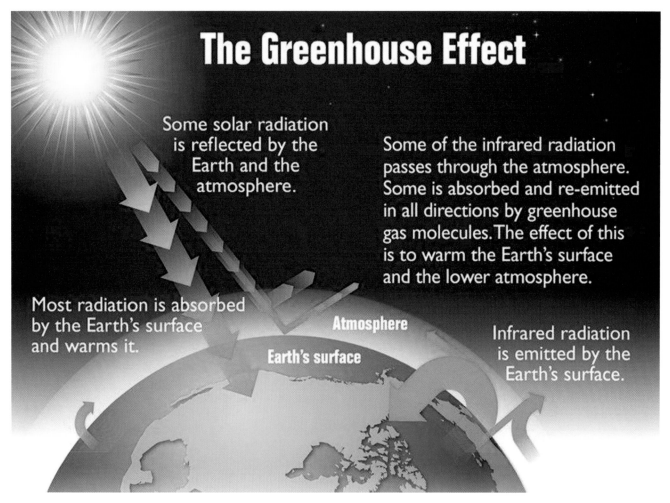

FIGURE 1.2 Total US Greenhouse Gas Emissions by Economic Sector in 2011
www.epa.gov/climatechange/ghgemissions/usinventoryreport.html

FIGURE 1.3 The Greenhouse Effect
www.epa.gov/climatestudents/basics/today/greenhouse-effect.html

The term "greenhouse gas" is a blanket term for compounds that exacerbate this situation. These gases are by-products of industry. Waste emissions from the burning of fossil fuels are the leading source of these gases, but they are not completely responsible. Other sources of greenhouse gas include the manufacture of hydrofluorocarbons (refrigerants), emissions from landfills, emissions from livestock, and off-gassing of chemicals.

The construction industry has only added to our current problem. Research shows that the construction industry impacts our global problem with residential buildings accounting for:

- 38.9 percent of total US energy consumption
- 38.9 percent of total US CO_2 emissions
- 13 percent of total US water consumption[4]

TRIPLE-BOTTOM-LINE APPROACH

We can answer the question "Why sustainable design?" with inspiration from the triple-bottom-line (TBL) concept (see Figure 1.4). This book is written in what appears to be the end stages of the worst economic crisis (recession) since the twentieth century's Great Depression. It is an exciting time. With the kitchen and bath remodeling sector experiencing a return to business growth, there is an opportunity to make this return to prosperity a green one. How do things look different now from four years ago? How will they look four years from today? The conversation about sustainable building, design, and remodeling practices is an evolving one.

At the end of the twentieth century, many companies were profiting at the expense of many workers and the natural environment. *People, planet, profit* is a business concept also known as the triple bottom line (TBL).

The term "TBL" first was used in 1994 by economist John Elkington. At the time, it was a revolutionary approach to *business as usual*. The TBL asks that businesses create three sectors with measureable outcomes to determine the success of the company. It states that it is not enough simply to look at the final success (profit) of the company as the one bottom line; one must also look at how the business affects the environment (planet) and how the business supports its community (people).

In this book, we examine ways to create sustainable kitchens and baths by understanding the need to become a steward of the environment. Creating a sustainable design practice means planning for benefit: saving your client money, paying homage to the environment, and designing healthy interiors that will enhance your clients' lives.

Event-Oriented Thinking, Systems Thinking, and the Butterfly Effect

There are a thousand hacking at the branches of evil to one who is striking at the root.

—Henry David Thoreau, *Walden*

The environment is a big issue—one country, one government, one community, one business, or one person cannot resolve all the issues, but if each one of us does our part, then change will occur. It will take a new way of thinking—a paradigm shift.

To make a paradigm shift, we must look at our attitudes, behaviors, and beliefs. This is not a linear process; it is a loop. Let's look at this in a different way:

Midterms are fast approaching, and you are getting a cold. Your homework is piling up, but there is a party this weekend, so you take cold medicine and head out. You spend the next three nights pulling all-nighters, take your midterms, and spend the next few days in bed very sick (see Figure 1.5).

This is event-oriented thinking. This process looks at the world in a linear fashion: A happens, then B, then C. Event-oriented thinking assumes that each event has a cause and that

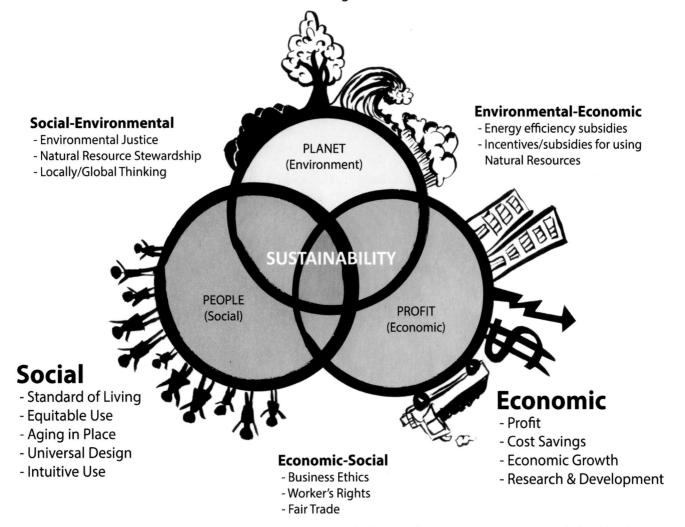

Environmental
- Recycle
- Indoor Air Quality (IAC)
- Water Conservation
- Natural Resource Use
- Waste Managment

Social-Environmental
- Environmental Justice
- Natural Resource Stewardship
- Locally/Global Thinking

Environmental-Economic
- Energy efficiency subsidies
- Incentives/subsidies for using
  Natural Resources

PLANET
(Environment)

SUSTAINABILITY

PEOPLE
(Social)

PROFIT
(Economic)

Social
- Standard of Living
- Equitable Use
- Aging in Place
- Universal Design
- Intuitive Use

Economic
- Profit
- Cost Savings
- Economic Growth
- Research & Development

Economic-Social
- Business Ethics
- Worker's Rights
- Fair Trade

FIGURE 1.4 The main parts of the triple bottom line are people, planet, and profit, but as this figure shows, there are subsets that further define the TBL. *NKBA*

changing the cause will correspondingly change the event. The rest of the system that produced the event need not be considered.

We can't solve problems by using the same kind of thinking we used when we created them.

—*Albert Einstein*

Now let's look at your cold in a new way.

Midterms are fast approaching, and you are getting a cold. After a few days of being miserable, you start thinking, "I seem to get a cold close to midterms often. Why is that?" You are

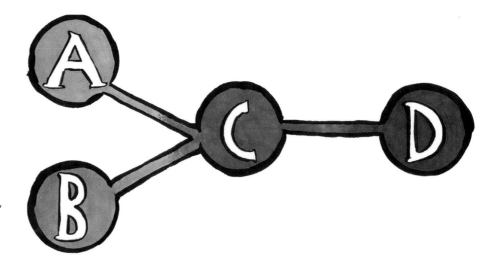

FIGURE 1.5 Event-oriented thinking says that everything can be explained by a chain of events: If A or B happens, then C will most likely occur—cause and effect.

NKBA

recognizing a pattern. So, what happens at midterms each time? Well, the amount of work is beginning to pile up, but you are still going out with your friends on Friday and Saturday, not eating well, and your exercise regime has gone by the wayside. Now you are seeing what is influencing the pattern. To make a change, you need to make a shift. What can you do to break the pattern? Perhaps you can only go out on Saturday if all your studying is done, plan your meals in advance, get a workout partner, and focus on your health.

You are on your way to break the cycle. This is systems thinking (see Figure 1.6).

System thinking is the process of looking at things as interdependent systems where one part influences another. Event-oriented thinking is linear cause and effect, but systems thinking is *circular* (a causal loop). Systems thinking is not reacting to a problem; rather, it encourages a more holistic approach to solutions.

The metaphor of the *butterfly effect* illustrates system thinking. A butterfly flaps its wings, and the small current has the ability to effect change as large as the path of a storm. The concept involves considering that small, almost imperceptible events can alter larger ones. It involves understanding that there is an interdependency of all events on the planet and that all circumstances are sensitive to one another. Much like the butterfly effect, systems thinking reasons that small events can be separated by time and distance and still affect one another.

This is the appropriate way to look at sustainability. Just changing your lamps to compact fluorescent bulbs (CFLs) or light-emitting diodes (LEDs) can be part of the solution; but as a designer, you have the opportunity to effect larger change. You can be part of the solution.

That's what this book is about—arming you with the knowledge and tools to effect change.

Imperceptible Change?

In a Pew Research poll conducted to determine Americans' views on global warming, it was found that while 67 percent of the respondents believe there is "solid evidence" for climate change, only 30 percent consider it an issue that the president and congress should address.

Why?

It has been suggested that our inability to deal with this issue is due to the way our brain functions. Daniel Gilbert, a professor of psychology at Harvard, suggests that because "global warming doesn't take human form," it is difficult for us to see it as an enemy. He further suggests that because global warming has occurred slowly, our minds have had time to normalize it.

In the nineteenth century, experiments were made using a frog and some water on the stove. If the frog was placed in uncomfortably warm water, it jumped out of the pan. However, if

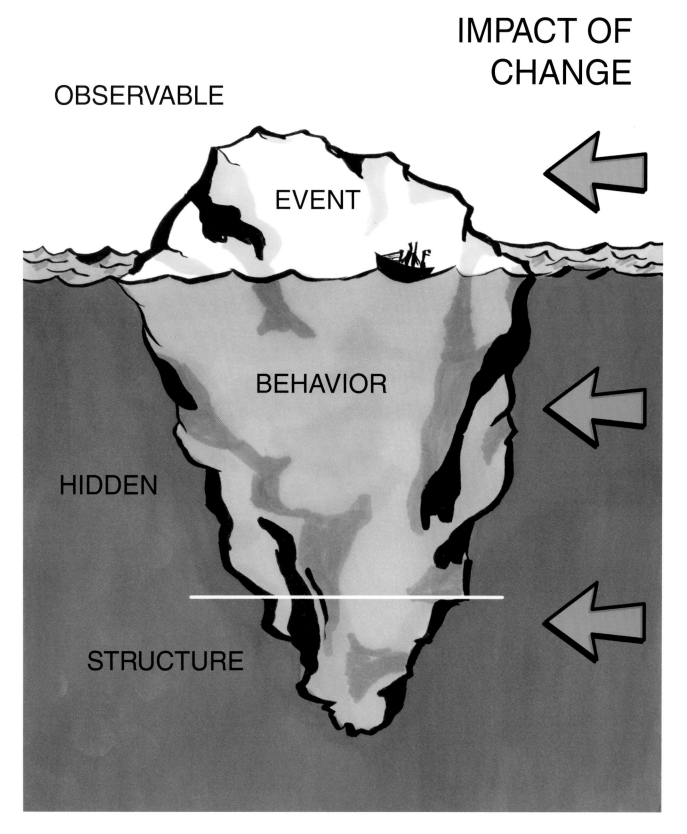

FIGURE 1.6 Systems thinking: To solve a problem, you need to assess what is happening at the base.
NKBA

the frog was placed in a pan of cool water and the water was heated very slowly, it was believed that the frog would not notice the change in the water temperature until it was, sadly, too late.

This story has become a cultural metaphor for the inability of user groups to "see" or understand gradual change. People don't feel an urge to change their behavior until it is too late.

Even if you have not been incorporating any sustainable design practices in your business, you don't have to embrace all of the concepts we will be presenting at once. Instead, find a concept that resonates with you (e.g., indoor air quality, buying local, energy efficiency, recycled content, water efficiency), and start there.

The Myth of Apathy

Dr. Renee Lertzman is a consumer researcher who uses her background in psychology and communication to advise on green issues from a behavioral perspective. "The Myth of Apathy" is reprinted from Dr. Lertzman's Web site (http://reneelertzman.com/the-myth-of-apathy/) with her permission.

We reprint Dr. Lertzman's words here as a means of discussing how the subject of sustainable living can be conflictual. When faced with so many habits to change and so many activities to modify, it is easy to become overwhelmed. More specifically, many individuals choose to do little or nothing because they believe in the all-or-nothing approach. The perspective this book is offering is to do *something*. In terms of kitchen and bath design, it may be specifying an alternative to an old water heater or using a material that is sourced locally. The goal is a paradigm shift first; behavior changes will follow.

The Myth of Apathy
By Dr. Renee Lertzman
The Conundrum

At this moment in time, there is no shortage of good ideas about how to make the world cleaner and greener.

We live in a time where there is an abundance of juicy good ideas, more awareness than ever about our ecological contexts. Information about biodiversity, creatures in the deep seas and remote corners of this planet, the fragility of our home. Information about the threats.

More information, period.

And yet, the riddle at the center of just about any sustainability effort is why more people are not taking action. People meaning "the public," elected officials, and all in between. Even more specific: people taking the actions that we know would have a good chance of mitigating the most severe threats facing our horizon, from climate change to overfishing to toxic contamination of air, water, and dirt. Actions that we know would do us all—plants, critters, humans—a lot of good.

For decades, the environmental movement has been situated as the naysayer, poised to pounce on anyone who would dare buy a battery farm chicken, buy cheap sweatshop clothes made with pesticide-saturated cotton, or take a short-haul flight. Worse still, those who dare to buy and drive large gleaming SUVs or buy extravagant McMansions. Flagrant consumption of finite resources and the ignorance of where our energy comes from is a veritable sin.

However, the image of the moralizing environmentalist appears to be changing. Marketing agencies and corporations are cottoning on to the fact that if we make green sexy, hot, and profitable, more people will "buy" into it (pun intended). Green sells. Yet in the move to commodify green as quickly as possible, something fundamental is overlooked, glossed over. It is as if we can somehow suture together the rifts inherent in our consumptive-based way of life, and all that led us to this point (yes, all of it, from the first coal mines carved out of Wales to the present moment), and smooth it all into one lovely, profitable, ideologically consistent, and seamless green dream.

While this vision is intensely appealing—as we generally want to avoid pain and struggle, and are drawn to comfort, ease, and pleasure like bees to honey—it is psychologically retrograde, emotionally confusing, and ideologically incoherent. Most of us are embedded in the very practices, desires, goods, textures, and sensations that contribute to our ecological ills.

It's the paradox at the center of an ecological consciousness, and one that runs to the heart of why people may do nothing to help save or protect our environment, despite our best wishes, hopes, desires, and dreams to do so.

Being green is attractive, desirable, and profitable. However, it is also potentially frightening and threatens what many of us hold to be central to who we are—how we construct meaning in our lives. Until we incorporate the whole picture into our vision of being sustainable, we are going to be fighting a battle. Flowing against a current. When, in fact, we can be flowing with the current—if we can acknowledge paradoxes, contradictions, and dilemmas these topics can bring up.

"Apathetic" is a description of a lack, a deficit, when something vital appears to be missing. We think of apathy as the central driver for public inaction in the face of serious issues, whether it is political injustice, ecological devastation, or plain wrongness in the world. Apathy is perceived commonly as an "enemy" of reform, political action, and up-take. It can also be seen as shorthand for "selfish," "ignorant" or "greedy"—attributes often ascribed to "the public" for not "doing enough" to protect our collective resources, fellow creatures, and planet.

In order to believe in apathy, and the studies that seem to suggest people don't really give a toss, we find some surprising assumptions about human psychology. Assumptions that require being challenged, including:

> If someone believes, feels, or values something, there is a necessary correlative, or "the face value myth."

> That we are aware of all of our thoughts, feelings, desires, fears, and conflicts at any given time and can adequately provide them on request. This is the "transparency myth."

(continued)

Humans have the capacity to quite literally turn off their feelings, sensations or responses to the world around them, or "the robot myth."

The "public" is largely passive, and what is required are ever more ingenious communication strategies to mobilize, inspire, cajole, threaten, frighten, or force specific actions. This can also be called "the sheep myth."

What all of these assumptions have in common is a particular conception of human psychology: that we are largely rational beings who are self-determined, transparent to ourselves and to others, and with the right levers and motivators, we can be enticed to take certain actions and avoid others. (And these levers and motivators can be in the form of a compelling campaign, reward scheme, or social acceptance.) That we are ultimately self-interested and focused on self-preservation more than anything else. It's a stunning image of human nature once you scratch the surface, and not a pretty one.

The alternative is not recourse to a Pollyanna fantasy that humans will always do what is right and just, for we know this not to be the case. A more compelling and arguably accurate conception of human nature may be one that assumes and presumes contradiction, ambivalence, paradox, and dilemmas. It takes on board that with change, there is often loss. And with loss, there is often mourning and melancholia. And with grief and loss, there can be space for creative engagement, participation, care and concern.

Dr. Renee Lertzman is an applied researcher, speaker, instructor, and strategic communications specialist who focuses on the deeper psychological dimensions of sustainability—charged issues requiring sensitive communications. Her work has been featured in the New York Times, *the* Guardian, *the* Ecologist, Time, Orion Magazine, *the* Sun *magazine,* Climate Access, *and on numerous other web sites and blogs. Used with permission.*

A Global Problem that Will Be Solved at the Local Level

Over 20 years ago, environmentalists recognized the need to address environmental destruction and the apparent climate change that was taking place. Because much of the destruction of the environment has to do with economic pressures, the International Council for Local Environmental Initiatives (now called ICLEI, Local Governments for Sustainability) was formed in 1990. The ICLEI believes that making positive changes to the environment will have more success if managed at a local level. The ICLEI has now grown to 14 offices in 84 countries. It is made up of 12 megacities, 100 supercities and urban regions, 450 large cities, and 450 small and medium-size cities and towns dedicated to sustainable development. The program set by the ICLEI varies by region to ensure that each local government is *served according to its local needs.*

Key points

- ICLEI is a nonprofit organization that helps local governments meet their self-defined sustainability, climate, and energy goals.

- ICLEI's tools, resources, and services help local governments save money, energy, and natural resources; create more livable communities; and address issues such as climate change.
- All ICLEI programs are voluntary, and often [they are] designed in collaboration with local governments.
- ICLEI does not seek to impose or mandate upon local governments any policies or initiatives, such as United Nations Agenda 21, the global environmental plan developed in 1992 at the UN Conference on Environment and Development—nor does ICLEI have any to do so.
- ICLEI is an independent nonprofit, and not part of the United Nations.[5]

The ICLEI works on initiatives to help small, local governments initiate programs that are designed to alter the path of climate change. One of the biggest subjects is local reduction of carbon. You may have noticed traffic lights being converted to LED, *light-emitting diode*, sources and city buses being fueled by bio-diesel or ethanol fuel. Many cities in the United States and around the world have signed up with programs to reduce their carbon production.

DESIGNING FOR BENEFIT

When the concept of sustainable design first became popular in the early 1990s, it was a "should"-based practice. Practitioners and their clients were "doing the right thing." Consumers were being asked to "go without" decent water pressure in their showers, utilize funky-flushing toilets, and select from limited materials. Sustainable design was, quite frankly, a drag. After all, kitchen and bath remodels are supposed to be enjoyable projects. They add to life, they enrich the activities we do that are closest to our human experience: food preparation and nourishment, bathing, toileting, and self-care. Remodeling these areas of the home is costly. For many consumers, it involves using equity that they are relying on to move forward in life.

It was cavalier of the early sustainable design paradigm to ask consumers to do without while, in many cases, spending more. Times have changed, and today the perspective with which to view sustainable design practice is designing for benefit. A kitchen or bath remodel created using a foundation of best practices can ensure that your client will have projects that will:

- Save money on energy bills.
- Save money on water bills.
- Save money on long-lasting materials.
- Offset the cost of the project with incentives.
- Be free of chemicals that can cause health problems.
- Benefit the local building community and strengthen community.

The view now is win-win for both the client and the environment.

Concepts to Consider

Kitchen and bath remodeling impacts the environment. Designers should consider the following truths and think about learning how to diminish or improve them:

Landfills are filled with construction and demotion waste.

Carbon emissions from the transport of goods and services related to remodeling is adding to climate change.

Carbon emissions from the manufacturing of materials have added to climate change and environmental problems.

Extraction of raw elements from nature causes damage to the earth's surface.

Clean water is becoming scarcer.

Until a few years ago, low-flow toilets (those using less than 1.6 gallons per flush) offered a feel-good incentive to clients who installed them. Unfortunately, they also offered reduced effectiveness. Which raises the question: what is the benefit of having a low-flow toilet if it must be flushed twice? Likewise, early versions of low-flow showerheads offered lower-quality showers. Such fixtures were not widely adopted. Even in areas with dwindling access to clean water, such as Phoenix, Arizona, or San Francisco, California, the discomfort of these water-saving devices made their use less than agreeable. Today, with new designs and technology, that has changed. Designers will have to communicate how these products have changed and improved with clients who may need convincing. One example is Kohler's low-flow toilet with updated technology that successfully flushes using 1.28 gallons of water.

The Problem with Carbon

In nature, the carbon cycle remains balanced. Decay from plant life releases carbon into soil while animals that eat the plant life release it in the form of CO_2. In their photosynthesis process to create food for their survival, living plants use CO_2 and release oxygen.

This would be the natural state of the carbon cycle were it not for human industry. Our use of fossil fuels for transportation, electricity, water purification, and agriculture means that too much carbon is being released into the environment.

An overabundance of CO_2 in the atmosphere is the leading cause of what scientists call the *greenhouse effect*. CO_2 reduces the atmosphere's ability to shield the earth's surface from radiation from the sun. This leads to rising temperatures and climate change that is unnatural for the planet.

When considering the impact of building and remodeling in relation to this unbalanced carbon cycle, we must look at what is used: new products (industry), trade of those products (transportation), and new appliances and systems (energy use).

The Problem with Landfill Waste

Currently, most residential construction waste is disposed of in a municipal solid waste landfill (MSWLF). In some states, these landfills are well maintained. In other areas, they are at capacity. Along with construction debris, these landfills also hold household waste, nonhazardous sludge, and industrial solid waste. Although they are regulated by the Environmental Protection Agency (EPA), these MSWLF, by their very nature, release immense amounts of methane gas into the atmosphere. The EPA is instituting measures to harness this gas. But such a mix of waste presents a serious problem. Many municipalities, such as Seattle, Washington, and Portland, Oregon, have taken measures to implement composting programs that will help to alleviate the amount of food waste in an MSWLF. The processing of that food waste to usable fertilizer helps to harness the embodied energy that remains in the waste.

The concept of embodied energy is important to understand. Every resource or manufactured object has embodied energy associated with it. Embodied energy is the sum of all the energy needed to source, create, and transport a good to where it is to be consumed. More often than not, there is embodied energy remaining after the good is removed or no longer in use. In order to prevent wasting that embodied energy, efforts should be made to recyle or reuse it.

Likewise, it is necessary to lessen the amount of construction and demolition (C&D) waste that makes its way to these landfills. According to the Deconstruction Institute, only 20 to 30 percent of C&D debris is recycled. C&D waste accounts for 30 percent of all solid waste in the United States (excluding road and transportation construction waste).

There are programs and incentives to help you reduce the impact of your clients' projects when it comes to C&D waste. This is discussed in detail in Chapter 3, "Sustainable Construction."

Hazardous Materials

Until congress passed the clean air act of 1970, not many people thought about the presence of hazardous materials inside their homes. Asbestos was banned as an ingredient in many building materials such as floor paper and insulation. The use of lead-based paint was banned in 1978. When remodeling in homes built before theses safety measures, the designer must take precautions.

Kitchen and bath designers have it tough. As rewarding as it is to create, design, and execute on-trend, high-quality spaces, sometimes these designers have to walk a fine line. The profession is, by its nature, one that creates, uses energy, and builds anew. The kitchen and bath industry has played a significant role in national and local economies, and it is important that it continue to do so.

It is an outdated mind-set that equates sustainable building practices with harming the economy. What is required is a willingness to change outmoded habits and to embrace new ways of doing things. In many municipalities, this approach is compulsory due to the implementation of new energy codes.

Designing for All Abilities

When considering how important the triple bottom line is to creating a balanced approach to sustainability, industry, and people, you also have to consider universal design. The *Rio Charter on Universal Design*, drafted in 2004, calls for inclusive design as a characteristic of environmentally conscious design.

The most numerous generation of the twentieth century in the United States and Canada, the Baby Boomer generation, began turning 55 in 2001. The United States census shows 76 million births between 1945 and 1962. The generation is sometimes characterized by a reimagining of tradition and a rejection of the social structure.

It makes sense, then, that independence is so important to members of this generation. The ability to stay in one's home has sparked a significant movement in interior design and remodeling: aging in place. To age in place, people need a supportive environment. Designers must learn how to create environments for clients who are older or have abilities that are not accommodated by the standard way of doing things. A custom kitchen and/or bath design is about a careful response to the needs and lifestyles of the users. A kitchen and bath designer understands the interior environment needs to accommodate users, not the other way around. This paradigm is the backbone of universal design. Universal design is composed of seven principles crafted to guide designers in creating supportive environments. We will focus on universal design and aging in place design because both perspectives are part of the sustainability movement: equality in use, planning for a longer span of time in the home, and being responsible for the safety of clients.

Rio Charter

1. The purpose of **Universal Design** is to serve needs and make possible social participation and access to goods and services by the widest possible range of users, contributing to both the inclusion of persons who have been prevented from interacting in society and to their development. Examples of such groups include: poor persons, persons marginalized for reasons of culture, race, or ethnicity, persons with different types of disabilities, very obese persons and pregnant women, very tall or very short persons, including children, and all those who, for different reasons, have been excluded from social participation.
2. We conceive of **Universal Design** as generating accessible environments, services, programs, and technologies that are equitably,

(continued)

safely, and autonomously usable by all individuals—to the widest extent possible—without having to be specifically adapted or readapted, based on the seven underlying principles, as follows:

- Equitable Use (for persons with diverse abilities);
- Flexibility in Use (by persons with a wide range of preferences and abilities);
- Simple and Intuitive (easy to understand)
- Perceptible Information (communicates necessary information effectively)
- Tolerance for Error (minimizes hazards of unintended actions);
- Low Physical Effort; and
- Size and Space for Approach and Use.

3. We acknowledge the value of the emerging concept of **Inclusive Development**, which attempts to expand the vision of development, recognizes diversity as a fundamental aspect in the process of socioeconomic and human development, claims a contribution by each human being to the development process, and rather than implementing isolated policies and actions, promotes an integrated strategy benefiting persons and society as a whole. Inclusive Development is an effective tool for overcoming the world's prevailing social exclusion and thus for achieving progress in eradicating poverty.

4. We conceive of **Sustainable Human Development** as a productive way of understanding social policies, considering the links between economic growth, equitable distribution of its benefits, and living in harmony with the environment.

5. We see that poverty and social exclusion affect millions of people worldwide, prevent human development and a decent life with quality—and that in Latin America and the Caribbean this situation affects over half of the population. We are also convinced that exclusion and poverty, together with inequality, diseases, insecurity, environmental pollution and degradation, and inadequate design, are public hazards affecting many people and threatening everyone.

6. Within the prevailing context of development based on exclusion, we pose the following challenges:

- How to apply the principles of Universal Design when there are people whose main concern is not "tomorrow," but uncertainty about their next meal, their housing, and the most basic health care?
- How to make Universal Design principles consistent with the fact that for the majority of the world, the concepts of "basic standards," "building codes," and "regulations" are non-existent?
- In these situations, what real meaning is there in services such as "the bathroom," "the kitchen," "the lobby," "the ramp," "the lighting," or "the acoustics"?
- And especially, how to add quality of life by applying Universal Design.

7. We emphasize that the current application of inadequate design to programs, services, and infrastructure generates inaccessibility and perpetuates conditions of exclusion for the future. We find it

unacceptable that public resources continue to be used to construct any kind of barrier.

8. We agree that Universal Design should become an indispensable component in policies and actions to promote development, in order for it to be truly inclusive and to effectively contribute to the reduction of poverty in the world.

9. We also agree that in order to make progress towards **Universal Design for Sustainable and Inclusive Development,** all new actions will require the following:
   - be planned with a balance between legal, human-rights, economic, technological, and local cultural issues;
   - meet the community's real needs;
   - include participation by stakeholders;
   - incorporate Universal Design criteria in order to prevent investments from generating extra costs for adaptations needed in the future;
   - apply locally available materials and technologies at the lowest possible cost;
   - plan for maintenance with local means; and
   - provide adequate training to allow increasingly extensive application of Universal Design.

10. We are convinced that in order for Universal Design to become an instrument at the service of Inclusive Development, it is necessary that all stakeholders in these issues (states and governments, private sector, civil society, civil society organizations, universities, professionals, and international and regional agencies) play active roles, in keeping with the following lines of action:
   - Governments should make efforts to achieve legal instruments for Universal Design to be applied permanently and as a cross-cutting component of national development plans and public policies.
   - The private sector should be attracted to apply Universal Design to products and services, and the theme should become a public interest matter.
   - Universities should promote Universal Design for training the professions related to this concept, fostering research that allows the expansion, application, and development of Universal Design.
   - Professionals directly related to Universal Design should furnish technical guidelines in order to achieve its more effective and efficient application, focused on local development and social inclusion.
   - The organizations currently most aware of the need for Universal Design should contribute to spreading the concept to other sectors of civil society and play an active role in social vigilance in order to make on-going progress in accessibility and inclusion through its effective application.
   - International and regional agencies should make progress in the legal framework with the support of international and regional technical standards and guidelines promoting the sustainable application of Universal Design at the service of Inclusive Development.
   - Multilateral lending agencies should make Universal Design a

(continued)

development issue and promote its advancement, practical application, research, and dissemination with economic resources and adopt it as a basic standard for designing projects and as a requirement for the approval of loans to countries.

11. We feel that all efforts and actions in this direction will be stronger and more effective to the extent that we move towards a common agenda for Universal Design and Inclusive Development and build alliances and partnerships between the different sectors and stakeholders. Yet it is still necessary to create networks to promote these issues, to contribute to their spread and constructive debate, and to empower the various efforts.

12. Finally, we hereby state that we are deeply convinced that if we work to build a world guided by the principles of Universal Design and Inclusive Development, it will be a better, more peaceful, more inhabitable, and more equitable world and certainly one with better quality of life.

Rio de Janeiro, December 12, 2004
Available at http://siteresources.worldbank.org/DISABILITY/.../
RioCharterUnivEng.doc (accessed June 20, 2014).

Being a Steward

What does it mean to be a steward of the environment? The life and work of sustainable design leader William McDonough is inspiring for any designer. In the early 1990s, McDonough took steps to create a new paradigm by which to evaluate the impact buildings and interior remodels have on the environment. McDonough's well-known book, *Cradle to Cradle*, explores the concept of complete recycling of building materials from structural members to carpet.[6] McDonough takes his inspiration from nature: There is a closed-loop system. Whatever materials are created are absorbed by the earth. Of course, the presence of landfills and barges of garbage show us that this is far from the truth when it comes to human consumption. From McDonough's book, a cradle-to-cradle (C2C) rating system was developed to help people make choices based on care for the environment. For many consumers, a C2C label on materials adds to their desirability. C2C ratings let consumers and designers know the environmental impact of materials. This labeling means that the product has undergone considerable testing and consideration. It is a voluntary labeling practice. Designers can find more information at the organization's website: www.c2ccertified.org.

Code Compliance

Code compliance is an important part of new construction and renovation. New construction and remodeling projects are subject to energy code compliance at the federal, state, and local levels. Scottsdale, Arizona, recently adopted the 2012 Federal Energy Code as its local code and became the first city in the southwestern United States to do so.

This book outlines conservation of materials, water, and power through specific construction practices. Leadership in Energy and Environmental Design (LEED) is a rating process that covers the residential sector as well as the commercial sector. Administered by the US Green Building Council (USGBC), it has awarded various rating levels to buildings since 1998. It is a participatory program and not mandated, as building codes are. LEED awards are a major goal and achievement for many architects and developers. There is a LEED for homes award, which we focus on in Chapter 2.

Marketability

Studies show that green design sells real estate. It is an accepted concept that remodeled kitchens and bathrooms add to the overall value for a home or condominium. Green design means that the remodel was done with value in mind. Many real estate agents recognize that green design is a marketable asset. As described in "An Interview with Susanne Clark," Suzanne Clark of the Suzanne Clark Group, a Keller Williams company, says her clients are looking for the values that green design showcases.

An Interview with Susanne Clark

Q: *So you're an Earth Advantage Certified Real Estate Broker. What does that mean exactly?*

SC: When I became certified, it was called STAR: Sustainability Training for Accredited Real Estate Professionals. It is a rigorous certification process available only to licensed real estate brokers. The education involves a deep understanding of how to communicate to homebuyers the benefits of purchasing a green home.

Q: *Does this involve remodeled homes?*

SC: Absolutely. My area of expertise involves historic homes that have been renovated and newer construction.

Q: *In your opinion, does a kitchen or bath remodel that is green focused add to the value of the home?*

SC: Updated kitchens and bathrooms always increase the value of a home. If the renovations are done with methods that decrease energy bills and water bills and provide for a healthy home environment, they are even more attractive to homebuyers.

Q: *Would you recommend that other licensed real estate agents become certified through Earth Advantage?*

SC: In the authors' market in Portland, Oregon, homebuyers are very interested in living a life that's easy on the environment. I would say, yes.

Q: *Thank you for your time, Suzanne.*

On the Horizon

The Appraisal Institute's *Residential Green and Energy Efficient Addendum* (Form 820.04) is available to aid in the evaluation of a home's overall appraisal value.[7] It gives an appraiser the ability to create a report that includes a home's certification (e.g., ENERGY STAR); LEED status; rating on the Home Energy Rating System (HERS) Index (see Figure 1.7); and note energy-efficient windows, appliances, and fixtures. It creates a very complete narrative and record of improvements a homeowner has made to a home that increases its desirability. This is just one example of how green building is no longer on the fringe but is very much becoming a mainstream concept.

The introduction of the Sensible Accounting to Value Energy (SAVE) Act to Congress in June 2013 is a sign that energy efficiency and saving money go hand in hand. The SAVE Act calls for a home's energy report to be part of underwriting policy. It allows potential borrowers to submit a qualified home energy report (see Chapter 3 for information on RESNET, Residential

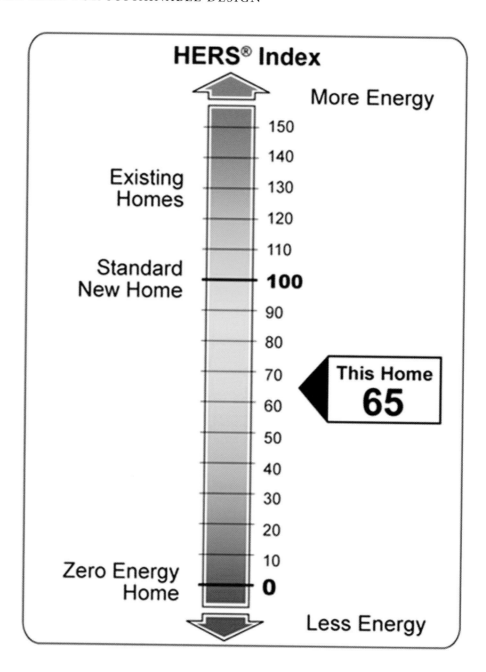

FIGURE 1.7 The HERS (Home Energy Rating System) Index measures the home's energy efficiency. It is the industry standard and nationally recognized for calculating a home's energy performance.

Image courtesy of RESNET, the Residential Energy Sources Network.

Energy Sources Network, and the HERS Index of a home) as part of the qualification process for a mortgage. Any improvements made to a home's energy efficiency will be taken into account in the loan to value equation when a potential buyer applies for a mortgage. According to a white paper release on the SAVE Act, it is projected to create 83,000 jobs in the green building and upgrade sector and to save $1.1 billion in energy costs. Whether through the SAVE act or other future legislation, a home's energy efficiency will soon be rewarded with financing incentives.

Goals

The goal of this book is to educate kitchen and bath designers on how participate in environmental stewardship. Once a designer, a builder, or a design student becomes confident in his or her own knowledge, then they "pay it forward," becoming agents of change as they design with an approach that includes preserving the environment.

To begin a dialogue on sustainable design, let's examine the four Rs of green design:

1. Reduce
2. Reuse
3. Recycle
4. Recover

Reduce

Construction Waste

According to the Institute for Local Self-Reliance, the construction and demolition industry in the United States creates 230 million tons of waste ever year. Much of this waste contains some reusable content. Likewise, some of the waste could be taken out of the landfill stream and recycled for its content. Careful deconstruction to remove building materials prior to a remodel and attentive construction techniques during construction are just two ways to reduce the amount of waste on a remodeling project.

Water and Energy Use

Helping clients choose to install ENERGY STAR–rated appliances and fixtures to diminish water use can result in lower bills for them. Some municipalities offer incentives for the installation these items. As a designer, learning to navigate these incentives and potentially getting rebates for clients will make you in high demand!

Reuse

Materials

Incorporating existing elements in your design or using building salvage are just two ways the reuse of materials (and thus, the saving of embodied energy) can work in a project.

Recycle

Material Content

Many materials now incorporate recycled content. In Chapter 5 "Materials," we cover what this means and how to research a material's environmental impact through a third-part evaluator.

Recover

Construction Waste

Chapter 3 covers careful construction techniques to help you navigate decisions regarding building material salvage.

Best Practices

Many business models are created around the concept of best practices. There are lists of best practices in management, marketing, and education. The concept of a best practices approach to green design and sustainable project management means adhering to proven methods, methods that are aligned with the triple bottom line. By creating a guiding template of best practices, designers will serve their clients' interests, save energy and resources, reduce waste, and plan for longevity and accessibility, and will be ahead of the game with each project undertaken. Best practices is really design programming which the National Kitchen & Bath Association (NKBA) is known to promote. The NKBA's extensive intake forms for kitchen and bath design aid designers in understanding precisely what is needed and desired in a project.

A best practices approach will also aid designers to communicate this information to clients. The approach offers a simple structure that outlines systems, construction, material selection, and product specification for a green renovation. For an example of best practices in construction, see Chapter 3.

What was at one time an exercise in dichotomy is now a much more holistic approach to kitchen and bath design. One doesn't have to choose between sustainable design and affordability, or green design and luxury. The earlier conversation of good versus bad, with little consensus on what either one means to a project, has been replaced by a new comprehensive approach. The list of the four Rs of sustainable design leads to the valuable design concept of best practices. This concept empowers designers and clients to create a road map during the design process. Sustainability in remodeling projects must start from the beginning. Without a firm foundation of knowledge about sustainability, the process will seem overwhelming and potentially more expensive.

In this book, we cover ways to create a best practice framework for your design process from predesign programming to construction install and beyond.

SUMMARY

In a recent kitchen and bath planning class taught by author Robin Rigby Fisher, CMKBD, the environment became the topic of conversation. The students and I discussed our part in the problem. Many students said they were concerned that the kitchen and bath design field only adds to environmental issues and expressed that they had begun to doubt their chosen educational path.

Yes, a career in the design industry may not be seen as a sustainable one, but by gaining a thorough understanding of the problems, learning various options in construction and business practices, and developing an in-depth knowledge of materials and their maintenance issues, we can impact the environment for good.

We also discussed that with careful planning, good design, and specifying the appropriate materials and their maintenance, we can help to make our clients' lives easier. Good kitchen design creates rooms that bring families together, makes it easier to eat healthier, and creates rooms that are easier to clean. Designs that consider how clients will live in their home in the future by incorporating universal design standards minimize the need for later renovations and allow people to live in their homes longer. Choosing materials for quality (they don't always have to be the most expensive) create longer-lasting kitchens and bathrooms with less waste.

Our goal for this textbook is to provide a sound background of the sustainable design challenge and the tools needed to lessen our industry's negative impact on the environment.

We may not change the world, but we can make a positive difference.

REVIEW QUESTIONS

1. What is the triple bottom line? Sketch a diagram. (See "The Triple Bottom Line Approach" page 4)
2. How can the four Rs of sustainable design be applied to kitchen and bath design? (See "Goals" page 18)
3. What are the seven principles of universal design? (See "Universal Design for Sustainable and Inclusive Development" page 15)

ENDNOTES

1. *Advancing the Science of Climate Change*. National Research Council. The National Academies Press, Washington, DC.
2. *Climate Change Indicators in the United States*. U.S. Environmental Protection Agency, Washington, DC.
3. J. G. Titus, E. K. Anderson, D. R. Cahoon, S. Gill, R. E. Thieler, and J. S. Williams. *Coastal Sensitivity to Sea Level Rise: A Focus on the Mid-Atlantic Region. U.S. Climate Change*

Science Program and the Subcommittee on Global Change Research. http://downloads. globalchange.gov/sap/sap4-5/sap4-5-final-all.pdf.

4. G. C. Hegerl, F. W. Zwiers, P. Braconnot, N. Gillett, Y. Luo, J. A. Marengo Orsini, N. Nicholls, J. E. Penner, and P. A. Stott, "Understanding and Attributing Climate Change." In *Climate Change 2007: The Physical Science Basis.Contribution of Working Group I to the Fourth Assessment Report of the Intergovernmental Panel on Climate Change.* S. Solomon, D. Qin, M. Manning, Z. Chen, M. Marquis, K. B. Averyt, M. Tignor and H. L. Miller (eds.), 663-745. Cambridge, UK, and New York, NY: Cambridge University Press, 2007.

5. ICLEI—Local Governments for Sustainability, www.iclei.org.

6. William McDonough and Michael Braungart, *Cradle to Cradle: Remaking the Way We Make Things* (New York: North Point Press, 2002).

7. www.appraisalinstitute.org/assets/1/7/ai-residential-green-energy-effecient-addendum-2.pdf, or see the fillable-form PDF version at www.appraisalinstitute.org/assets/1/7/Interactive820.04-ResidentialGreenandEnergyEffecientAddendum.pdf.

What Defines Sustainability?

The conversation about what defines green building has changed dramatically in the last decade. Rather than focusing on reducing and going without, the new perspective is designing for benefits. With the addition of building science and access to third-party evaluators, green design is defined now as a benefit to clients: conservation of energy and resources, better-performing appliances, and tax incentives to remodel or build new in this format for sustainability.

Learning Objective 1: Explain the criteria that make a product or a technique sustainable.

Learning Objective 2: Describe the impact energy codes have on your project beyond your jurisdiction.

Learning Objective 3: Apply knowledge of the importance of third-party evaluators.

Learning Objective 4: Recognize how green design can save your client money.

This chapter defines sustainability as it relates to the building industry. The Energy & Environmental Building Alliance (EEBA) defines sustainable houses in their "Houses that Work" program as buildings that have improved performance and profitability. The EEBA, like the Home Builders Association and other home building associations, is focusing its interests on educating designers and builders in new sustainable building techniques. However, "Houses That Work" is the educational arm of the Building American Program of the US Department of Energy (USDOE). "Houses that Work" provides up-to-date education on building science and code compliance for designers, builders, and consumers.

As a kitchen and bath designer, you have added responsibility because the areas you are designing are the parts of the home that use high amounts of both energy and water and have a big impact on indoor air quality. How do you begin to look at the sustainable building industry? What makes a product or a construction method more sustainable than another?

The sustainable characteristic of a product, construction method, wall type, or appliance (just to name a few) is an equation. It is the culmination of research into various aspects of sustainability and then weighing those aspects against each other while at other times viewing them as a group. The aspects to observe are:

- Embodied energy
- Carbon footprint

FIGURE 2.1 Embodied energy is determined by the amount of energy used in the production of a product from a raw resource through leaving the factory.

- Environmental health (including indoor air quality)
- Renewable resources
- Renewable energy

EMBODIED ENERGY

Simply put, *embodied energy* is the totality of energy necessary to create a product. It is the process of measuring the amount of energy that is involved in the production of a material from the extraction of the raw material through the fabrication of the finished product (prior to arriving on the project site) (see Figure 2.1). Embodied energy is expressed in the *mega joules* (MJ; units of expended heat) needed to make 1 kilogram of product created by the energy needed to make the same 1 kilogram of product. It is not a straightforward sum, but the concept of embodied energy is crucial to understanding how much impact the creation of a product has on the environment. Embodied energy is discussed in more detail in Chapter 5.

Let us look at granite and its embodied energy. Granite is quarried from the earth (extraction of raw materials). The process of removing granite requires drills that are fueled by diesel or gas (both fossil fuels), and then the block of granite is transported to a fabrication plant. The transportation could be relatively close to the quarry or quite far away; the fuel needed for transportation must also be taken into account. Once the granite block arrives at the processing facility, it is sawed into slabs, polished, and packaged for shipment to its country of destination. All of the resources used in the processing facility, including plant operation and maintenance and creation of the packaging material, are included in the calculations. This entire timeline is defined as *cradle to gate*. Chapter 5 defines the different stages of a product: *cradle to gate*, *cradle to site*, and *cradle to grave*.

At this point the embodied energy calculation is complete.

Since embodied energy is present in all materials, incorporating products with recycled content or salvage materials in your projects will decrease the total embodied energy and drive your finished project closer to the sustainable goal. Incorporating deconstruction techniques (Chapter 3) over the usual demolition-to-Dumpster™ method will further minimize the embodied energy in future products.

Carbon Footprint

The environmental impact of each product you specify goes beyond its embodied energy. Carbon footprints are the measurements of the CO_2 and methane (CH_4) emissions created by a specific event, product, or population. These gas emissions are referred to as greenhouse gases, which are the leading cause of climate change in our atmosphere. The carbon footprint is the measurement of the global warming potential (GWP) of a product. The idea of naming the total impact of an activity (be it a airplane trip or the creation of a product like vinyl flooring) comes from theories by Mathis Wackernagel and William Rees. The theories begin with the *demand* an activity makes on the environment and ends with a metric of how long it will take the environment to *recover* from that activity.

Carbon footprints are categorized into two types: direct and indirect. Direct carbon footprints are the emissions you create when you drive your car or turn on your cooktop. Indirect carbon footprints are harder to see. They come from the production of products you specify, such as vinyl flooring, or items you use or the coffee cup you purchased on the way to your first meeting.

The average US household creates 48 tons of CO_2 emissions per year; that is five times greater than households in the rest of the world. Transportation (driving, flying) is our largest creator of CO_2 emissions, followed closely by housing (construction, heating, and daily operations). Food production is third on the list.[1]

The carbon footprint paradigm is controversial. Obviously, those of us in the United States, Canada, and Europe consume more energy than our neighbors in South America and Africa. However, this is changing. The presence of a fully global economy has shifted the responsibility of resource preservation to a global perspective.

The Emissions Gap Report 2012 (created by the United Nations Environment Programme [UNEP] and the European Climate Foundation) stated that unless we make a drastic change in the world's behavior, CO_2 emissions are going to continue to rise. Scientists have determined that emissions could rise to 58 gigatonnes (Gt) by 2020, far above the 44 Gt projected to keep the global temperature rise below 2 degrees Celsius this century.

Achim Steiner, UN Under-Secretary General and executive director of UNEP, said:

> There are two realities . . . there are many inspiring actions taking place at the national level on energy efficiency in buildings, investing in forests to avoid emissions linked with deforestation and new vehicle emissions standards alongside a remarkable growth in investment in new renewable energies worldwide.

> Yet the sobering fact remains that a transition to a low carbon, inclusive Green Economy is happening far too slowly and the opportunity for meeting the 44 Gt target is narrowing annually.[2]

The time for action is *now*!

Environmental Health

The World Health Organization first used the term "sick building syndrome" in the mid-1980s. This began the very real concern over the indoor air quality (IAQ) of a building. Many factors contribute to the health of a building's air: heating and cooling systems, proper ventilation (air exchange), and the presence of volatile organic compounds (VOCs) in building materials. A VOC is a carbon-based gas that is highly pressurized in normal interior temperatures. This means it will *off-gas*, or move to places of lower concentration, thus increasing the toxicity of the air.

Mold is major cause for concern in creating a healthy environment. Mold in its various forms is present in all interior environments. It is of particular concern in wet locations, such as bathrooms. Basements and buildings in wetter climates often are contaminated with mold. Not all molds create health problems, but the ones that do can do considerable harm to the inhabitants of a space.

The presence of mold is of special concern for users who are either very young or older or have decreased immunity. A building cannot be considered sustainable if it creates health problems for its inhabitants.

RENEWABLE RESOURCES

Renewable resources are any natural resources that replenish themselves through the passage of time either through reproduction or through naturally recurring processes.

Today natural construction materials are making their way into traditional projects more often. Cork and linoleum flooring are long lasting, easy to maintain, have lower embodied energy, and have lower off-gassing emissions than petroleum-based flooring options. Clay-based plasters are being installed on walls in new kitchens and baths.

Advantages of incorporating renewable resources in construction include those listed next.

- Added value—many are better insulators (straw bale) and less toxic (either low or zero VOCs).
- Reduced embodied energy. Dimensional lumber has a much lower carbon footprint than cement.
- Fewer nonrenewable resources are needed in the production. Cork flooring uses less oil in its production process than does the manufacturing of vinyl flooring.
- Less impact on the natural world.

A more comprehensive list of natural resource materials is available in Chapter 5.

Water is considered a renewable resource but with only 3 percent of the world's water being potable (drinkable) and our ever-increasing population, its sustainable status is quickly fading. (see Figures 2.2 and 2.3). According to the UNEP, by 2025, Africa and most of West Asia will be experiencing severe water scarcities.

In the United States, Canada, Australia, and Europe, *all* water delivered to buildings is potable. Considerable energy is used to treat, deliver, and retrieve water.

Each home generates three types of wastewater. Fresh or potable water is considered *white*; water from dishwashing, sinks, and laundry is labeled *gray*; and wastewater from toilets is *black* (see Figure 2.4). Many municipalities have created standards for small and large-scale collection and reuse of graywater. Graywater can be safely used for irrigation, keeping it out of water treatment plants and returning it directly to our groundwater.

Techniques for the conservation of water and the collection and use of graywater are discussed in Chapter 3.

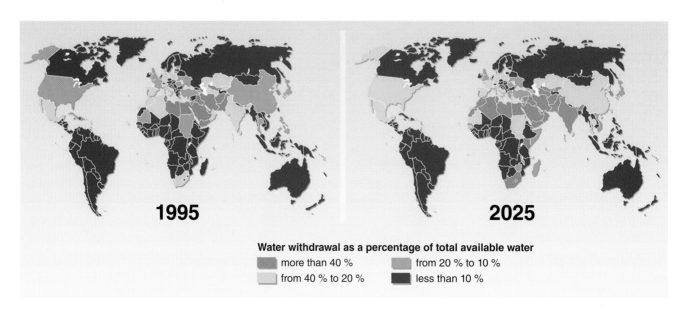

FIGURE 2.2 UNEP Vital Water—Availability of fresh water.

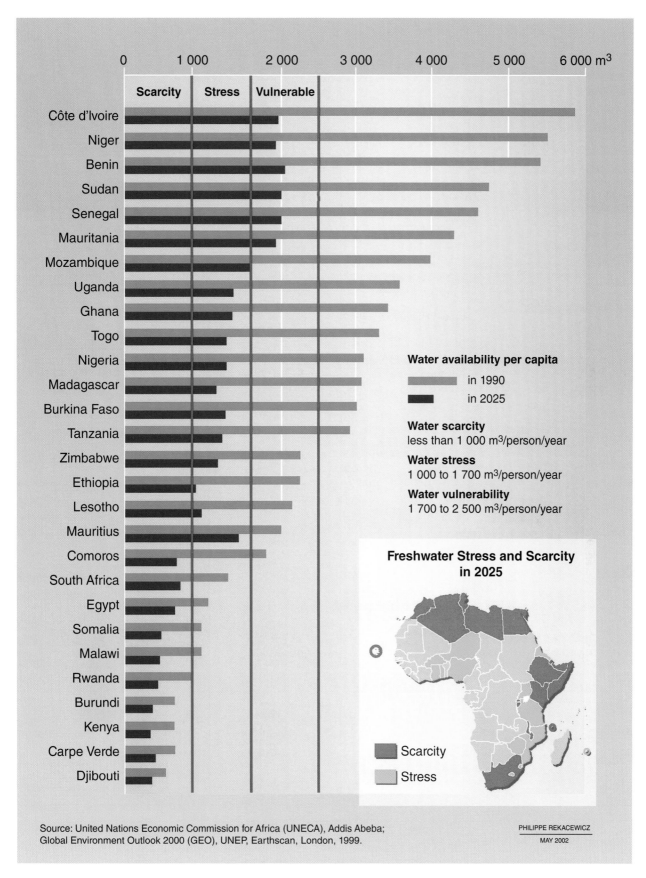

FIGURE 2.3 UNEP Freshwater Stress and Scarcity. The UNEP estimates that by 2025, the entire continent of Africa will be dire straits in regard to access to fresh water.

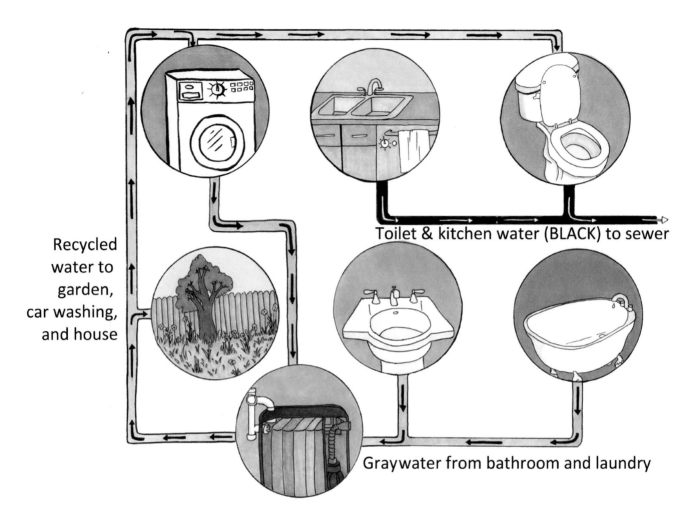

Recycled
water to
garden,
car washing,
and house

Toilet & kitchen water (BLACK) to sewer

Graywater from bathroom and laundry

FIGURE 2.4 Graywater and blackwater. In many jurisdictions, systems for the reclamation of graywater in the home are available to homeowners.

Renewable Energy

Renewable energy is defined as a continually replenished supply of energy created from wind, rain, sun, tides, waves, and geothermal sources. The US Energy Information Administration (USEIA) estimates the world's generation of energy from renewable energy sources to be at 19 percent of the world's energy. That number is expected to increase to 23 percent by 2035.[3]

Technology in heating, ventilation, and air conditioning (HVAC); windows; and insulation in combination with stringent energy and building codes have resulted in homes that are more efficient. As a result, we have seen a drop of 11.6 percent in total energy consumption in residential homes between 1993 and 2009 (www.eia.gov/consumption/residential/) (see Figure 2.5).

Although this is a step in the right direction, the United States is still the largest consumer of energy. With almost 50 percent of our demand coming from homes, more must be done.[4]

Designers today have more opportunities at their disposal to help create a kitchen or bath that is not only beautiful and sustainable but also energy efficient.

You can begin by knowing what type of power your local power company supplies. In Portland, Oregon, for example, Portland Gas and Electric (PGE) offers clients green power

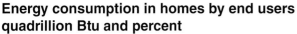

**Energy consumption in homes by end users
quadrillion Btu and percent**

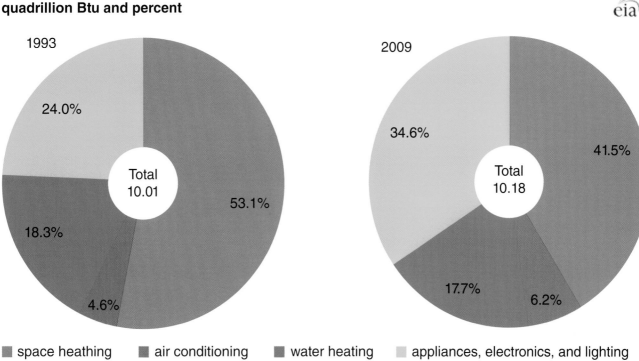

FIGURE 2.5 USEIA Residential Energy Consumption Survey (RECS)

options for electricity. Customers have the opportunity to select from wind, wave, or solar power. Many utility companies offer similar programs. Mandatory green power utility options are currently offered in 11 states. You can find out if your clients have this fossil fuel conserving opportunity by visiting the USDOE web site at www.energy.gov.

Technology is available for retrofitting existing homes with alternative energy sources. Solar (or photovoltaic) panels allow the homeowner to capture some or all of the home's energy needs from the sun. Credits are then registered through a policy called net metering.

Net metering is designed for the consumer who owns alternative renewable energy sources, such as wind or solar power. Excess energy is sent back to the public grid. This policy gives clients retail credit for the energy they generate.

For aggressive energy savers, it is possible for a home to generate all the energy it needs and more. This is called a net-zero or carbon-neutral home (see Figure 2.6).

There is considerable wasted energy in a home. It can be in the form of air leaks, hot water waste, and duct work that is not insulated. The goal is to optimize sources of heat and cooling so that the energy is not wasted. Consider the warm air that leaves a home from a dryer vent or the warmed water from a shower that goes down the drain. Simple, effective steps can save this energy for your clients without breaking the bank. Specific measures you can take to minimize this wasted energy are outlined in Chapter 3.

For the new-construction project, a successful design option for energy efficiency is capturing heating and cooling from passive sources. Solar collecting is a passive energy collecting activity, as is daylighting for illumination and solar gain via windows or thick walls.

According to the Passive House Institute (www.passivehouse.us), a home designed according to its guidelines will have heating and cooling costs that are 10 percent of a conventionally designed home. While still experimental in the United States, Passive House building techniques (thick, insulated walls; virtually airtight construction; careful air exchange; double- and triple-paned windows; a reliance on passive energy; alternative heating and cooling) are

FIGURE 2.6 This home, built by Neil Kelly, is the first residential LEED-certified home built in Oregon. It is a net-zero home.
Courtesy of Neil Kelly

becoming part of local codes in some European countries. Even if a fully passive house approach to a new home or addition is not feasible, you can learn from the innovative approaches this paradigm sets forth (see Figure 2.7). The institute states that the goals and standards of the passive house movement are "quality construction, unparalleled levels of comfort, superior air quality, lasting energy savings, user-friendly operation as well as increased structural longevity and integrity" (www.passivehouse.us/passiveHouse/PassiveHouseInfo.html).

While on the subject of renewable energy, it is worth discussing the subject of food waste and recycling.

In 2011, the United States produced 36 million tons of food waste that went into our country's landfills (see Figure 2.8). As food waste decomposes, it creates CH_4 gas (a greenhouse gas that is more powerful than CO_2). As of the time of writing this book, over 150 communities across the United States and Canada have implemented food-composting programs (see Figures 2.9 and 2.10); leading the way are San Francisco, California; Seattle, Washington; San Antonio, Texas; Portland, Oregon; New York City, New York; and Toronto, Canada.[4]

Cities that have curbside composting programs provide households with receptacles for all food waste. Space planning for these receptacles is an important part of a kitchen designer's job. Even clients living in areas without food-composting programs have many composting options. For example, all-in-one composters, such as the Earth Machine, make garden composting very easy.

Many cities have some type of curbside recycling programs. In Portland's program, people can include food waste with their yard waste. Glass is separate; paper goods, plastics, and

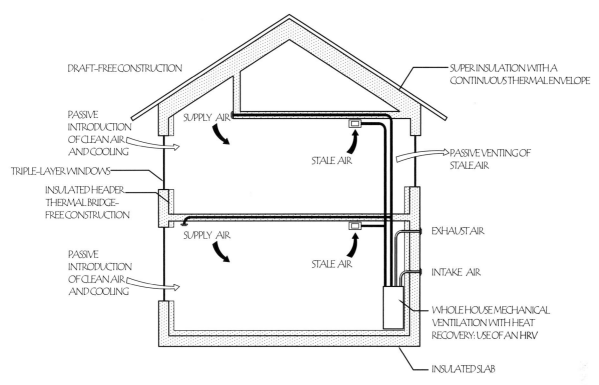

DRAFT-FREE CONSTRUCTION

SUPER INSULATION WITH A
CONTINUOUS THERMAL ENVELOPE

PASSIVE
INTRODUCTION
OF CLEAN AIR
AND COOLING

SUPPLY AIR

TRIPLE-LAYER WINDOWS

STALE AIR

PASSIVE VENTING OF
STALE AIR

INSULATED HEADER
THERMAL BRIDGE-
FREE CONSTRUCTION

PASSIVE
INTRODUCTION
OF CLEAN AIR
AND COOLING

SUPPLY AIR

STALE AIR

EXHAUST AIR

INTAKE AIR

WHOLE HOUSE MECHANICAL
VENTILATION WITH HEAT
RECOVERY: USE OF AN HRV

INSULATED SLAB

FIGURE 2.7 Passive House construction techniques can save homeowners "60–70% of overall energy expenses without the addition of active technologies like photovoltaics or solar thermal hot water systems." (www.passivehouse.use/passiveHouse/FAQ.html) *NKBA*

FIGURE 2.8 Landfill

FIGURE 2.9 Curbside composting program in Portland, Oregon
Creative Commons-Share-Alike, Photo by Tim Jewett

FIGURE 2.10 Home composting unit

cans go together. Cities vary in how the recycling is collected. Research and careful planning for recycling collection in a kitchen will allow your client to have a seamless cooking experience. Chapter 3 includes case studies on recycling.

Knowing the Codes

The International Residential Code (IRC) is a far-reaching set of standards in the form of residential codes. The codes stipulate regulations for single-family homes and duplexes of three stories or less. The code addresses construction, plumbing, mechanical, fuel, energy, and electrical provisions for these residences.

The International Energy Conservation Code (IECC) is similar to the IRC in that the IECC mandates energy conservation through efficiency in building design, mechanical systems, lighting systems, and the use of innovative building techniques.

Currently, different states have adopted different versions of the IEEC. You can find your state's compliance in Figure 2.11.

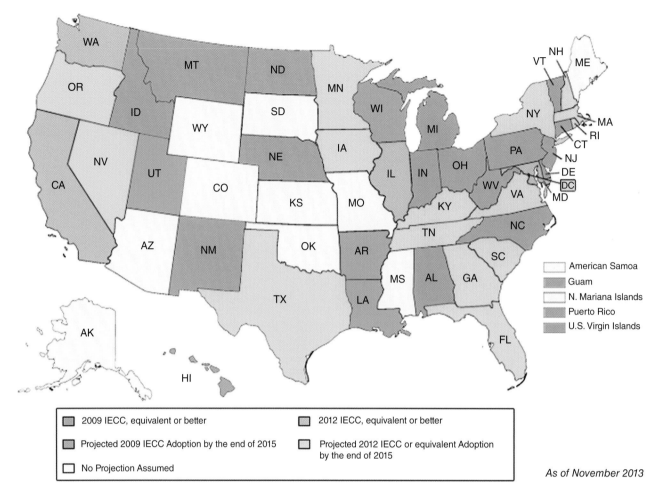

2009 IECC, equivalent or better

2012 IECC, equivalent or better

Projected 2009 IECC Adoption by the end of 2015

Projected 2012 IECC or equivalent Adoption by the end of 2015

No Projection Assumed

As of November 2013

FIGURE 2.11 USDOE map of residential code compliance

Courtesy of US Department of Energy

Being aware of the energy codes and how they apply to your project is a requirement for all designers. Furthermore, you must be vigilant in regard to changes in the codes, as they impact your project. If you work in multiple jurisdictions (even county to county), there may be different requirements. Note that some states have adopted the 2012 version of the IECC while other states have not.

Case Study: Meritage Homes

C. R. Herro, vice president of energy efficiency and sustainability at Meritage Homes, is a trailblazer when it comes to combining profitability and sustainability. Although most of your kitchen and bath projects will be remodel projects, it is worth looking at this pioneer in the new-construction business. "If you build beyond code, your home has great resale potential," believes Herro. Meritage Homes is based in Scottsdale, Arizona, but builds throughout the United States. The company has made a name for itself by building ENERGY STAR–certified homes. These items come standard on Meritage homes:

• Spray foam insulation throughout the home

- Careful attention to air intake to provide for healthy IAQ
- Programmable thermostats
- Weather-sensing irrigation
- Low-flow toilets, faucets, and fixtures
- ENERGY STAR–certified appliances
- E-2- or E-3-rated windows
- Highly efficacious lighting in all parts of the home

Extra solar panels can be purchased to bring the home close to a net-zero energy use. The face of Meritage's commitment to sustainable design is C. R. Herro. He approaches customer education by showing that homes built to save resources can save people money. A home built with the listed techniques also provides for a more comfortable home, with more constant temperatures, and quiet heating and cooling systems. When you visit a Meritage home, it does not *look* green, except for the solar panels on the roof. It looks like a new home with architectural styling that matches the neighborhoods.

The company is not resting on its accomplishments. Each spring, on Earth Day (April 22), Meritage introduces a new advanced building technique. Experimental initially, the goal is to integrate the new technique into the company's home-building processes within five years.

AFFORDABLE COMFORT PERSPECTIVE

Affordable Comfort, Inc. (ACI) is a leading resource in the practice of building high-performance homes. The organization offers networking opportunities for designers and builders interested in green building. Originally started as an advocate for the interests of the HVAC professionals, the ACI now is concerned with education. It promotes local organizations and events. Its perspective is one of improving a building and remodeling methodology that has not changed in decades.

Think about an incandescent light bulb. It represents technology that is very old—light generated from fire. When we consider what has been accomplished with other light sources, we have to ask ourselves, "Why not consider other building techniques?"

Green Alliances and Programs

There are many organizations that promote sustainable building practices. The four organizations and programs listed next are included because of their proven ability to affect real change in the building arts.

CalGreen. This is the building initiative for the state of California. CalGreen is considered the leading clearinghouse on water-saving and energy-saving guidelines.

Energy and Environmental Building Alliance (EEBA). This nonprofit organization is dedicated to education in green building techniques. The EEBA's vision statement reads: "A world where everyone can live in a healthy, safe, durable, energy efficient home." The EEBA is specifically concerned with the study of building science and how an understanding of the building science paradigm will result in more ecological buildings. The EEBA also sponsors the "Houses That Work" educational program that can be completed online by those interested in green building.

Leadership in Energy and Environmental Design (LEED). This program often is considered the gold standard when it comes to sustainable building certification. The LEED program is administered and monitored by the United States Green Building Council (USGB).

Pacific Northwest National Laboratory (PNNL). One of many USDOE laboratories, PNNL has studied climate change and currently is setting new standards for efficiency minimums.

FIGURE 2.12 C2C logo

Third-Party Evaluators

Greenwashing is an accepted term today. As a designer, what does it mean to you? At its core, it probably means something is deceptive. Without specific restrictions in so many areas—demolition/deconstruction, specification of alternative construction methods, specification of green materials, and the use of energy-saving/resource-saving fixtures and appliances, it is difficult to know where to look for guidance.

Next we present a list that, although it is not exhaustive, is a place to begin in order to achieve a sustainable project.

C2C

The C2C clearinghouse (www.c2ccertified.org) aligns itself with the work of William McDonough, coauthor of *Cradle to Cradle* referred to in Chapter 1 (see Figure 2.12). Products are rated across five categories (material health, material reutilization, renewable energy and carbon management, water stewardship, and social fairness) and awarded one of five levels (basic, bronze, silver, gold, or platinum) (see Figure 2.13). The methodology for rating has been in effect since 2005, and currently over 400 products have achieved C2C certification. Products that have been certified include building materials, interior design products, personal and home care items, paper and packaging, fabrics and textiles, and more.

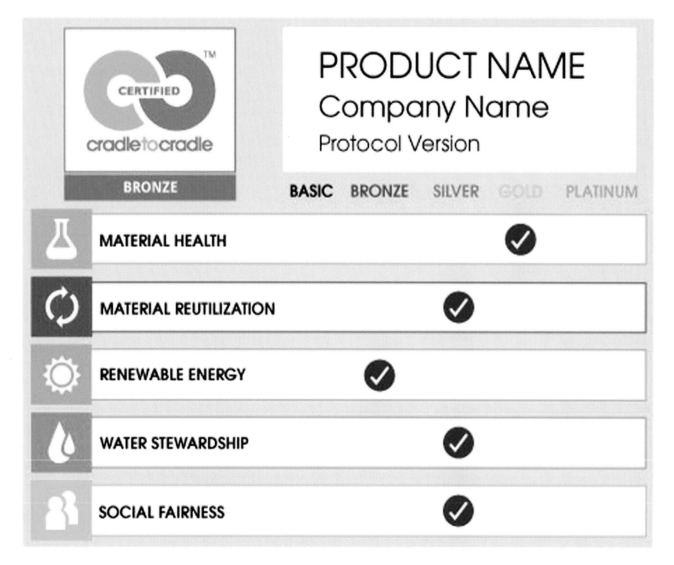

FIGURE 2.13 C2C Five-Category logo

GREENGUARD

GREENGUARD (www.greenguard.org) is part of Underwriters Laboratory (UL Industries). (see Figure 2.14). This certification concerns itself with promoting healthy indoor air quality. Certified products and materials must meet strict guidelines regarding chemical off-gassing.

FIGURE 2.14 GREENGUARD logo

ENERGY STAR

ENERGY STAR (www.energystar.gov) is a voluntary program funded by the US Environmental Protection Agency (EPA) (see Figure 2.15). It is nationwide and offers many different benefits and certifications to help designers, builders, and homeowners make sustainable decisions about homes. Interested parties can access information about products, energy-saving strategies, tax incentives for existing homes, and how to locate and purchase new homes that have an ENERGY STAR rating.

Earth Advantage

Earth Advantage (www.earthadvantage.org) (Figure 2.16) got its start in the Pacific Northwest. It certifies buildings for sustainable building credentials. This organization is behind the Sustainability Training for Accredited Real Estate Professionals, which was showcased in Chapter 1. Earth Advantage certifies both new residential projects and residential remodels based on five pillars: energy, health, land, materials, and water. The organization offers *per pillar* and *full certifications.* An Earth Advantage certification will add value to your project and increase the resale value of your client's home. Earth Advantage is a regional third-party certifier. To find one in your area, contact the EEBA.

FIGURE 2.15 ENERGY STAR logo
US Department of Energy

Forest Stewardship Council

The mission of the Forest Stewardship Council (FSC) (Figure 2.17) is to "promote environmentally sound, socially beneficial and economically prosperous management of the world's forests."

The FSC has established a set of 10 principles and 57 criteria that include these ten principles:

PRINCIPLE #1: COMPLIANCE WITH LAWS AND FSC PRINCIPLES. Forest management shall respect all applicable laws of the country in which they occur, and international treaties and agreements to which the country is a signatory, and comply with all FSC Principles and Criteria.

PRINCIPLE #2: TENURE AND USE RIGHTS AND RESPONSIBILITIES. Long-term tenure and use rights to the land and forest resources shall be clearly defined, documented, and legally established.

PRINCIPLE #3: INDIGENOUS PEOPLES' RIGHTS. The legal and customary rights of indigenous peoples to own, use, and manage their lands, territories, and resources shall be recognized and respected.

PRINCIPLE #4: COMMUNITY RELATIONS AND WORKER'S RIGHTS. Forest management operations shall maintain or enhance the long-term social and economic well-being of forest workers and local communities.

PRINCIPLE #5: BENEFITS FROM THE FOREST. Forest management operations shall encourage the efficient use of the forest's multiple products and services to ensure economic viability and a wide range of environmental and social benefits.

PRINCIPLE #6: ENVIRONMENTAL IMPACT. Forest management shall conserve biological diversity and its associated values, water resources, soils, and unique and fragile ecosystems and landscapes, and, by so doing, maintain the ecological functions and the integrity of the forest.

PRINCIPLE #7: MANAGEMENT PLAN. A management plan—appropriate to the scale and intensity of the operations—shall be written, implemented, and kept up to date. The long-term objectives of management, and the means of achieving them, shall be clearly stated.

FIGURE 2.16 Earth Advantage logo

FIGURE 2.17 Forest Stewardship Council

PRINCIPLE #8: MONITORING AND ASSESSMENT. Monitoring shall be conducted—appropriate to the scale and intensity of forest management—to assess the condition of the forest, yields of forest products, chain of custody, management activities, and their social and environmental impacts.

PRINCIPLE #9: MAINTENANCE OF HIGH CONSERVATION VALUE FORESTS.—Management activities in high conservation value forests shall maintain or enhance the attributes which define such forests. Decisions regarding high conservation value forests shall always be considered in the context of a precautionary approach.

PRINCIPLE #10: PLANTATIONS. Plantations shall be planned and managed in accordance with Principles and Criteria 1–9 and Principle 10 and its Criteria. While plantations can provide an array of social and economic benefits, and can contribute to satisfying the world's needs for forest products, they should complement the management of, reduce pressures on, and promote the restoration and conservation of natural forests.[5]

Bottom Line: How Remodeling Sustainably Can Save Your Client Money

The conversation about green building has changed significantly in the past ten years. What was once an exotic or novel approach to energy conservation is now a popular option. Residential solar power, for example, is more popular than ever. There are many homeowners in the United States who sell their surplus energy back to the power companies (i.e., net zero). But many clients, rightfully so, will want to know what the payback is for installing solar panels, or on-demand hot water heaters, or changing out old windows. To assist you in collecting data based on your clients' criteria, look at the Web site called www.find-solar.org.

It makes sense that clients will want to know what their *payback period* will be. The payback period equals the initial cost of the technique divided by annual energy savings due to this technology, technique, or methodology.

We use the term "simple payback" for the equation:

$$Simple\ payback = Total\ cost/Annual\ savings$$

Admittedly, calculating simple payback periods can be difficult. This is due to many factors, the first being climate. In the relatively temperate Northwest, it is hard to find a payback period that is less than 30 years for replacing old windows, but in the cold north of Alberta, Canada, the payback period can be 10 to 15 years for windows with low U-value. The U-value of a window determines a window's insulating performance. The lower the U-value the better the window performs at keeping heat in a home.

The second point regarding simple payback numbers is that they destroy the idea that the house is a system and the total energy efficiency of a home is a sum of many smaller energy-saving upgrades. Installing photovoltaic panels is an excellent way to gauge energy savings because you can meter the energy that is created in wattage. Sealing outlets in exterior walls, insulating exterior walls, and installing sealed insulated can fixtures for lighting are great measures, but it is very hard to get a firm metric on the amount of energy (from heat transfer) that is saved.

Replacing windows can save clients money on heating bills. In colder climates, the cost recouped is more evident. In Figure 2.18, you can see the amount of money a change to double-paned, thermally improved windows can make on heating bills. This case study is in Minneapolis, Minnesota, where homeowners can expect to save 16 percent on their heating bills when thermally improved windows are specified.

Although the amount of money saved might not be enough to consider replacing all the windows in a home, it shows that when replacement windows or new windows are specified on a remodel, they should be the most thermally insulated that the project can afford.

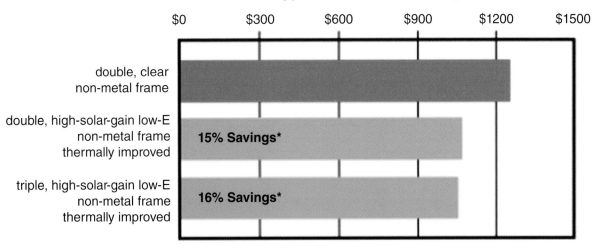

* Compared to the same 2600 sf 2-story existing house with clear, double glazing in a non-metal frame, equally oriented with typical shading.

FIGURE 2.18 Heating costs for existing construction
Efficient Windows Collaborative

You can use *incentivized programs* to help clients offset the cost of green building upgrades. The incentives can be cash rebates or tax deductions. A great place to start is with the Web site for the Database of State Incentives for Renewables and Efficiency (DSIRE) at www. dsireusa.org. This database can help you source various incentives that can help state by state.

The *value* of thermal comfort, health, and well-being in an interior environment can be assessed. Interiors that have cleaner air; fewer pockets of cool, drafty air; and more daylight make users feel more comfortable. It is impossible to put a number on the delight created by a sustainable design. Sticking to a budget and respecting the cost of a project is paramount to the success of the project and the career of a designer. At the same time, clients can feel solidarity with the green building movement. There is real value in the feeling of being included in the local and global efforts to do good for the environment. Help your clients imagine the value of a quiet, healthy home that saves them money over time. Help them to visualize saving embodied energy in the materials they choose for the project. This is an important part of green design and of becoming a steward of the environment.

SUMMARY

Green remodeling is very different from new construction, but the goals are the same. In fact, remodeling an existing home is, by nature, much greener than purchasing a new home. Embodied energy is conserved, as is land. Follow these four steps to begin your project:

1. Get an energy audit from a Residential Energy Services Network (RESNET) certified advisor and get the Home Energy Rating System (HERS) number for your client's home.
2. Make a plan.
3. Set priorities; this includes setting a budget.
4. Stay focused on making the project green throughout the process.

REVIEW QUESTIONS

1. What does it mean to *design for benefits* rather than to *design for conservation*? (See "Case Study: Meritage Homes" page 34)

2. What version of the IECC does the state you live in follow? You can find out at www.energycodes.gov/adoption/states. page 34.

3. Why is it important to get information from a third-party evaluator? (See "Third-Party Evaluators" page 36)

ENDNOTES

1. Christopher Jones and Daniel Kammen, "Quantifying Carbon Footprint Reduction Opportunities for U.S. Households and Communities." *Environmental Science and Technology* 45(9): 4088–4095. doi:10.1021/es102221h. Retrieved May 4, 2012

2. UNEP News Centre, "Greenhouse Gas Emissions Gap Widening as Nations Head to Crucial Climate Talks in Doha," (November 21, 2012), www.unep.org/newscentre/default.aspx?DocumentID=2698&ArticleID=9335#sthash.ydajtphH.dpuf.

3. US Department of Energy, "Energy Efficiency Trends in Residential and Commercial Buildings," (October 2008), http://apps1.eere.energy.gov/buildings/publications/pdfs/corporate/bt_stateindustry.pdf.

4. UNEP News Centre, "Greenhouse Gas Emissions Gap Widening as Nations Head to Crucial Climate Talks in Doha."

5. https://us.fsc.org/mission-and-vision.187.htm.

Sustainable Construction

Sustainable construction methods can vary greatly. Some of these construction methods are responses to state energy codes. California leads the way with its adoption of the 2012 International Energy Conservation Code (IECC) code and its own CalGreen initiative. (CalGreen is a shortened name for the California Green Building Standards Code.) CalGreen is the first state-wide green building code in the United States. Established in 2010, it was revised in 2014 with considerable changes in the residential building sector (www.bsc.ca.gov/Home/CALGreen.aspx).

In this chapter, we outline how to create your own list of best practices for a sustainable approach to the construction of your kitchen and bath projects. These best practices are inspired by progressive codes, such as CalGreen and others. There are many incentive programs to encourage implementation of these measures and upgrades. These incentives can help offset the cost of the project. As a designer, part of your scope of work on a project can include the navigation of incentives.

Learning Objective 1: Apply building component ratings to a remodeling project.

Learning Objective 2: Identify the basic building science of remodeling projects.

Learning Objective 3: List the best practices for individual projects to facilitate the creation of a sustainable remodel.

It is important to achieve a basic understanding of building science. The term "building science" can be defined as the study of how a building operates in terms of energy efficiency. Basic calculations are used to create rating systems for building components: windows, walls, and roofs for example. Knowledge of these rating systems will allow you to understand more precisely how a building will perform and, thus, save energy.

All sustainable construction methods are concerned with accomplishing four things:

1. Energy conservation
2. Material conservation and material use that is environmentally responsible
3. Water conservation
4. Healthy indoor air quality (IAQ)

Home Energy Rating System

As a sustainably minded designer, you will want to get your client's home energy efficiency rating. This can be easily done by contacting a certified Home Energy Rating System (HERS) rater in your area. HERS is maintained by Residential Energy Services (RESNET), and is available in the United States and Canada. There are various tests that a HERS rater will perform. The audit observes how well the house performs as a system. Where are there air leaks? How well to do the walls insulate from the outside? At the end of the audit, the rater will produce a report with a list of suggestions to increase the energy efficiency of the home. How important is HERS? HERS provides specific data on the energy efficiency of a home. Many real estate listings include a HERS rating in the listing. The Appraisal Institute's new form, Form 820.04: Residential Green and Energy Efficient Addendum, includes the HES, or Home Energy Score, achieved with a HERS audit as part of the overall sustainability character of a property. Around the United States, various organizations promote HERS testing and knowledge; one such organization is the Northeast Energy Home Energy Rating System Alliance (NEHERS), which promotes HERS testing and knowledge in New England, New Jersey, and New York. NEHERS advocates for the use of the HERS test for all residences. The organization creates educational opportunities for real estate agents, designers, and builders. Although you are most likely working with only part of an existing home, having a HERS rating conducted for your client's home is the beginning of the conversation regarding insulating walls and ceilings and changing out energy-wasting windows. It is a great place to begin, as people can see exactly how efficient (or inefficient) a home is. The lower a house is on the HERS scale, the closer it is to net-zero energy use. A net-zero home creates as much or more energy than it consumes over one year.

Plan your sustainable project from a holistic perspective. This means getting all of the information you can about the existing conditions before you begin. It means educating yourself on overall approaches and setting goals prior to focusing on details.

When planning for a kitchen or bath remodel, you should begin with the big picture, such as the siting of a new addition to an existing home, and work down to the details such as specifying water-conserving toilets.

Best practices covered in this chapter:
1. Practice clean site management, including on-site recycling, and the creation of a healthy construction site.
2. Site your project for passive daylight, warmth, and cooling.
3. Plan for window location and the specification of windows with low U-value for energy conservation.
4. Specify of alternative wall types with high R-value construction to reduce heat loss.
5. Insulate outlets in walls appropriately to prevent air loss.
6. Plan carefully for the heating and cooling of new and renovated spaces.
7. Plan for the conservation of water and a look into the use of gray water.
8. Recommend on-demand water heaters to reduce energy draws.
9. Use deconstruction techniques rather than demolition to preserve embodied energy in materials and appliances with some use still in them.
10. Specify sustainable construction materials.
11. Design with lighting techniques that align themselves with energy conservation.
12. Look at the ENERGY STAR program and other sources of information on appliances and fixtures.
13. Plan for environmental stewardship: Establish recycling centers in the kitchen and cities with recycling/composting programs.

This list serves as an outline for the chapter, but it also can serve as an outline for your project. What will your best practices be? What will you add to or remove from this list?

THE PATH YOU TAKE—BEYOND CODE

There are many builders, architects, and designers who work beyond their state's energy code requirements. In Chapter 2 we quoted C. R. Herro of Meritage Homes, who said the company builds for projected code requirements; this is known as *future proofing*. When you follow

FIGURE 3.1 This kitchen by Green Hammer Design Build, based in Portland, Oregon, is made with locally made cabinets and reclaimed wood.
Courtesy of Green Hammer Design Build

the best practices outlined in this chapter, the resulting project will be one that surpasses local code compliance.

Green Hammer Design Build, located in Portland, Oregon, takes inspiration from passive house design along with a practice of making the soundest environmental building decisions it can make. (See "Interview: Alex Boetzel of Green Hammer Design Build.") The company's kitchen remodel can be seen in Figure 3.1. Its practice is constantly evolving as the company seeks to employ new techniques in green building.

Interview: Alex Boetzel of Green Hammer Design Build

Q: *How long have you been with Green Hammer?*

AB: Nine years.

Q: *From the looks of your website, you are busy.*

AB: Yes, we have many new residential and commercial projects currently.

Q: *We notice some beautiful solid wood cabinetry and furniture in your conference room. Did Green Hammer build these?*

(continued)

AB: We have a wood shop in the middle of our operations. We began as carpenters and have expanded to architectural and interior design, but we always come back to our dedication to fabrication of high-quality, custom, sustainable designs.

Q: *You have some enormous pieces of wood in your shop.*

AB: A few of those trees are from right around urban Portland. For natural reasons they had to be felled, and we were called in by the city to see if we were interested in using them. One is 150 years old.

Q: *What is Green Hammer's mission?*

AB: We are dedicated to creating buildings that are inspired by nature. Our presence as a design-build firm means that a client can achieve a green project from design inception to finished project.

Q: *Do the projects that Green Hammer builds begin with an energy code evaluation?*

AB: We design far beyond what a code states we should do. We look at concepts of passive house and net-zero homes as starting points and go from there.

Q: *If you had one thing to say to an emerging designer, what would it be?*

AB: Any measure toward green building is a step in the right direction. Don't hesitate to take the steps to make the most "green project" you can. It does make a difference to the environment.

Clean Site Management

Recognize that most of your kitchen and bath projects will be remodeling projects. Construction dust and debris can be harmful to the installers but also to the inhabitants of the home. Be sure to seal all ducts to the rest of the home from the renovation site. Provide adequate ventilation when painting and other finishing tasks take place to keep the IAQ as healthy as possible.

Every job site should maintain on-site reclamation areas for scrap construction materials. Pieces of framing lumber and plywood scrap should be collected and taken to a facility where they can be incorporated into new material.

Before recycling construction waste, identify who will accept it. This is important in designating types of waste to separate and in making arrangements for drop-off or delivery of materials.

The next list, taken from the "Construction Waste Recycling" portion of the Sustainable Sources website (www.sustainablesources.com), describes what can be recycled from a construction site.

- Appliances and fixtures
- Brush and trees
- Cardboard and paper
- Lumber and plywood (in reusable form)
- Masonry (in reusable form or as fill)
- Metals
- Plastics—numbered containers, bags and sheeting
- Roofing (in reusable form)
- Windows and doors

Work with the general contractor to install leftover insulation in areas where it is needed rather than throwing it away. Ask that the job site be cleaned every day and that work areas be well labeled and organized.

The donation of salvaged materials is discussed later in this list of best practices.

Siting Your Project

Depending on the location of your project, the direction of openings in the building envelope can greatly augment or hamper your attempts at getting good passive heating, cooling, and daylighting. In the northern hemisphere, the north-facing direction receives less direct light than the south-facing direction. East-facing walls benefit from morning light; west-facing walls benefit from afternoon light. In warmer parts of the northern hemisphere, the southern direction can be a source of heat gain (desired) in the winter and (undesired) in the summer. Figures 3.2 and 3.3 show the different paths of the sun depending on the hemisphere you are in.

Rarely does an existing space have windows and doors that are appropriately placed for any good application of the NKBA's planning guidelines. Paths of circulation in older homes often include movement to basement spaces and the backyard, which greatly hampers the design application of planning guidelines.

When planning for a new addition, consider these four points:

1. Warming from the prevalent west or east direction
2. Cooling from the northern or southern directions. In North America, for example, north-facing windows are sources of *cool* daylight for most of the year.
3. Southern exposure in the northern hemisphere can promote great passive daylight and warmth in the winter months but will need to be mitigated in the summer months.
4. Consider prevalent wind directions. From which direction does the home need protection? From which direction can the home harness passive cooling in warm months?

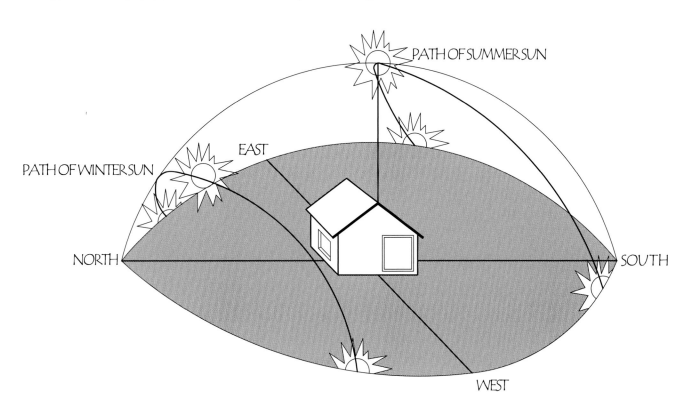

FIGURE 3.2 This diagram shows the sun's northern hemisphere path.
NKBA

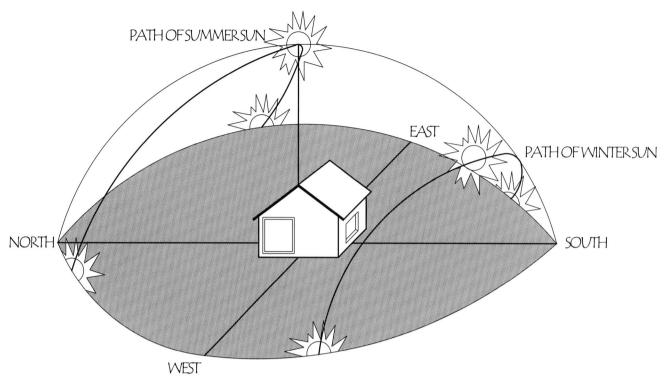

FIGURE 3.3 This diagram shows the sun's southern hemisphere path.
NKBA

Daylighting

Sustainable design needs to include daylight harvesting. The term "daylight harvesting" refers to the practice of maximizing the natural light entering the home. When planning for a kitchen or bath design project, a designer must consider both task illumination and ambient illumination. Task illumination is concerned with optimizing the amount of light so that a task can be performed easily; ambient light is concerned about overall light levels. Access to natural light creates balanced circadian rhythms. Every living thing has a circadian rhythm that follows the amount of daylight and responds to the sun's presence. Healthy circadian rhythms have been credited with better moods (particularly in months with less sunlight), better sleep, and better nutrition. The hormone melatonin that is stimulated by exposure to daylight is responsible for the better moods. The vitamin D created by exposure to daylight is responsible for the better nutrition. Interruptions of the circadian rhythm due to lack of daylight/sunlight have been blamed for conditions such as insomnia and depression. Good amounts of daylight in an interior mean that there is less reliance on electric sources. Daylight is a passive source of illumination; therefore, it is something we are really interested in having in our interiors. You can harvest daylight during daytime hours by installing windows above countertops but below upper cabinets. Figure 3.4 shows how to design the countertop work surface so that it is illuminated throughout the day, reducing the need for electric lighting. There are two examples of this. The Breeze-Kondylis kitchen (Figure 3.5) has windows installed in this way, while the Carriage Way house (Figure 3.6) has glass block to provide this type of daylighting while also providing privacy.

Solar

A zero-energy home or a net-zero home creates as much power as it consumes. When considering a green approach to any project, the installation and use of a passive and renewable energy source should be at the top of the list. There are a few different approaches to harnessing solar energy, but the two we examine are solar collecting and the use of a photovoltaic system.

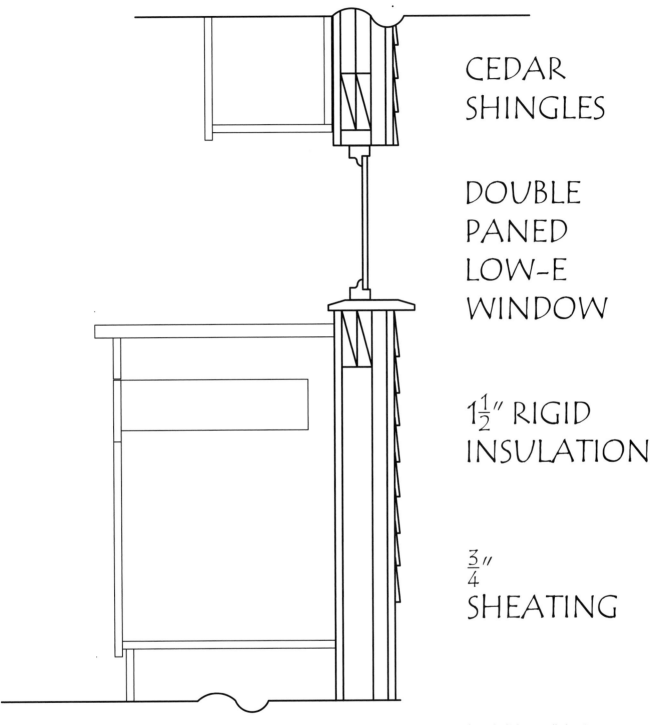

CEDAR
SHINGLES

DOUBLE
PANED
LOW-E
WINDOW

$1\frac{1}{2}''$ RIGID
INSULATION

$\frac{3}{4}''$
SHEATING

FIGURE 3.4 Consider designing a window that will provide passive lighting onto the kitchen countertop from daylight. Install electric sources, such as light-emitting diode (LED) under-cabinet lights for illumination as needed.
NKBA

One of the most popular solar collecting methods is solar hot water. It is important to understand that this is an assistive method for most parts of the world; it is not the main source of hot water for most homes. A solar collector warms the water in its tankand then stores it in a tank separate from the conventional hot water heater. A simple monitor notes the temperature on the solar tank. When the temperature dips during cooler months, the hot water system relies on the conventional hot water heater. Solar hot water systems are straightforward

FIGURE 3.5 Windows between the upper and lower cabinets in the Kondylis-Breeze kitchen provide passive lighting during daylight hours.
NKBA

FIGURE 3.6 Glass block between the upper and lower cabinets in this kitchen provides passive lighting during daylight hours.
NKBA

and relatively easy to install. Consider consulting with a builder well versed in sustainable building systems.

A home cannot become a net-zero home without creating its own energy. Photovoltaic panels (or solar panels) are installed on a home's roof to collect radiant energy from the sun. Location is important. Climates with considerable sunlight do much better with fewer panels than those in wetter climates. This does not mean that a net-zero home is not possible in Seattle, Washington. It just means that more higher-performance panels will be required.

WINDOW SPECIFICATION

It is important to understand the climate in which your project is to be constructed. In the Northwest, where it rains most of autumn, winter, and spring, it is easy to consider that "more is better" when it comes to daylight. But before you design for a north-facing picture window in the breakfast area of your client's kitchen, ask yourself, "What type of daylight is coming in?" For example, in the Northwest, light from the north is very cool and gray. Choosing colors for the interior can warm the quality of the light.

When looking for windows, you should specify those with a low U-value. U-value is a measure of heat loss through a building component, such as a wall, floor, roof, door, or window. Windows are where we see U-value used the most because window manufacturers publish the U-values for their products. Also, thanks to the ENERGY STAR program designers can easily select a suitable product. The National Fenestration Rating Council (NFRC) publishes ratings to help with the selection of windows. Most windows achieve a U-value between 0.20 and 1.20. The lower the U-value, the more energy efficient the window is.

Windows should also protect your clients from heat gain. In the Northwest, this is not too great an issue, but in the late summer months, heat through windows is felt even in that climate, particularly through windows with southern and western exposures. The solar heat gain coefficient (SHGC) is a number between 0 and 1. The lower the number, the better the window is at reducing solar heat gain and creating thermal comfort for your clients. Figure 3.7 shows a window energy label from the NFRC. A lower SHGC means less energy will be needed to cool the interior during warm weather. Figure 3.8 shows how the U-value and the SHGC work on a home's exterior.

Both U-value and the SHGC are required to be published for all windows that are endorsed by the Energy Star program. The ratings are an important place to begin when specifying new windows. Interestingly, according to the NFRC, another value, air leakage (AL), is an optional rating. As a designer you will want to get an idea of the AL rating of the windows you are specifying. Like the other two window ratings, a lower AL is preferred and falls between 0.1 and 0.3 for most windows.

Replacing windows on a remodeling project can be a tough decision to make. Due to the expense of new windows and their installation, homeowners can decide to utilize the existing windows. This is, of course, unfortunate, as older windows are big sources of interior heat loss and heat gain. For this reason, many incentive plans have been established to help offset the cost of window replacement. The Efficient Windows Collaborative (www.efficientwindows .org) provides a list of incentive plans to help client save money.

WALLS AND INSULATION

Green building focuses on how well a building performs. Earlier green building techniques tended to focus only on creating energy and saving resources. These are great concepts! But when you add building methods that can keep your energy in and the climate you are protecting against out, you have a much better chance of lightening the load of a home's energy consumption. Green builders use this saying: *Build tight and ventilate right.*

World's Best Window Co.
Series "2000"
Casement
Vinyl Clad Wood Frame
Double Glazing•Argon Fill•Low E
XYZ-X-1-00001-00001

ENERGY PERFORMANCE RATINGS

U-Factor (U.S. / I-P)	Solar Heat Gain Coefficient
0.35	**0.32**

ADDITIONAL PERFORMANCE RATINGS

Visible Transmittance	Air Leakage (U.S. / I-P)
0.51	**≤0.3**

Manufacturer stipulates that these ratings conform to applicable NFRC procedures for determining whole product performance. NFRC ratings are determined for a fixed set of environmental conditions and a specific product size. NFRC does not recommend any product and does not warrant the suitability of any product for any specific use. Consult manufacturer's literature for other product performance information.
www.nfrc.org

FIGURE 3.7 The labeling from the National Fenestration Rating Council explains the U-value and SHGC of windows to help consumers make decisions.
Courtesy of National Fenestration Rating Council

Recently, great developments in alternative exterior wall construction methods mean that there are a few ways to create well-insulated walls. Whichever you choose, the important factors will be the same: Reduce air leaks, increase the R-value or insulation in your walls, and specify a system that works with your client's budget.

The R-value over an area such as a wall or a ceiling is a determination of thermal resistance. Depending on where your project is located, you can determine what the local code is for

Understanding the NFRC Label

National Fenestration Rating Council®

Solar Heat Gain Coefficient measures the amount of OUTDOOR heat that can enter a room. The lower the number, the lower the potential for wasted cooling expenses.

Air Leakage measures how much air will enter a room through the product. The lower the number, the lower the potential for draft through the product.

U-factor measures the heat from INSIDE a room that can escape. The lower the number the lower the potential for wasted heating expenses.

Visible Transmittance measures how much natural light can come into a room -- a HIGH number means more natural light.

This image mirrors the four sections of the certified NFRC Label, providing the consumer with visual illustrations of what the label ratings mean. More in-depth information on the NFRC Label and purchasing the best possible windows, visit
www.WindowRatings.org

FIGURE 3.8 How U-value and SHGC affect the thermal and energy efficiency within a residence
Courtesy of National Fenestration Rating Council

the R-value required on your project. But in keeping with the perspective of kitchen and bath design and the subject of remodeling, insulation retrofits are an important part of your client's project. See the return on investment discussion in Chapter 2.

Green Wall Construction

To begin the topic on alternative walls, we'll look at Meritage Homes again. On Earth Day 2013, Meritage Homes established a pilot program called MGV5 that created six homes using insulated concrete panels (ICPs). This was groundbreaking for three reasons:

1. The houses looked like other houses in the area.
2. The ICP panels were created nearby (local economy, less transport fuel necessary).
3. This type of wall is superior to conventional wall construction in energy efficiency.[1]

Insulated Concrete Panels

ICPs are prefabricated (made off-site) wall components. The panels are made of structural steel reinforcement, concrete sheathing, and expanded polystyrene foam in the middle of those two sheets (see Figure 3.9). An ICP wall system is very well insulated, and the installation time is much shorter than that of a traditional stick framing wall system. In much the same way commercial buildings are built with a tilt-up wall construction system, an ICP wall system comes to the site ready to install. You can see this in Figure 3.10. This method is particularly

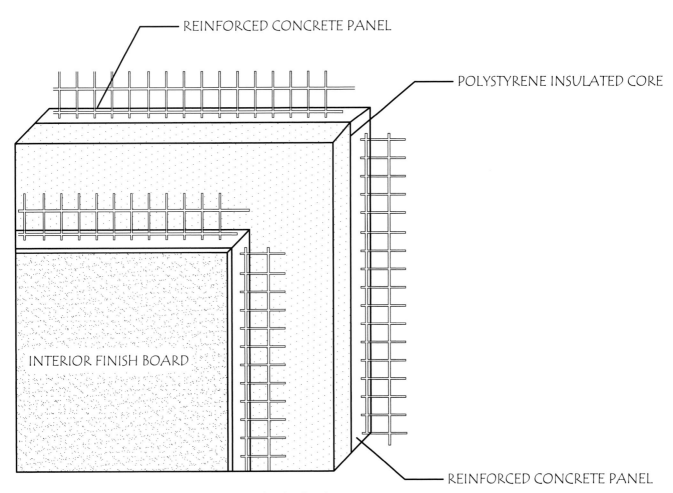

FIGURE 3.9 An insulated concrete panel is heavily insulated and ready to go.

NKBA

FIGURE 3.10 ICPs delivered to a job site make construction go quickly and efficiently.
Courtesy of Meritage Homes

helpful when remodeling in wetter climates or during cooler months when the time frame to enclose the building is shorter. To find a contractor who can help with the installation of an ICP wall system, research green builders in your project's area. Installer experience is an important part of your project's success.

Structural Insulated Panels

Structural insulated panels (SIPs), like ICPs, are prefabricated wall units made custom for each project. They are a sandwich of oriented strand board (OSB) on either side of a layer of expanded polystyrene foam or EPS. (See Figure 3.11 to understand how a SIPs wall is constructed.) The formaldehyde level of the OSB used should be checked. SIPs panels boast many of the same attributes of ICP panels but tend to be more affordable and lighter in weight. Check with a green builder about this wall system, which can cut construction time and energy costs for clients.

Advanced Framing

The term "advanced framing" refers to methods that improve on conventional wood-stud-and-sheathing construction, which is the predominant way our homes and our additions are

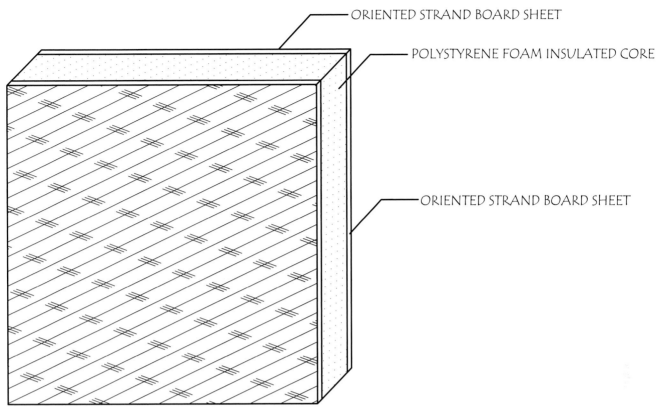

ORIENTED STRAND BOARD SHEET

POLYSTYRENE FOAM INSULATED CORE

ORIENTED STRAND BOARD SHEET

FIGURE 3.11 Structurally insulated panel cross-section
NKBA

created. Figure 3.12 diagrams one method of advanced framing. Some ideas that fall under the category:

- Use wood members carefully to maximize the material and minimize waste.
- Use 2- by 6-inch studs spaced 24 inches apart (saves more wood than 2- by 4-inch studs spaced 18 inches apart and allows for more insulation).
- Apply rigid insulation to the outside to prevent conductivity in exterior walls.
- Utilize staggered-stud construction to increase the mass of an exterior wall and improve the insulation of the interior
- Use recycled steel studs (but with rigid insulation on the exterior to cut down on conductivity).
- Recognize that wood is a resource that should be conserved wherever it is possible. Consider the use of engineered wood products over large dimensional lumber that requires the felling of larger, older (and rarer) trees.

Regardless of when your client's home was built, the best advice you can give when considering energy savings is to increase the insulation in the home. Adding insulation to existing, older homes greatly increases the R-value of walls and reduces the number of heat exchanges in the space and the entire home.

Traditional batt or fiberglass insulation is familiar and very affordable. It is easily rolled over attic floors (when floors are not in use) or into cavities between studs in exterior walls. This is the traditional way of insulating an exterior wall (see Figure 3.13).

Blown-in insulation (see Figure 3.14) is relatively easy and is commonly done to existing structures. Cellulose-based products have less off gassing than the petroleum-based foam used in foamed-in insulation. If you are looking for a product with recycled content, some options use recycled denim fiber that has been treated with fire retardants and insecticides. Do your research; refer to Chapter 5 and a third-party evaluator, such as the Pharos Project Index (www.pharosproject.net), for information about how green a product is.

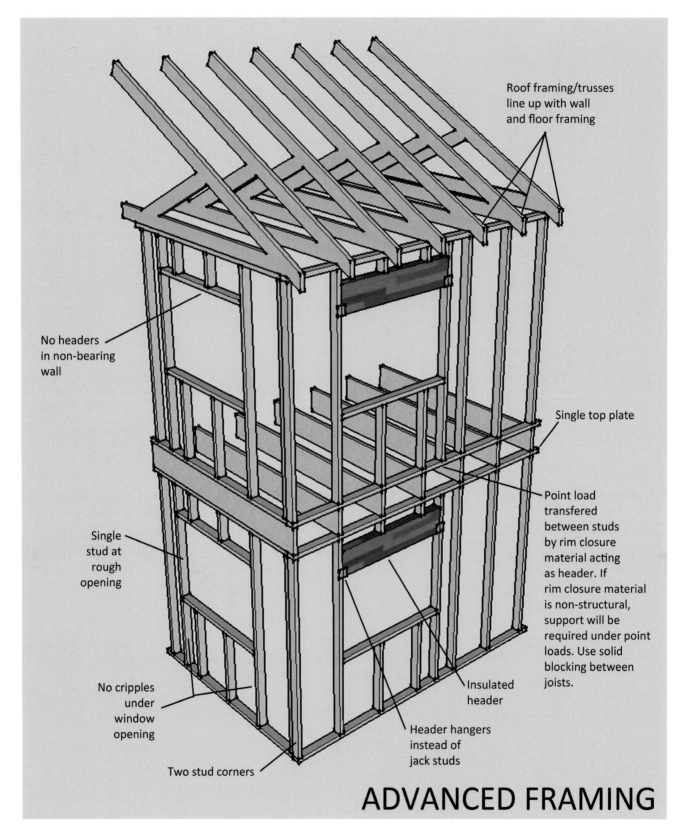

Roof framing/trusses line up with wall and floor framing

No headers in non-bearing wall

Single top plate

Point load transfered between studs by rim closure material acting as header. If rim closure material is non-structural, support will be required under point loads. Use solid blocking between joists.

Single stud at rough opening

No cripples under window opening

Insulated header

Header hangers instead of jack studs

Two stud corners

ADVANCED FRAMING

FIGURE 3.12 This approach to advanced framing shows insulation at the window headers and a conservative use of materials. *NKBA*

FIGURE 3.13 Wall with batt insulation

NKBA (Photo by Amanda Davis)

FIGURE 3.14 Blown-in insulation installation using recycled cotton
NKBA (Photo by Amanda Davis)

FIGURE 3.15 CertainTeed spray-foam insulation installation
Courtesy Spray Polyurethane Foam Alliance

Like blown-in insulation, foam insulation goes into existing walls with relative ease, as shown in Figure 3.15. Its ability to conform around nooks and crannies makes it an ideal product for reducing leaks in and around electrical outlets, windows, and door frames. By nature, foam insulation does not permit airflow, so IAQ in nonvented spaces can become poor. This is important to consider in attics, for example. Foam does not become compressed over time, as do batt and blown-in types of insulation. There are tax incentives for installing foam and other types of insulation in a remodel.

It is very important to reduce the number of air leaks in a home. The loss of warm air in the winter and cooled air in the summer is just wasted energy, pure and simple. In the 1980s, the use of plastic house wrap became popular to reduce the number of air leaks and create a tight building envelope. What resulted was buildings that were very tight but lacked controlled air exchangers. This resulted in *sick building syndrome* for many homeowners: increased allergies, chemical sensitivity, and fatigue. Coupled with the use of toxin-producing materials, such as conventional carpet, homes became incredibly toxic environments. (See Chapter 4, "Indoor Air Quality.") Today green building shores up homes with walls that have an R-value that exceeds that of the local code and utilizes air exchangers that will bring fresh air into the home and send stale air out. This approach keeps the conditioned air inside, where it is meant to be.

Wall Outlet Insulation
The insulation of outlets in the wall is part of the weatherization process necessary for a high-performance remodel. Traditionally, large holes are left behind the faceplate of an

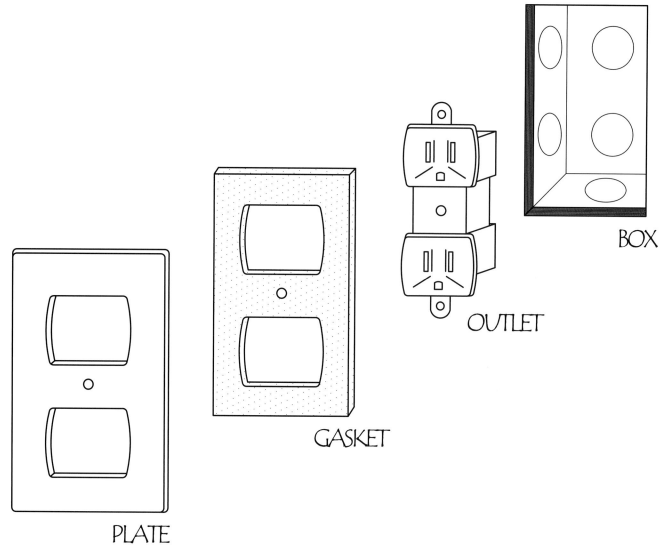

PLATE

GASKET

OUTLET

BOX

FIGURE 3.16 Wall plate, gasket, outlet, and box
NKBA

electrical outlet or a light switch. The technique in Figure 3.16 shows how to prevent air flow at an outlet. Weatherizing an outside wall against heat loss through outlets and switches is easily done by installing a gasket around the electrical box.

Take the insulation against heat loss (or cool-air loss in warmer months) a step further and use caulk or spray-foam insulation to seal the gaps around the electrical box and the finish wall prior to installing the faceplate.

HEATING AND COOLING

The highest energy draw in the home is energy used to create climatic comfort in the interior. This takes the form of heat in the cold months and cooling in the warm months.

A HERS rating includes an audit of your client's heating and cooling systems. An old furnace, particularly one in a detached garage funneling warmed air across uninsulated metal ductwork, will be tagged for an upgrade. Interesting enough is the fact that a detached garage is best for IAQ within a home. (Parking a carbon-monoxide-producing machine within a home is worth rethinking.) There is more to planning and advising clients on how to heat and cool their new kitchens and bathrooms than just one, simple answer. Budget can and should play a role. Understanding zonal heat is important as well.

According to the RESNET website, a home with a HERS index of 70 is 30 percent more energy efficient than a standard new home.(www.resnet.us/hers-index). Conversely, an older home with a rating of 130 is 30 percent more *inefficient* than a standard new home.

According to the *LEED for Homes Reference Guide*, duct leakage accounts for 15 to 25 percent of total heating and cooling use in new homes.[2] If all ducts are contained within the insulated interior of the home, duct leakage is not considered an issue. Duct leakage becomes an issue when ducts are located in crawl spaces or within any uninsulated area.

Consider recommending a radiant heat system in renovated areas if appropriate. A radiant-heated floor can be constructed using a mat of conductive filaments under the finished floor. Conductive flooring materials, such as ceramic tile, work best. Do your research to ensure that use of a radiant system does not invalidate the warranty for various flooring materials.

Zonal heating and cooling is a concept whereby interiors are designed with user-controlled areas to provide custom thermal comfort and to conserve energy. Consider this concept when designing your project. Place thermostats for individual zones in easy-to-reach locations, typically near the light controls.

There are whole house systems that can aid in this zonal thermal control plan. Consult with a specialist to get an idea of pricing and other information. Whole-house systems can be used to control lighting, music, and communication within the home.

Heat pumps are heating and cooling devices that replace conventional forced-air furnaces and traditional air conditioners. A heat pump transfers heat from a colder area to a hotter area using mechanical energy. Heat pumps are engineered to be much more efficient than forced-air systems because they work with the existing air in the space rather than creating new warmed air. They can often be a great solution when running new ductwork to an addition proves difficult.

Heat Recovery Ventilators

Most homes have a simple exhaust system installed: fans in spaces where the air needs to be replaced, such as bathrooms and kitchens, serve to pull used air out of the home. But what about that air being conditioned? It is wasteful to send cooled air out of the home in the summer and warmed air out in the winter. The focus on high performance in a building or addition means fewer air leaks and a tighter home. Conventional means of ventilation (already in question in regard to performance) are not enough to keep good air coming in and poor air going out. A heat recovery ventilator (HRV) can provide recover between 60 and 80 percent of heat from warmed air. The concept is that as the cool air moves in to the home (during cooler months), it is warmed against the used but much warmer stale air. The process is reversed in the summer months. It is a straightforward method of optimizing conditioned air. This process can be seen in Figure 3.17.

Energy Recovery Ventilators

Like the HRV, an energy recovery ventilator (ERV) helps to condition fresh air as it moves into the home, whether it is to be cooled or warmed. An ERV takes it a step further and traps energy from the humidity of the air exchange. Traditionally ERVs have been recommended for use in warm, tropical climates; they are a great help to the cooling system, which does not have to work as hard to get the moisture out of the cooled air it is delivering to the interior. The management of humidity by an ERV will support any furnace, which could extend the life of a forced air system.

Chapter 4 discusses the benefits that ERVs can bring to IAQ.

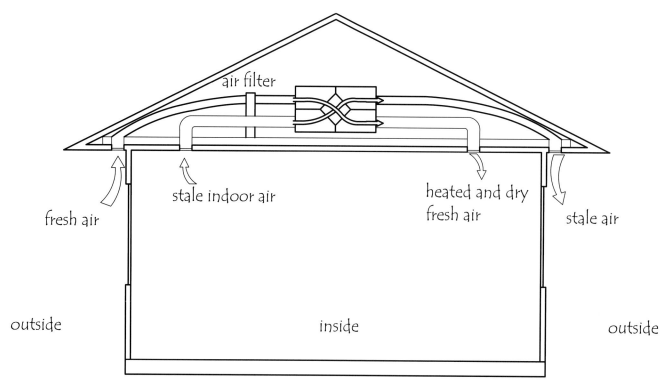

FIGURE 3.17 Air exchange with a heat recovery ventilator
NKBA

WATER CONSERVATION AND DISTRIBUTION

According to the Environmental Protection Agency (EPA), 36 states face water shortages at the time of this book's publication. Single-family homes use more than half of the available treated water in the United States. And according to their website, an average family can easily consume more than 300 gallons of water a day.[3] You can see the breakdown of water use in a typical home in Figure 3.18.

The EPA sponsors the WaterSense program to aid designers and consumers in the selection of water-saving plumbing fixtures, particularly toilets. WaterSense is a great nonprofit third-party evaluator. According to their website, the average American home (presumably with two toilets) can save 13,000 of gallons of water a year.[4] The site offers easy links to see if the municipality in which your project is located offers any rebate to add incentive to your choice for replacing and installing water-saving devices. The city of Hillsboro, Oregon, for example, offers a rebate of $75 per toilet replaced or installed up to two toilets. That's $150 that can be used elsewhere in the project, and it really helps to motivate clients.

As mentioned in Chapter 1, first-generation low-flow toilets were problematic, but thanks to new designs and technology from companies such as Kohler and Toto, the current generation functions as well as old toilets did.

WaterSense also labels bathroom sink faucets and showerheads. Look for the WaterSense label to help you make choices in your project.

In addition to saving water, you will want to consider the distribution of water in your project. New innovations in cross-linked polyethylene (PEX) plastic tubing makes it a great alternative to copper pipe installation. PEX saves money because it does not need to be welded. It can be maneuvered around stubborn structural obstacles and it can easily work with a boiler if you want to consider a radiant heating system for your client. Another problem with copper pipe is that it is very conductive; it loses heat easily.

On-demand heated water is one of the most important steps a person can take to creating a greener project. Conventional tank water heaters continually heat between 20 and 80 gallons

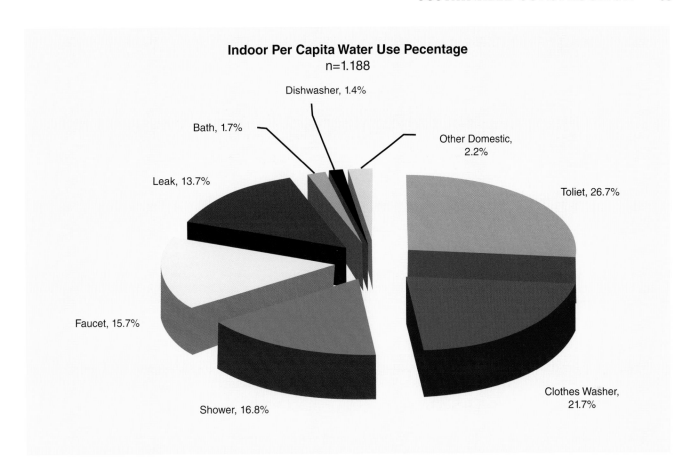

FIGURE 3.18 Water use in the home
Courtesy of Water Research Foundation

of water for consumption when needed. This means that the water is being heated at night and when the users are away on vacation. This is a huge waste of energy. A tankless or on-demand water heater heats water only when demand is there. Such heaters are mounted to a wall, which frees up floor space. Although the initial cost is considerable, clients will save up to 30 percent of energy costs from heating water. Also, in a large remodel, you can place more than one tankless water heater close to where it is needed. This will cut down on waste of cold water in the pipes that needs to be sent down the drain in order to get to the warmed water.

Still want to use a tank-style water heater? Ask for a California Builder's model, which is heavily insulated to reduce heat loss. Also be sure to look for the energy factor (EF) on the appliance. Tank water heaters are rated by their EF. Look for an EF close to 1. This is published information, much like the number you will look for regarding window selections.

One very simple way to cut down on energy loss in plumbing is to insulate the hot water pipes, especially if they run in unconditioned spaces.

The use of graywater is currently not widely practiced by many green designers and builders. Although most plumbing codes do not allow it, there is a movement to plumb ahead for it in new construction. As mentioned in Chapter 2, water that has already been used in laundry, showering, and dishwashers defines gray water. Today some municipalities allow it to be used for irrigation. Not surprisingly, water-starved areas like Arizona have guidelines on the books for consumers who want to use gray water to water their yards and gardens.[5]

Collecting rainwater for irrigation is an excellent way to harvest a natural resource that can help maintain a garden or a yard. Many at-home chefs have herb and vegetable gardens. Figure 3.19 shows a water cistern in Portland.

FIGURE 3.19 Garden rainwater cistern
Duehmig-Greisar Residence, Portland, OR. Photo by Amanda Davis

FIGURE 3.20 This Caroma Profile smart toilet uses graywater from hand washing to flush.
Courtesy of Sustainable Solutions

Currently graywater–fed toilets are in the experimental stages. A specialized toilet comes with a repository for water used to wash hands (Figure 3.20). The toilet captures the used or graywater from an integrated sink and faucet combination. The wastewater fills the tank and is used to flush the toilet.

Point-of-Use Water Heaters

How long do you wait for warm water to reach your shower: thirty seconds? an entire minute? Even with a low-flow shower head that has a 2.5-gallon-per-minute (gpm) flow, that 30 seconds means 1.25 gallons down the drain. Shower every day, and that adds up to 465 gallons per person in the home annually. It isn't just a poorly functioning water heater that is to blame. Uninsulated hot water pipes and long runs from the water heater (even with an on-demand tankless fixture) to the bathroom add to the wasted water. Consider speaking with your client about a point-of-use hot water heater, which creates hot water instantly while your main water heater gets to work. These are discussed at length in Chapter 5.

Trapping Heat

When you consider the amount of energy required to warm the water that is delivered to our showers and tubs, washing machines, and dishwashers, it makes little sense not to try to recover some of the energy remaining as heat in the wastewater. One of the simplest and most straightforward energy-gleaning techniques is a drain water heat recovery system (DHR) (see Figure 3.21). A DHR is comprised of a heat exchanger that wraps around the cold water supply to the hot water tank. The heat of the wastewater is transferred to the cold water source, which raises the temperature of the water before it enters the hot water tank. A DHR can be used with a conventional tank water heater or a tankless one. (A point-of-source water heater is discussed in Chapter 5.)

DECONSTRUCTION

According to the deconstruction services at the ReBuilding Center in Portland, Oregon, a non-profit organization that specializes in reused building materials, the implementation of deconstruction over demolition on a remodeling project is one-to-one cost. Many believe the practice of deconstruction far exceeds the cost of a Dumpster. What is deconstruction and why is it a good idea?

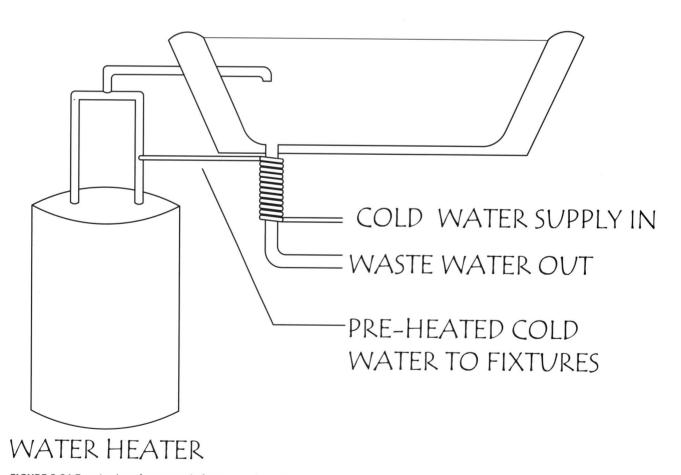

COLD WATER SUPPLY IN

WASTE WATER OUT

PRE-HEATED COLD WATER TO FIXTURES

WATER HEATER

FIGURE 3.21 Trapping heat from water before it goes down the drain
NKBA

According to the Deconstruction Institute, *deconstruction* is defined as follows:

> Deconstruction is a process of building disassembly in order to recover the maximum amount of materials for their highest and best reuse. Reuse is the preferred outcome because it requires less energy, raw materials, and pollution than recycling does in order to continue the life of the material. As a consequence of deconstruction, there are also many opportunities for recycling other materials along the way.[6]

The recovery of building materials can be done by local deconstruction services. It is crucial to preserve the embodied energy of these materials. Habitat for Humanity is behind the ReStore program that provides deconstruction and salvage services for consumers and builders. There are ReStore locations in every state in the United States. ReStore is also represented in Canada, Guam, and Puerto Rico.

According to Metro, a government agency in Portland, Oregon, that aids in the disposal of materials taken from construction sites, Oregonians created 3 million tons of garbage in 2012. Twenty percent of that was construction and demolition waste. That is 600,000 tons of waste from our related professions. If the state fabricators, designers, architects, and builders were to reduce this amount by just 10 percent, 60,000 tons of waste could be diverted from landfills, and the embodied energy of that waste could live on in new projects.[7]

Look for local sources and salvage yards that perform this important task for any project. You should be able to secure a free estimate that will aid you and your client in making budgetary decisions. Although the materials and other items that are recovered from your project likely will not be exchanged for cash, the company should provide donation values that your clients use as tax write-offs.

In cases where your project's contractor can utilize regraded lumber, you can save embodied energy by using building materials that have been salvaged from other places. The new opening in Figure 3.22 shows a header created from salvaged lumber. To be used in this manner, lumber must be regraded by an engineer. Check with your local building salvage yard to ask about this important building material.

Donation of Salvaged Materials

As described, your project's implementation of deconstruction will render building materials that can be reused in other projects. Habitat for Humanity ReStores sell toilets, sinks, cabinetry, and all kinds of building materials and components that are removed from existing homes (see Figure 3.23). What about old appliances or materials that are not accepted by a salvage yard? In Portland, Metro works to ensure that the embodied energy in these old components and materials can be put into a recycling system. In your project's area, find an organization that specializes in this kind of information.

Lead

Lead was a common component in paint and adhesives prior to 1978. The federal government banned the use of lead-based paint in 1978; some states banned its use before then. If your project is in a home built before 1940 there is an 87 percent chance that there is lead in the home. If the project was built between 1960 and 1977, there is only a 24 percent chance of lead in the home. If your project in in a home that was built before 1978, your client's contractor must be in compliance with the EPA's 2010 measures to curb lead poisoning.[8] The measures are part of Subpart E–Residential Property Renovation. This EPA requirement outlines specific activities that must be conducted during a residential renovation to create an environment that is devoid of lead-based paint hazards. Lead dust can collect on surfaces when lead paint, even from many decades ago, is disturbed. The measure stipulates that contractors must be certified and trained in the implementation of lead-safe work practices. Additionally, contractors doing work (including, but not limited to, renovation, repair, and painting) on projects that are determined to have lead on the site are to be EPA certified. These requirements became fully effective on April 22, 2010.

FIGURE 3.22 New opening framed with salvaged lumber
NKBA

FIGURE 3.23 Salvaged cabinetry donated from a remodeling project: This cabinet can be reused in a storage room or garage.
Courtesy of Habitat for Humanity ReStore, Portland, Oregon; photo by Harvey Thomas

Lead poisoning affects everyone but is particularly damaging to small children, whose developing bodies are more susceptible to lead poisoning. Due to their small size, poisoning is possible with low levels of lead inhalation or ingestion. Children's height also places them around lead-containing dust at windowsills, and they may pick up paint chips and ingest them.

To be certified, contractors must complete the Lead Safe Program. (Figure 3.24). You must be able to advise your client on how to find a contractor who is familiar with the construction of older homes and the hazards of lead on a project. A Lead Safe–certified contractor will take the important steps to minimize dust on a project and keep the building site as clean as possible. From the EPA's website (http://cfpub.epa.gov/flpp/searchrrp_firm.htm), you can locate a Lead Safe–certified contractor in your project's area.

FIGURE 3.24 The EPA provides certification for lead removal work.
Courtesy of EPA

Lighting Choices and Design

Planning a well-designed and beautiful lighting scheme is important for any kitchen or bath project. To put all the time, money, and labor into a beautiful renovation only to have it improperly illuminated is a terrible waste.

Kitchen and bath lighting is both crucial for the functional aspects of the space as well as the aesthetics. No other rooms in the home (other than a hobby shop with power tools) poses a greater risk for injury than kitchens and bathrooms. This next section gives designers pointers on how to plan for energy and resource conservation in you lighting scheme.

Lamping is important for energy conservation. Where author Amanda Davis, NCIDQ, teaches, the school plans for 10 percent or fewer of lamps (the industry term for "bulb") to be halogen or incandescent. (Halogen is a high-performance option in the incandescent family.) This means, for example, that you should reserve the use of incandescent lamping for your accent layer: where a piece of art needs fine illumination with a great point source or some flattering, warm light at the bathroom mirror. In all other places, you should use high-efficiency sources: fluorescent, LED, and in some places, ceramic metal halide (which today are used only in track applications because of the need for an attached ballast). There is concern over the presence of mercury in fluorescent sources. Proper disposal of fluorescent lamps is necessary to prevent contamination of landfills, surface soil, and water. For this reason, many green-minded designers do not use fluorescent sources. Look at Figure 3.25 for different lamp shapes and technology. Figure 3.26 is an excellent example of using passive daylighting in a bathroom by designing a skylight into the room.

Residential lighting should look to the retail sector, where commercial energy code restrictions have curtailed the use of incandescent lighting and new, innovative, and flattering sources are employed.

Controls and the placement of controls are just as important as lighting choices. Preset dimmers that allow for a constant 10 percent decrease in the amount of light output (lamps discharged at 90 percent or less) will lengthen the life of any lamp and reduce landfill waste. Placing controls in easy-to-reach places will encourage users to turn lights off when not in use. Motion sensors are great for walk-in closets and storage areas of the home where the area is not illuminated for long.

Last, consider your fixture choices. It's back to ENERGY STAR for sourcing green choices in fixtures. All ENERGY STAR sources are lamped with fluorescent, LED, or ceramic metal halide lamps. The program lists hundreds of compliant fixtures, and many have recycled content in them such as recycled steel.

Lamp choice, control placement, the use of dimmers, and the selection of green fixtures will add to the sustainability approach in your project.

FIGURE 3.25 LED lamps are energy efficient and have the longest life of all electric light sources used residentially.
Creative Commons 3.0, Geoffrey.landis at en.wikipedia

FIGURE 3.26 Daylighting in a bathroom
Courtesy of Squaredeal Remodeling, Portland, Oregon

SPACE PLANNING

A kitchen dedicated to sustainable practices will look just about the same as any kitchen but will have a few characteristics that set it apart. In the NKBA Professional Resource Library volume *Kitchen Planning* there is thoughtful discussion of the importance of creating a layout that encourages recycling and composting. Specific space planning layouts are provided.

Recycling programs vary from city to city so plan the recycling center accordingly. For example, some cities require that glass be separated from other materials while some municipalities allow all items go in the same container, to be sorted later at transfer station.

Specific bins and accessories for recycling and composting are available from cabinetry companies.

Recycling Center

The two most important considerations for locating the recycling center are ease of use and ease of removal. Do your clients have any physical limitations that would get in the way of taking out the recycling? Be mindful not to specify bins that are too large. It is better to have to make more trips to the main container or sidewalk than risk injury from lifting an overly heavy container.

Note that in Kitchen A shown in Figures 3.27 and 3.28, the recycling center is located near the door to the garage. The dimensions are small and are contained in a 24-inch-wide cabinet. There is room for three bins: garbage, glass, and combined.

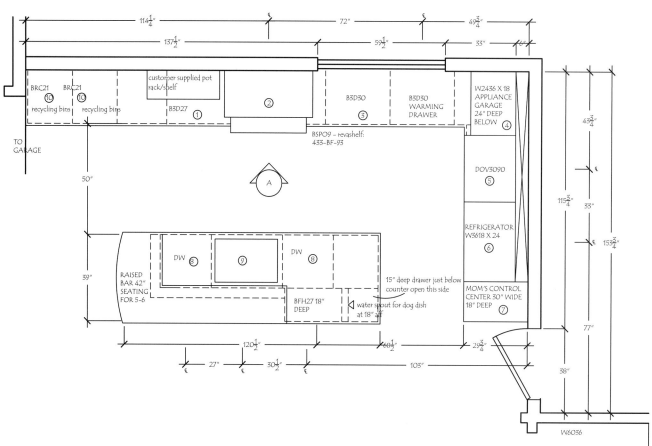

FIGURE 3.27 Floor plan Kitchen A
NKBA

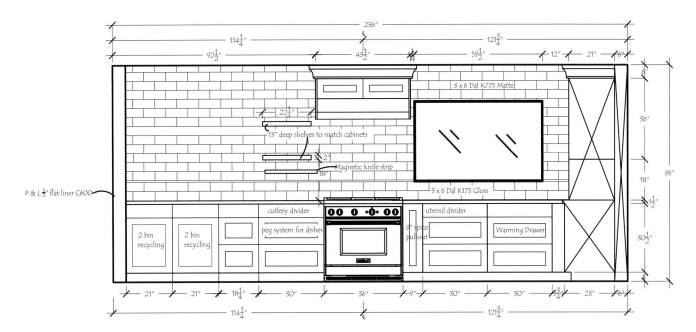

FIGURE 3.28 Elevation Kitchen A
NKBA

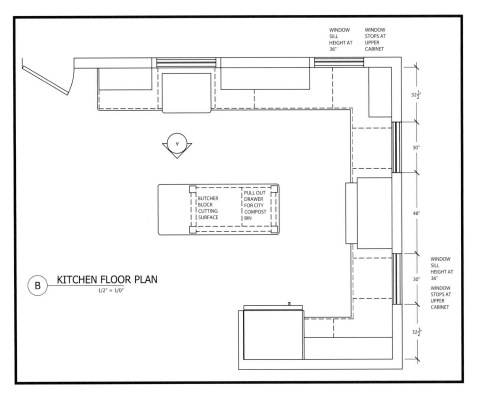

FIGURE 3.29 Floor plan Kitchen B
NKBA

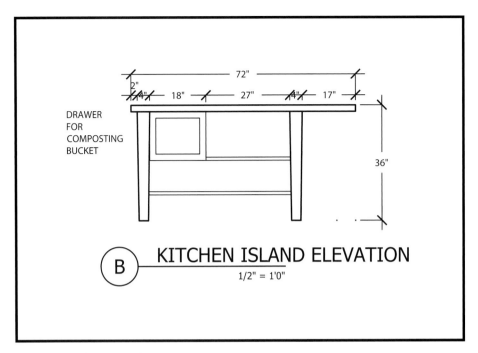

FIGURE 3.30 Elevation Kitchen B
NKBA

Recycling Center Plus Composting

Kitchen B, shown in Figures 3.29 and 3.30, has the recycling center conveniently located near the cleanup/prep center. The interior dimensions of the cabinetry are larger than the example in Kitchen A. The bins are small and are contained in a 24-inch-wide cabinet. There is room for three bins: garbage, glass, and combined. The city in which this kitchen is located provides for curbside composting. The city provides bins for composting that are 14 inches long by 9 inches wide by 10 inches high. The drawer in the island was designed with a depth that could accommodate the bin. This is a great location as food scraps can be placed directly in the bin. The island is topped with a butcher block counter material.

SUMMARY

The construction and remodeling sectors of our economy have an opportunity to move in a sustainable direction with a focus on designing for benefit, not austerity. Designing with the perspective of saving materials, saving energy, and saving water means saving money for your client. As designers move ahead with careful choices and responsible practices, it is more important than ever that we see ourselves as stewards of the environment. This stewardship demands that we be educators. Education is the best tool our industry has to be more mindful of the environment. Recommended building codes are a place to begin. Stay involved in the sustainable design community by attending webinars or other learning opportunities offered by nonprofit organizations, such as 365GreenExpo, the NKBA, or the National Association of Home Builders (NAHB), which are dedicated to sustainable design education.

There is a real opportunity to create a specialization in a field that is quickly becoming the expected norm. Designers who spend the time to educate their clients to future proof their home are simultaneously future-proofing their careers.

REVIEW QUESTIONS

1. What is a HERS rating, and why is it important? (See "Home Energy Rating System" page 62)
2. What does the term "future-proofing" mean? (See "The Path You Take–Beyond Code" page 44)
3. What does it mean when a house is "net zero" in energy use? (See "Solar" page 48)
4. What are two criteria for determining the energy-conserving character of windows? (See "Window Specification" page 52)
5. List two advantages to using SIPs or ICP walls on an addition or new construction. (See "Green Wall Construction" page 56)

ENDNOTES

1. "Meritage Homes' MGV5 Pilot Include Solar and SIPs Option" (May 1, 2013). Available at www.greenbuildermedia.com/blog/meritage-homes-mgv5-pilot-include-solar-and-sips-options; accessed June 20, 2014.
2. US Green Building Council, *LEED for Homes Reference Guide* (Washington, DC: US Green Building Council, 2009), p. XX
3. See under "Water in Daily Life" at www.epa.gov/watersense/our_water/water_use_today.html; accessed June 13, 2014.
4. See www.epa.gov/WaterSense/products/toilets.html.
5. Arizona Department of Environmental Quality, *Using Gray Water at Home: The Arizona Department of Enviromnmental Quality's Guide to Complying with the Type 1 General Permit.* Publication No. C 10-04 (February 2011). Available at www.azdeq.gov/environ/water/permits/download/graybro.pdf; accessed June 13, 2014.
6. Bradley Guy and M. E. Rinker, *A Guide to Deconstruction* (Gainsville, FL: The Deconstruction Institute, 2003), p. 7. Available at www.deconstructioninstitute.com/files/learn_center/45762865_guidebook.pdf.
7. www.oregonmetro.gov.
8. See www2.epa.gov/lead/lead-renovation-repair-and-painting-program-rules.

Indoor Air Quality

Learning Objective 1: List the pollutants that degrade the indoor air quality of a home, and recognize the health hazards they pose to the inhabitants.

Learning Objective 2: Calculate the appropriate amount of cubic feet per minute (CFM) of air movement to specify for a range/cooktop you are installing in a kitchen.

Learning Objective 3: Define "makeup air," and differentiate between types of mechanical systems to aid in creating a healthy home and when a makeup air system is required for your project.

INDOOR AIR QUALITY—WHY SHOULD WE CARE?

According to the American Lung Association, "Poor indoor air quality [IAQ] can cause or contribute to the development of infections, lung cancer, and chronic lung diseases such as asthma. In addition, it can cause headaches, dry eyes, nasal congestion, nausea, and fatigue. People who already have lung disease are at greater risk."[1]

Poor IAQ affects our health and contributes to the structural degradation of our homes. Consider these points:

- According to the US Environmental Protection Agency (EPA), indoor air pollutants have been ranked among the top five environmental risks to public health.[2]
- Cases of asthma grew by 4.3 million from 2001 to 2009, costing the United States approximately $56 billion in 2007 (or approximately $3,300 per person affected). Asthma is triggered by environmental factors, such as IAQ, smoking, mold, and infections.[3]

Consumer demand for homes with cleaner, healthier air has driven the EPA to establish the airPLUS certification as an add-on to an ENERGY STAR certification for a house. The airPLUS certification takes into account radon mitigation, pollutants from combustion, and the prevention of infestation by pests. But most of all, the airPLUS certification looks to minimize the presence of mold and poor levels of humidity in the home by requiring the sealing and conditioning of all crawl spaces and basements.

Causes of Poor IAQ

Poor IAQ is a result of many factors: off-gassing of chemicals in building materials found in adhesives, laminated woods, fiber boards, and cleaning supplies as well as molds and mildews that grow due to overly tight construction and poorly designed heating, air conditioning, and ventilation systems.

The most common indoor pollutants are:

- **Biological.** Caused by molds, bacteria, viruses, pollen, animal dander, and particles from dust mites and cockroaches. These factors may cause infections, provoke allergic reactions, or trigger asthma attacks.
- **Radon.** Radon is a naturally occurring radioactive gas that moves through the ground and enters the home through cracks and other holes in the foundation. According to the National Cancer Institute, radon is the second leading cause of lung cancer in the United States with an estimated 15,000 to 22,000 radon-related lung cancer deaths each year.[4]
- **Asbestos.** Asbestos is a nonflammable silicate mineral. When inhaled, it causes asbestosis (scarring of the lung tissue), lung cancer, and mesothelioma. It is found in many products in the home, including roofing and flooring materials and insulation.
- **Combustion pollutants.** Sources include fuel-burning stoves, furnaces, fireplaces, heaters, and water heaters. The most dangerous are both colorless and odorless gases: carbon monoxide (CO) and nitrogen dioxide (NO_2). CO interferes with the delivery of oxygen to the body, resulting in fatigue, headaches, confusion, nausea, dizziness, and even death. NO_2 irritates the mucous membranes in the eye, nose, and throat; can cause shortness of breath; and can promote infections.[5]
  - Many jurisdictions require the installation of carbon monoxide detectors for any home with fuel-fired appliances or an attached garage. Be sure to confirm with your local jurisdictions to determine if this is a code requirement.
- **Formaldehyde.** Formaldehyde is a common material found in many adhesives and bonding materials in the home. It is found in carpets, upholstery, particle board, and plywood paneling. When released into the air, it may cause coughing; eye, nose, and throat irritation; skin rashes; headaches; and dizziness. Formaldehyde is discussed at length in Chapter 5, "Materials for Sustainability."
- **Other pollutants.** Found in household cleaning agents, furnishings, pesticides, herbicides, paints, solvents, hobby products, and personal toiletries.

As a kitchen and bath designer, it is your responsibility to understand where these pollutants come from and how they can be minimized or eliminated from your client's home. Education is the key to being a successful designer.

Moisture and Mold

We walk a fine line when it comes to moisture in our homes. A house that is too dry can cause dehydration, respiratory illnesses, skin irritations, and static electricity; a house that is too moist is a breeding ground for mold, dust mites, and more. Mold can cause the degradation of a home's structural system, costing homeowners thousands of dollars in unnecessary repairs.

Moisture enters our homes naturally through atmospheric humidity, cooking, bathing, laundry, and breathing. (The average person produces approximately three pints of water every day just by breathing.) It also enters houses through cracks and openings in the home and from leaks. All of these activities and conditions raise the humidity levels inside our homes.

For the health and comfort of the inhabitants of a home, the goal is to maintain a relative humidity (RH) between 25 and 60 percent. Complete consensus on the lower limit has not been reached; however, there is consensus that the lower limit of RH will not go above 25 percent. This range is the current recommendation within the American Society of Heating, Refrigerating and Air-Conditioning Engineers (ASHRAE). There is an emerging consensus that indoor RH should never rise above 60 percent.

What exactly is RH? Basically, it is an indication of how moist the air is in relation to the current temperature. The warmer the air is, the more moisture it can hold; conversely, the colder the temperature, the drier the air. When RH reaches 100 percent, the water vapor in the air turns to water, and condensation is formed.

Maintaining a comfortable RH range is easier in the warmer months than in the winter months. In the winter, dry air enters the home through cracks and openings in the building, which results in a lower RH inside the home. When the RH drops below 30 percent, inhabitants may start to experience static electricity and dry mucus, which may result in nosebleeds, infections, and other respiratory ailments.

An elevated relative humidity (70 percent or higher) may lead to problems with mold, corrosion, decay, and other moisture-related deterioration. This level of RH creates an environment conducive to the growth of dust mites.[6]

The RH can change from room to room, even within a room, based on the air circulation. If it is cold outside and the exterior walls are not insulated, the RH at the exterior walls may be lower than at the interior walls. This situation reverses in the warmer months, with the RH being higher at the exterior walls. Locating soft furniture and bookcases close to exterior walls and carpets can raise the RH in a room and contribute to mold growth.

There are many methods for maintaining healthy RH in the home. Some methods include air conditioners and whole-house dehumidification or humidification (depending on the location of the home). It is best to consult with your heating, ventilating, and air-conditioning (HVAC) contractor to determine the best course of action for your client.

Radon

Radon is an odorless, colorless, naturally occurring radioactive gas that is present nearly everywhere. It is released from the normal decay of uranium, thorium, and radium found in rocks and soil. Radon usually exists at very low levels outdoors; it becomes a problem as it seeps into homes that lack adequate ventilation (see Figure 4.1). Levels of accumulated radon in a home may substantially increase the risk of lung cancer.

FIGURE 4.1 How radon enters a home
NKBA

There is a very easy way to determine if the house suffers from radon exposure: Test it. Two types of tests are available: short-term and long-term detectors. Short-term detectors measure levels for a minimum of 2 days to a maximum of 90. Long-term detectors measure the concentrations for more than 90 days. Most states have a map to determine if the area of the home is susceptible, but it is important to note that each home should be tested individually. Just because the house next door tested negative does not indicate that the home you are working on will test negative also. Tests, which are inexpensive and effective, are available through the Radon Information Center's website (www.radon.com). Many municipalities offer free radon test kits.

There are several methods to lower high radon levels (over 4 picocuries per liter [pCi/L]) in a home. The most used method is a vent pipe system and fan (also called a soil suction radon reduction system). This pulls radon from beneath the house and vents it to the outside. Sealing cracks and openings in the foundation is the most effective and cost-efficient method for safeguarding a house from radon. Similar methods are also available for crawl spaces.

Consult a contractor who is trained in fixing radon problems. A qualified contractor will be able to assess the project and offer the most cost-effective and efficient method of remediation.

Asbestos

"Asbestos" comes from the Greek word for inextinguishable. It is a mineral fiber, detectible with a special type of microscope. Asbestos is a highly effective and inexpensive fire retardant and thermal and acoustical material that was used in home construction from the early 1940s through the 1970s.

Asbestos has been used in in a myriad of materials throughout the home, including:

- Roofing and siding shingles
- Insulation (in homes built between 1930 and 1950)
- Paint and Sheetrock compound (although this was banned in 1977)
- Plaster
- Some vinyl floor tiles
- Backing of sheet vinyl
- Adhesives
- Some linoleum
- Insulation wrap on hot water and steam pipes
- Oil and coal furnaces and exterior door weather stripping
- Window caulking and glazing
- Walls and floors around wood-burning stoves

Asbestos is a serious health hazard that can lead to an increased risk of lung cancer and other lung diseases. Two of the most serious asbestos-related conditions are mesothelioma, a cancer of the lining of the chest and the abdominal cavity, and asbestosis, a condition where the lungs become scarred with fibrous tissue.

The risk of lung cancer increases as exposure to inhalation of asbestos fibers continues. Health risks are greater for those who smoke. Symptoms usually do not appear until 20 to 30 years after the first exposure.

Exposure to the fibers is what creates the health risks. Asbestos in good condition should be left alone. It is most hazardous when it is *friable*, which means it is easy to crumble and release the harmful fibers into the air. If you suspect that a home contains asbestos, it is important to note this in your home survey.

Existing asbestos products in good condition should be inspected periodically for signs of wear or damage. Once those products are disturbed, fibers may be released into the home and inhaled by the occupants.

Although visual inspections are not sufficient to determine if asbestos is present in a home, certain conditions should make you aware of the potential presence of asbestos.

Conditions that should arouse the suspicion of potential asbestos presence:
- Home built prior to 1981
- Built-up flooring in kitchen or bathroom (see Figure 4.2).
- Asbestos insulation on pipes in basement (see Figure 4.3).

FIGURE 4.2 Built-up flooring in a kitchen. The black glue is an indicator of the presence of asbestos.
NKBA

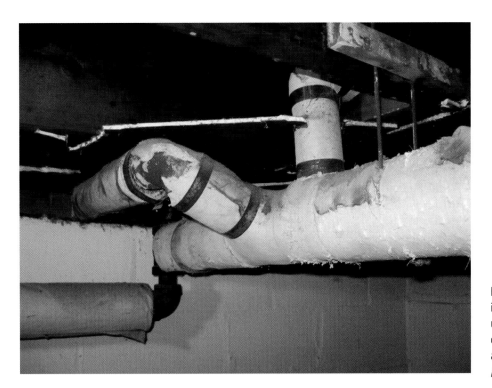

FIGURE 4.3 As long as the insulation is in good shape, it can remain undisturbed. If you notice *any* peeling or flaking, bring in an asbestos abatement professional.
NKBA

If any of these conditions are present, it is best to have a trained asbestos abatement professional come into the home to take samples for testing. If the tests come back positive, then a trained professional should be in charge of all asbestos removal.

Combustible Air Pollutants

Combustible pollutants are created when gas is used for cooking or heating. Pollutants also come from cleaning products, aerosols, and nail polish, just to name a few.

Combustible air pollutants and their health effects are detailed next.

Carbon monoxide (CO) is a colorless, odorless, and tasteless gas; sources include:

- Malfunctioning gas appliances
- Improper use of gas stoves
- Wood-burning and kerosene heaters
- Charcoal grills and idling cars in enclosed garages
- Polluted outdoor air

Health effects of carbon monoxide include:

- Headaches
- Fatigue
- Queasiness
- Poor vision and concentration
- Heart pains
- Death at very high levels

Nitrogen dioxide (NO_2) is a colorless and tasteless gas with a sharp odor. Sources of NO_2 include:

- Gas ranges
- Malfunctioning gas appliances
- Wood burning and kerosene heaters
- Charcoal grills
- Automobiles

Nitrogen dioxide has these adverse health effects:

- Lung damage
- Lung disease after long exposure
- Respiratory infections

Particulate matter (PM) refers to liquid or solid particles found in the air. The EPA has determined that particles larger than 2.5 and smaller than 10 micrometers are responsible for adverse health effects, as they have the ability to reach the lower regions of the respiratory tract. Concerns for human health include adverse "effects on breathing and respiratory systems, damage to lung tissue, cancer, and premature death. The elderly, children, and people with chronic lung disease, influenza, or asthma are especially sensitive to the effect of particulate matter."[7]

Sources of PM include:

- Tobacco smoke
- Wood-burning and kerosene heaters
- Charcoal grills
- House dust
- Incense burning
- Polluted outdoor air

PM has the following adverse health effects:

- Nose, throat and eye irritation
- Emphysema
- Bronchitis
- Allergies
- Asthma

- Respiratory and ear infections
- Lung cancer

Polycyclic aromatic hydrocarbons (PAHs) is a group of approximately 10,000 compounds, including benzo(a)pyrene, benzanthracene, benzo(b)fluoranthene, fluoranthene, and naphthalene.

Sources of PAHs include:

- Tobacco smoke
- Wood-burning and kerosene heaters
- Charcoal grills
- Self-cleaning ovens

Health effects of PAHs include:

- Lung, stomach, bladder, and skin cancers
- Nose, throat, and eye irritation

Proper ventilation is the key to minimize the harmful effects of combustible air pollution. Details about how to size your ventilation are covered later in this chapter. The most important advice to give to clients is that they use their mechanical ventilation when cooking, every time.

For homes with gas furnaces, hot water tanks, fireplaces, and any other nondirect or *naturally vented* gas appliances, installation of a spillage alarm is recommended (see Figure 4.4). Spillage indicators or alarms are designed to notify the inhabitants if excess CO is being

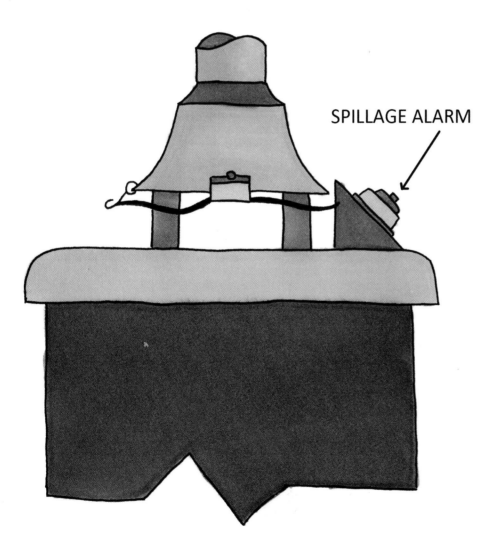

SPILLAGE ALARM

FIGURE 4.4 Spillage alarm on a hot water heater with atmospheric venting
NKBA

released in the home, either from backdrafting (more about this under "Improving Indoor Air Quality") or malfunctioning appliances. Spillage alarms are inexpensive to install. They must be tested and have their batteries replaced every year for optimum efficiency.

Formaldehyde

Formaldehyde (urea-formaldehyde [UF]) is a chemical that is used in many adhesives and found in building materials, such as pressed wood and composite products (i.e., particle board, plywood, oriented strand board [OSB], and medium-density fiberboard [MDF]). It is also a by-product of combustion of unvented, fuel-burning appliances, such as gas cooktops and kerosene space heaters. Additionally, it may be found in some paints and coating products as a preservative. The World Health Organization (WHO) and the state of California (Proposition 65) have classified formaldehyde as a known carcinogen. It also is a bronchial irritant and asthma trigger and has been connected to chemical sensitivity.

By 2012, the tighter regulations on formaldehyde emissions from composite wood products established by the California Air Resources Board exceeded the standards set forth by the majority of European countries and Japan. Although these regulations do not eliminate use of formaldehyde during product manufacturing, they do make formaldehyde-free alternatives much more cost-competitive.[8]

Improving Indoor Air Quality

As construction techniques have improved, our homes have become tighter, minimizing natural air flow and increasing the risks of indoor air pollution. As a kitchen and bath designer, you need to be armed with options to increase the quality of the air within your client's home.

According to the EPA, there are three basic strategies to improve indoor air quality:

1. Source control
2. Improved ventilation
3. Air cleaners[9]

Source Control

The best way to improve IAC is to try to eliminate the pollutants. For example, asbestos can be removed, encapsulated by covering with Sheetrock, or painted over with an elastomeric paint. Specifying adhesives and paints with low volatile organic compounds (VOCs) and building materials with non-UF will improve the IAC of your client's home.

We discuss source control further in Chapter 5.

Improved Ventilation

Increasing the amount of outdoor air that can enter the home is another way to improve the IAC. There are three general methods of ventilation:

1. Natural ventilation (passive)
2. Mechanical ventilation (active)
3. Combination of ventilation types (mixed mode)

Air Cleaners

Mechanical air cleaners are designed to remove air pollutants from the home. Pollutants typically fall into two categories: particulate matter and gaseous. Air cleaners are designed to remove certain types of pollutants but not all. If a client is considering a mechanical air cleaner, consult your HVAC expert for the best system for the home.

Natural Ventilation (Passive)

Natural ventilation usually requires no mechanical means (i.e., fans) to move air. Although just opening a window may seem like an acceptable way to ventilate a home, the effectiveness of natural ventilation depends on many factors:

- Climate
- Initial design (are the windows easy to operate and located properly?)

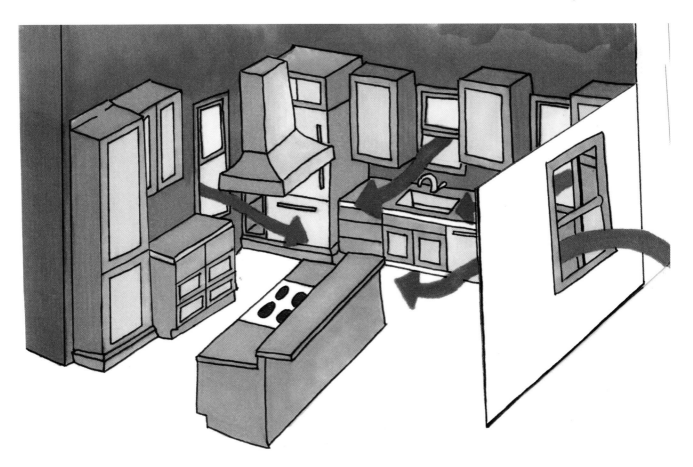

FIGURE 4.5 Natural ventilation

- Surrounding environments (neighbors, traffic, etc.)
- The homeowner

A study conducted by the California Energy Commission and the California Air Resource Board found that 32 percent of homeowners did not use their windows during the study period.[10] (Many homeowners stated that they never opened their windows or doors for ventilation because of their concerns about security/safety, weather, noise, dust, and odors.)

Natural ventilation systems rely on pressure differences to move fresh air through the building. Pressure differences are caused by wind, temperature, and humidity. The largest factor in the success of natural ventilation is the size and placement of the openings in the home. When homes are located on the coast, many are designed with large ocean-facing windows to take advantage of cooling sea breezes. In drier climates, natural ventilation (such as operable skylights or clerestories) draws the heat out to prevent heat buildup during the day or night.

When considering the location of windows in a kitchen or bathroom, it is best to think of airflow as a circuit, with air moving in and out of a room. Transoms, windows, louvers, grilles, or open floor plans are all part of the circuit (see Figure 4.5).

Mechanical Ventilation (Active)

As a designer, it is your job to create an environment where your clients are comfortable. Part of your job is to specify materials and equipment that will assist in maintaining a comfortable range of relative humidity and properly exhaust indoor pollutants. Consider advising your clients to install a heat recovery ventilator (HRV) or an energy recovery ventilator (ERV) in their home.

An HRV is not a heater; it is a ventilator. It helps to recover heat a home loses through natural venting such as wall grilles, vents, and so on. It works with your existing heating system and usually is installed in an attic, basement, utility room, or adjoining garage. An HRV works by tempering incoming air (heating during the cooler months and removing heat during the warmer season).

An ERV is recommended in warmer, more humid climates. It is not a dehumidifier, but it transfers the moisture from the incoming humid air to the stale indoor air that is being vented to the exterior. ERV are a ducted whole-house system.[11]

These units benefit air quality in four ways:

1. They increase the air exchanges in the home. With a tighter-built, energy-efficient home, there are fewer natural heat exchanges.
2. They are less noisy than whole-house fans installed in the attic.
3. Energy is captured from the conditioned air leaving the home.
4. They may help a forced air system last longer by preconditioning the air before it reaches the furnace.

KITCHEN VENTILATION

Many designers (and clients) believe that the hood vent is the ugly stepsister of the kitchen appliances. Clients are excited about their professional-style range, built-in refrigerator, and incredibly quiet dishwasher but not so excited about the vent fan. We authors believe, however, that the hood vent is the *most important* appliance in the kitchen.

The purpose of kitchen ventilation is to remove HOGS from the kitchen. HOGS are heat, odors, grease, and smoke. The average family of four in America (the average American family cooks 1.5 meals per day) creates 3 *gallons* (11 liters) of grease per year. Yes, that's 3 *gallons* (11 liters) of grease per year! Codes now require a mechanical ventilation source in the kitchen so, if your clients do not want that grease on their cabinets, walls, ceilings, and furniture, they must *use* the hood vent.

Ventilation moves air. The movement of air is measured in cubic feet per minute (CFM). The number of CFM to specify is based on the type of cooking unit your client desires. Standard slide-in ranges and most electric cook surfaces need fewer CFMs, whereas gas cooking surfaces may require more CFM to adequately vent.

Table 4.1 shows only the *absolute minimum* requirements for venting in a kitchen. This minimum rate *does not apply* to professional-type ranges. For these types of ranges, it is strongly suggested to consult the manufacturer's recommendations. To get a rough idea of the size of ventilation your project will need, use these calculations:

Step 1: Measure the length (L), width (W), and height (H) of the kitchen. Determine the volume (V) of air by multiplying them together.

$$L \times W \times H = V$$
$$Example: Room\ is\ 8 - feet\ wide \times 10 - feet\ long \times 8 - feet\ high = 640$$

Step 2: Multiply V × 15 to determine cubic feet of the room:

$$V \times 15 = Cubic\ feet$$
$$Example: 640 \times 15 = 9600$$

TABLE 4.1 CFM Minimum requirements per hood location

Location	Required Minimum Ventilation Rate per Linear Feet of Range (at high speed)	Minimum Ventilation Rate per Linear Feet of Range (at low speed)
Wall	100 CFM	40 CFM
Island	150 CFM	50 CFM

Source: Home Ventilating Institute (www.hvi.org/publications/HowMuchVent.cfm)

Since CFM is measured in minutes, divide cubic feet by 60.

$$Example: 9600/60 = 160$$

Step 3: Determine the BTUs (British thermal units) produced by the cooktop. Average electric cook top produces 3,000 Btu per burner; gas produces 18,000 Btu per burner.

Example: For our example, use a six-burner gas cooktop.

$$6 \times 18,000 = 108,000$$

Step 4: Multiply by 0.01

$$Example: 108,000 \text{ by } 0.01 = 1,080.$$

Step 5: Add to this number the results from Step 2

$$Example: 1,080 + 160 = 1240 \text{ CFM}$$

Step 6: Next, determine the length of ducting that will be used. There is a detail chart, but for our purposes, add 1 CFM for every foot of straight pipe, 20 CFM for every elbow and turn, and 40 CFM for exterior caps.

Example: We have 7 feet of pipe and 1 elbow.

$$1240 + 7 + 20 + 40 = 1307 \text{ CFM ventilation fan required for this range}$$

Electric cooking appliances are not rated in Btus. They are rated in watts to Btus. To determine the Btus of an electric cooking surface, you first have to convert to watts:

1 watt = 3.412412 Btu/hr

10 watt = 34.121416 Btu/hr

100 watt = 341.214163 Btu/hr

1000 watt = 3412.14633 Btu/hr

Once you have done the conversions, proceed through steps 1 through 6 listed previously to determine the correct CFMs required to appropriately vent your client's kitchen.

It is important to note that the size of the fan motor required also is affected by the number of bends in the ducting. Consider drinking milk out of a straw. With a straight straw, it is pretty easy. Now bend the straw—it becomes a little harder to drink the milk. What if you drink out of a straw that is excessively long? Is it harder to drink? As more ducting and bends are added, it is harder for air to flow freely. As a result, the longer the ducting, the more power the ventilation hood will require.

Current codes require minimum ventilation for bathrooms, kitchens, and laundry rooms, but they are still a minimum. Codes further define ventilation to achieve a specific number of air changes per hour.

Our codes are changing, and with each change, the minimum requirements for ventilation increases. The NKBA and these authors recommend that, for the health of your clients, you err on the side of more ventilation.

Even the NKBA *Kitchen & Bathroom Planning Guidelines* only reference the International Residential Code (IRC) code requirements for minimum ventilation (see Figure 4.6). To determine the appropriate ventilation requirements for your project, it is best to communicate with your appliance specialist and your HVAC contractor. You can also perform the previous calculations to determine the best ventilation for your project.

Codes are constantly changing. As new research and building practices are developed, our codes are revised to reflect those changes. At the writing of this book, the International Code Council (ICC) is working on 2015 IRC. The state of California (a leader in sustainable and green design) has adopted the California Indoor Ventilation Minimum Best Practices Guide (based on Ama). This guide requires the ventilation system be shown on plans including "note blocks, sheet notes, schedules, or other means of written communication that describe the requirements for ventilation airflow, fan selection, and room location, and duct sizing for whole-building ventilation and local ventilation exhaust." California also requires that the table shown in Table 4.2 be included on plans in case ducting sizes need to be modified on the project site.[12]

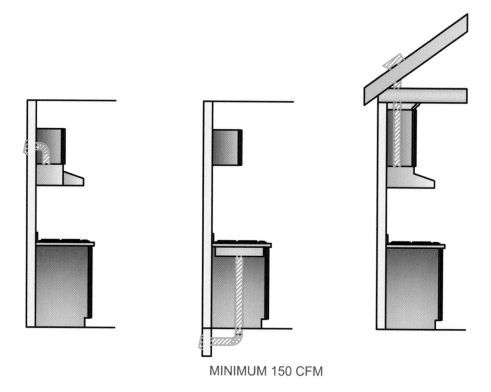

FIGURE 4.6 NKBA Kitchen Planning Guideline 19: Cooking Surface Ventilation

MINIMUM 150 CFM

BATHROOM VENTILATION

Over the years, it has become common practice (although completely wrong) to vent a bathroom into the attic space. This has resulted in many homes being infected with mold. The IRC 2009 clearly states, if mechanical ventilation is used, it must be "exhausted to the outside."[13] Although today we do have a code requirement for bathrooms, mechanical venting is, unfortunately, not the only option. As long as you have an operating window of at least 3 square feet (0.27 square meters) of which 50 percent is operable, mechanical ventilation is not required.

Let's discuss this further.

First of all, bathrooms are used for bathing, and bathing creates moisture, *lots* of it! It makes sense that in a home where IAC is a concern, proper ventilation must be considered. The

TABLE 4.2 Prescriptive Duct Sizing Requirements (based on ASHRAE 62.2)

Duct Type	Flex Duct				Smooth Duct			
Fan Rating (CFM at 0.25 in. w.g.)	50	80	100	125	50	80	100	125
Maximum Allowable Duct Length (ft)								
Diameter (in)	Flex Duct				Smooth Duct			
3	X	X	X	X	5	X	X	X
4	70	3	X	X	105	35	5	X
5	NL	70	35	20	NL	135	85	55
6	NL	NL	125	95	NL	NL	NL	145
7 and above	NL	NL	NL	NL	NL	NL	NL	NL

California Energy Commission, *Indoor Ventilation Minimum Best Practices Guide* July 2010

Note: water gauge (w.g.) is the same as water column (w.c.).

X = not allowed, any length of duct of this size with assumed turns and fittings will exceed the rated pressure drop.

NL = no limit on duct length of this size.

This table assumes no elbows. Deduct 15 feet of allowable duct length for each turn, elbow, or fitting. Interpolation and extrapolation in the table is not allowed. For fan rating values not listed, use the next higher value. This table is not applicable for fan ratings >125 CFM.

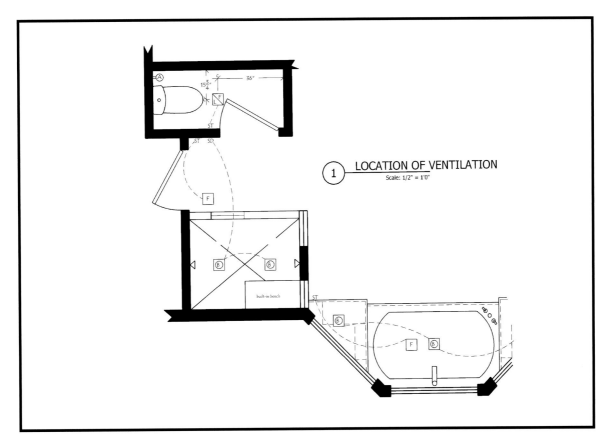

LOCATION OF VENTILATION
1
Scale: 1/2" = 1'0"

FIGURE 4.7 Location of ventilation in a bathroom
NKBA

current code requires only 50 CFM intermittently or 20 CFM continuously, but this is a *minimum*. There are calculations to determine the best ventilation sizing for a bathroom over 100 square feet, or you can use this guide, as suggested by the Home Ventilating Institute (HVI):

Bathtub	50 CFM
Shower	50 CFM
Toilet	50 CFM
Jetted tub	100 CFM

For enclosed toilet rooms, an operating window or a 50-CFM ventilation fan is required.

It is best to place the fans in the ceiling, as hot air, humidity, and odors rise. A compartmentalized bathroom may require more than one fan. Each fan should be switched independently with a minimum of a 20-minute timer.

As shown in Figure 4.7, there are two options regarding ceiling ventilation installation:

1. **Several-fans option.** Use 50-CFM fan over the tub, one in the shower, and one over the toilet. This method is very effective as it will provide ventilation where and when it is needed. A word of caution, however: The ventilation system may cause a wind chill and should not be used directly over the bathing area.
2. **Single-fan option.** Install one 150-CFM fan. The air will be pulled through the entire room and exhausted at a central location. This method is the better choice when all of the fixtures required for ventilation share the same space.

With the windows closed, exhausted air will be replaced by makeup air from adjacent rooms or through forced air system registers. The HVI recommends exhaust points be located away from the supply air, so as not to pull supply air out of the room. Bath doors should be undercut at the base to allow makeup air to enter the bathroom (see Figure 4.8).

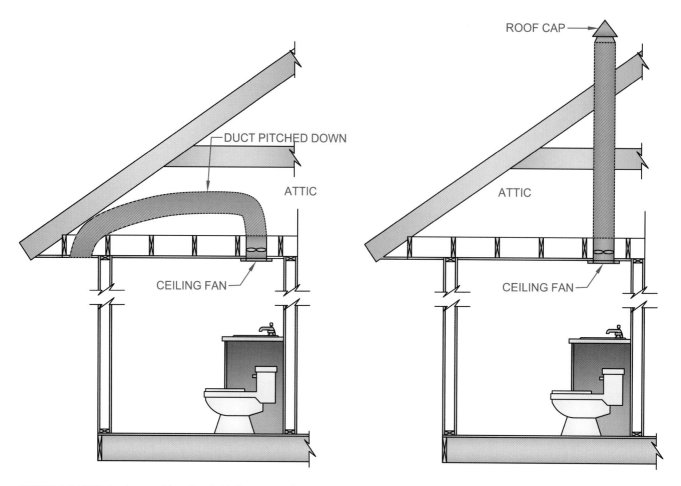

FIGURE 4.8 NKBA *Bathroom Planning* Guideline 26: Ventilation
NKBA

Ventilation for Laundry Rooms

Currently, there is no code requirement for ventilation of laundry rooms for remodeling projects. However, according to guidelines from Leadership in Energy and Environmental Design (LEED) and the EPA's Indoor airPLUS Program standards, "Conventional clothes dryers shall be vented to the outdoors. Electric condensing dryers are not vented and shall be plumbed to a drain according to the manufacturer's instructions."[14]

Noise Created by Ventilation

Although this chapter is about IAQ, not noise pollution, this is a good time to discuss fan noise.

Ventilation fans are measured in *sones*. A sone is a measurement of perceived loudness. The lower the sone rating of a vent fan, the more comfortable the listening environment is for the occupants. One sone is equivalent to the sound of a refrigerator. If a sone is doubled, the noise is also doubled; therefore, the lower the sones, the more comfortable the environment. If clients perceive a fan to be loud, they will be hesitant to use the system, and then mold can grow. Not a good situation for IAQ. Manufacturers are constantly working to create fans with the correct CFM to vent properly with minimal noise.

Clients should be made aware that a fan is a motor attached to a hollow metal tube. Even if the vent fan is extremely quiet, there will be sound of vibration and of air moving through the ducting. It is very important for you to educate clients on the benefits of the system and to remind them that the fan is on for just a brief time while bathing or cooking. Remind them that by not using their vent fan, they have a much higher chance of creating an environment conducive to mold growth or the deposition of up to 3 gallons (11 liters) of grease per year around their beautiful new kitchen.

MAKEUP AIR

What exactly is makeup air, and why is it a factor in a healthy home?

Today's building technology is creating homes that are tighter and more energy efficient. As a result of this tightness, less air is leaking in (or out) of the home. As we introduce larger ventilation units into the home, adverse pressure balance is created. We know that the purpose of ventilation is to pull HOGS and pollutants out, but as this occurs, it is also pulling *fresh air* out of the house. This can lead to additional problems, such as backdrafting of combustible equipment, radon introduction, or door operation problems.[15]

IRC energy codes since 2009 require makeup air. What follows is a basic primer to assist in the understanding of this new requirement. It is the responsibility of the designer, along with the HVAC tradesperson, to determine which system best satisfies code requirements and client budgets. It is the further responsibility of the designer to adequately educate clients on the system's application in their home.

Makeup air is required for any kitchen ventilation that exceeds 400 CFM. For many kitchens, this will not be an issue, but when it does apply, it will increase the cost of the project. As of 2013, additional costs average $300 to $3,000, and may cost more depending on the project and local jurisdiction code requirements.

Addressing the client's budget as early as possible in the design process is paramount to the overall success of the project. Since the appliance selection must be made early in the process as well, the makeup air requirements, and their impact on the budget, also should be addressed at this time. As the designer, you can help your clients determine if a professional range (which has both higher ventilation requirements and the additional cost of a makeup air system) is best for both their cooking style and the overall cost of the project.

The installation of a mechanical ventilation system will cause the pressure inside the home to change. Two events cause changes in building pressure: naturally occurring phenomena and mechanical systems operations.

Naturally Occurring Phenomena

The two naturally occurring events that affect building pressure and air movement are wind and stack effects.

As wind blows against the exterior of a home, it creates a pressure imbalance around the home (see Figure 4.9). The wind side experiences positive pressurization and the leeward side (downwind side of the home) experiences negative pressurization.

Natural ventilation relies on wind and the *chimney* or *stack* effect to keep a home cool and remove indoor air pollutants (see Figure 4.10). The stack effect is created by the temperature changes between the inside and outside of the home. In the winter, the warm air (which is lighter than the cold air outside) rises to the top of the home. As it rises, the warm air draws in cold air from the lower level of the home through cracks and openings. The reverse of this process happens in the summer, when the cold air falls and pulls the outside hot air in from the upper floors.

There is a point where the pressure is balanced. This point is called the neutral pressure plane (NPP).

Mechanical Systems Operations

When mechanical ventilation is engaged, the pressure differences become larger and more unbalanced. Kitchen exhaust is one of the greatest causes of this imbalance. The fan requires a constant source of air to exhaust. If the home is tightly constructed, the fan has no air to draw; it will start pulling air from unhealthy areas of the home, such as the basement, furnace, and chimney flues (see Figure 4.11).

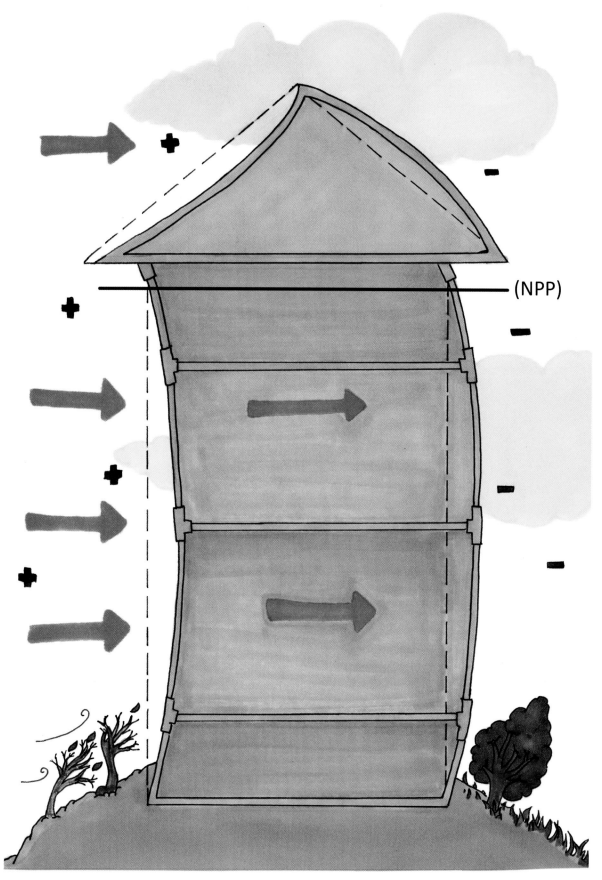

FIGURE 4.9 Wind effect on a home

(a)

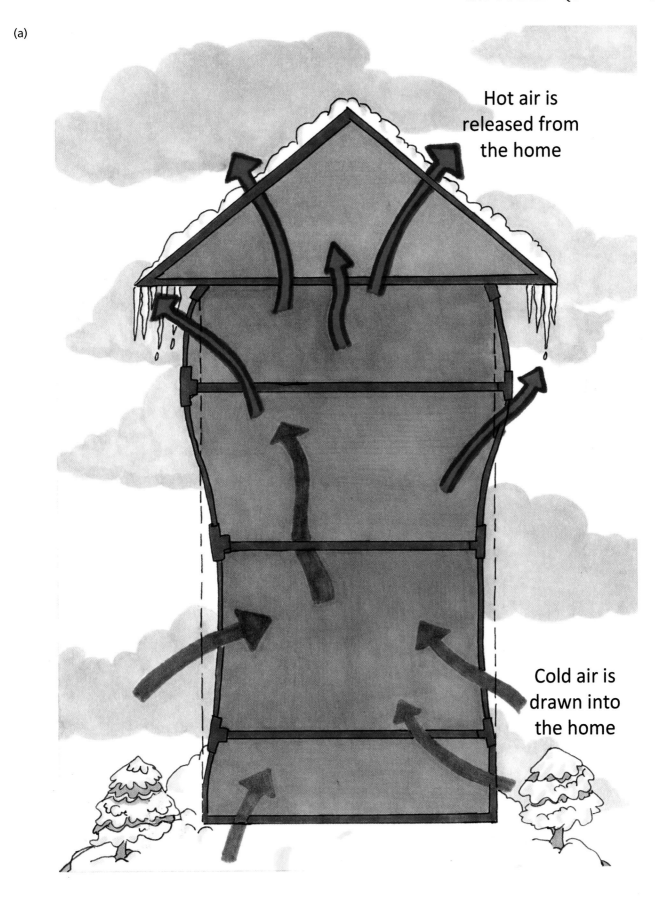

Hot air is released from the home

Cold air is drawn into the home

FIGURE 4.10 a. The stack effect on a home in the winter; b. The stack effect on a home in the summer

(b)

FIGURE 4.10 (*continued*)

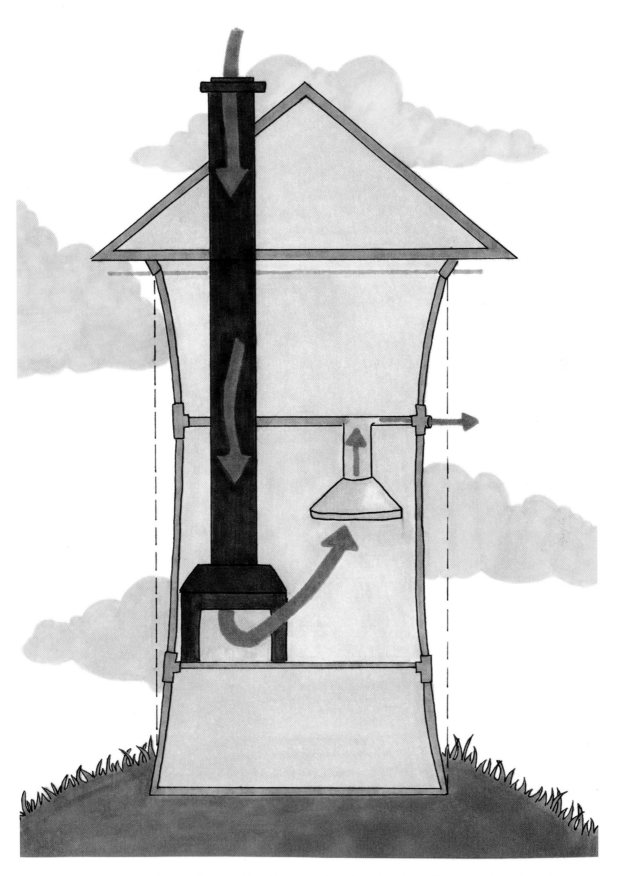

FIGURE 4.11 In a tight home, the kitchen ventilation could pull hazardous fumes from the chimney, furnace, and hot water systems.

To determine the rate of pressure imbalance, it is best to consult with your HVAC specialist, who has many methods and models for estimating how leaky or tight the home is. The most accurate of these methods is a blower door test (see Figure 4.12). In many jurisdictions around the country, blower door tests are mandatory for many type of remodeling projects.

When homes are more airtight, HVAC and energy costs may be reduced, but there is an increased risk for the home becoming depressurized, which can cause backdrafting. This leads to the code requirement of makeup air. The trend toward professional-style ranges with higher Btus requires ventilation systems capable of exhausting 600 to 1200 CFM of air. In chapter 3 we discussed Heat Recovery Ventilators (HRV) or Energy Recovery Ventilators (ERV). These items are *not* makeup air units. Their purpose is to bring in a balanced air flow, but they do not supply air.

Blower Door Tests

Blower door tests are used to measure the tightness of a home. They can also be used to test the airtightness of ducting and to help locate air leaks in a home.

There are three components to a blower door:

1. A calibrated, variable-speed fan that creates a range of airflows to pressurize and depressurize the home
2. A manometer—a pressure measurement instrument that measures the change in pressure in the home
3. A mounting system that attaches to the door or window

Once the blower door fan is installed in an exterior doorway, all the interior doors are opened and all exterior doors and windows are closed. Dampers on fireplaces should be closed and all mechanical vents, such as the kitchen hood vent and bathroom vents, are turned off. A pressure tube runs from the outside of the house to the inside to measure the indoor/outdoor pressure change. A baseline differential is then taken.

The blower door test forces air through all of the holes in the house (including windows and doors). The tighter the house, the less air is needed from the blower door fan to create a change in the home's pressure.

Problems with Depressurization: Backdrafting

When the mechanical ventilation is activated, causing the house to become depressurized, air will be pulled from any area of the home.

This may exacerbate the draw of radon into the home; other pollutants (such as carbon monoxide [CO]) may be pulled from garages, mechanical rooms, and storage spaces. In addition, air infiltrating from the outdoors may cause drafts. Other common indicators of depressurization include exterior doors that are difficult to open, exhaust fans that don't work properly, and drafts around doors and windows. All of these problems are more pronounced during the cold season when windows are kept closed.

Backdrafting is the worst effect of depressurizing. In backdrafting, negative house pressure overpowers the upward draft of a combustion appliance's chimney or vent. This causes the flow of hazardous products of combustion to reverse and reenter the house, as illustrated in Figure 4.11.

It is for these reasons that the 2009 IRC included the requirement for makeup air. The threshold for the makeup air requirement is 400 CFM; however, no data substantiates that threshold. Besides establishing this requirement, the IRC has offered little guidance as to how makeup air is to be provided. The only requirement is that a fan shall be "automatically controlled to start and operate simultaneously with the exhaust system." [16] For this reason, the kitchen and bath designer should consult with their contractor and HVAC expert as to the best path to take for each project.

Makeup Air Options

A home with a properly installed makeup air system replaces the air that is expelled by the home's exhaust system. Maintaining properly balanced pressure between the inside and outside of the home provides the these eight benefits:

1. Improves indoor air quality
2. Promotes proper operation of the home's exhaust systems

FIGURE 4.12 Blower door in use

Kmcrady (Own work) CC-BY-3.0 via Wikimedia Commons

3. Reduces the infiltration of cold outdoor air and drafts through opened doors
4. Eliminates suction pressure at exterior doors
5. Decreases load on existing HVAC systems
6. Lowers energy costs
7. Maintains a more comfortable and productive home environment
8. Supplies conditioned air that may be heated, cooled, humidified, and dehumidified

The purpose of introducing makeup air to the home is to ensure a safe, comfortable, and efficient home. But how is this done?

There are two methods for the introduction of makeup air: engineered openings and mechanical systems.

Engineered openings (see Figure 4.13) are essentially screened openings in the house that allow fresh air to enter. This is the least expensive solution. Since fresh air enters the home unconditioned, care must be taken in the location of this system for the comfort of the home's occupants.

Advantages of engineered openings
- Inexpensive
- Little impact to the HVAC system, as the fresh air mingles with the ambient air prior to returning to the central HVAC system

Disadvantages of engineered openings
- Drafts may occur if location is not well planned
- Effectiveness may vary based on location of opening
- Most effective with lower CFM requirements

To maintain the comfort level of the home, an engineered opening should be installed in an area that is consistently warm, such as behind a refrigerator. It is very important that the final location is placed as far from the thermostat as possible.

HVAC-integrated makeup air systems (see Figure 4.14) add unconditioned air directly into the central air handler. The air mixes with the return air and is tempered before returning to the central conditioning unit where it is filtered and distributed into the home.

Advantages of HVAC-Integrated Units
- Relatively inexpensive
- Existing HVAC unit filters and conditions air
- Air is evenly distributed throughout the house

Disadvantages of HVAC-Integrated Units
- Adds additional load to existing HVAC unit
- Existing HVAC unit may not be designed to handle additional loads and may have to be upgraded or replaced

Supplementary makeup air conditioning equipment (see Figure 4.15) is best when large amounts of makeup air are required. This system adds a stand-alone makeup air heater and dehumidifier to the HVAC-integrated unit.

Initial Investigations Required by the Designer

It is important to determine the type of fuel the client currently uses in the home to heat the house and water. It is equally important to determine if any of this will change before, during, or after the renovation. There are many factors that must be determined to accurately estimate and design a successful kitchen remodel.

First, you must do some initial sleuthing. Ask to look at the existing furnace, hot water heater, clothes dryer, and fireplaces in the home. Where are they located? In the garage? Basement? Attic? What type of fuel do they use? If they are all electric, makeup air may not be a major issue in your design, but if one or more burn fossil fuels, you must do additional sleuthing.

After confirming that fossil fuels are used, you must confirm the type of venting for each unit. There are basically three types of venting: atmospheric, direct, and power.

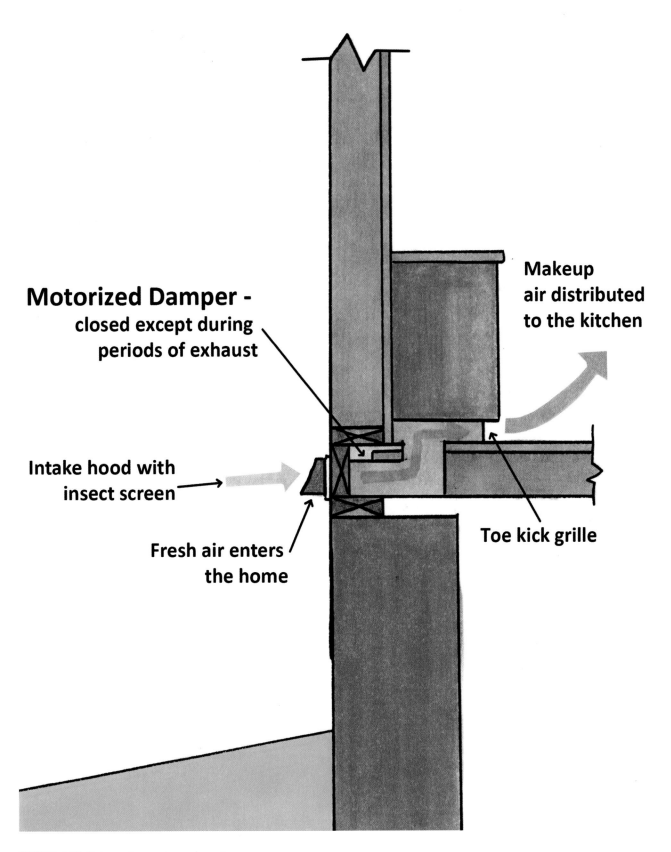

Motorized Damper -
closed except during
periods of exhaust

**Makeup
air distributed
to the kitchen**

**Intake hood with
insect screen**

Toe kick grille

**Fresh air enters
the home**

FIGURE 4.13 Makeup air—engineered opening

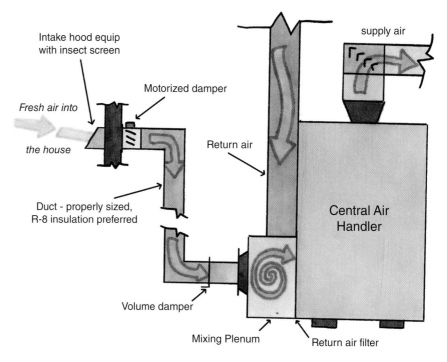

FIGURE 4.14 Makeup air, integrated system: When the motorized damper is opened in this typical HVAC-integrated unit, air enters through an opening that is ducted to the central air handler.

TYPICAL HVAC-INTEGRATED MAKEUP AIR SYSTEM
when the motorized damper is open, air enters through an opening which is ducted to the central air handler

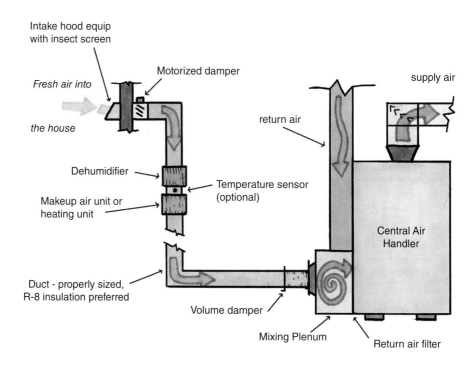

FIGURE 4.15 Supplementary makeup air conditioning equipment: This unit is similar to the HVAC-integrated system but includes a dedicated heating and dehumidifying unit.

SUPPLEMENTARY MAKEUP AIR CONDITIONING EQUIPMENT
similar to the HVAC-Integrated system, but includes a dedicated heating and dehumidifying unit

FIGURE 4.16 Water heater with direct vent
Courtesy of Rheem

Atmospheric venting (also called gravity venting), as illustrated in Figure 4.4, is the most common type of venting for both hot water heaters and furnaces. Lower in cost than direct venting, it works by integrating the stack effect. The pressure outside of the vent is higher than the pressure inside the vent, causing the exhaust gases to rise up and out of the house. The downside to this type of venting is that, in addition to pulling warm air out of the home, it increases the opportunity for backdrafting of exhaust gases into the home.

Fireplaces, furnaces, and hot water heaters typically are located next to an exterior wall through which they are vented in *direct venting* (see Figure 4.16). The double-walled vent permits combustion air to be drawn from the outside of the home, eliminating the risk of backdrafting of noxious fumes into the home.

Many direct vent units incorporate a small electric blower to force the exhaust gases out of the house through a flue; this is known as *power venting* (see Figure 4.17). Direct vents and atmospheric vent units rely on gravity, thus requiring a vertical vent. Power vents may be vented horizontally, giving more options for installation. This type of venting prevents any possibility of backdrafting.

When Is Makeup Air a Factor in Your Project?

The most important takeaway about makeup air is that it ensures the health and safety of the homeowner. When you begin your consultation on a new project, be sure to confirm these four points:

1. Determine the type of fuel the furnace and hot water heater are burning. Make a note whether the home is burning fossil fuels (oil, gas, or liquid propane [LP]) or if the house uses electricity.
2. Determine the venting type of the furnace and hot water heater. Are they direct vented or atmospheric?

FIGURE 4.17 Water heater with power vent

Courtesy of Rheem

3. Does the home contain fireplaces? How are they vented? Atmospheric or direct vent?

4. What style of cooking surface is preferred: electric? gas?

As the design process progresses, you will need to:

• Determine the length of a venting run and total amount of bends that will be required for the new cooking surface.

• Calculate (don't guess) the accurate amount of CFMs required to effectively vent the new cooking surface.

• Check the location of the garage and see if it is attached to the house.

The IRC 2009 section M1503.4 on ventilation clearly states that "makeup air systems shall be equipped with a means of closure and shall be automatically controlled to start and operate simultaneously with the exhaust system." This requires a motorized damper that prevents air from entering the system when the ventilation is not in use. Consultation with your HVAC contractor will help to determine which system will be best for your project.

SUMMARY

Many of today's kitchen and bath designers are not only designing beautiful spaces but are educating their clients about how to make their homes healthy and long lasting. Code requirements regarding IAC are only going to become more restrictive; it is the designer's job to integrate this science of indoor air quality with the client's needs, wants, and desires.

REVIEW QUESTIONS

1. List the common indoor pollutants, and explain how they enter the home. (See "Causes of Poor IAQ" pages 79–82) What are the three strategies to improve IAC? (See "Improving Indoor Air Quality" page 86)

2. Define "relative humidity." How does relative humidity affect the livability of the home? (See "Moisture and Mold" pages 80–81)

3. Explain why natural ventilation is an important factor in the overall design of a kitchen or bath. (See "Natural Ventilation [Passive]" pages 86–87)

4. Explain "makeup air" and its importance to a home's indoor air quality. Explain how makeup air can impact a project's design? (See "Makeup Air" page 93)

5. Define the term "friable." What steps should a designer take to remove this condition from the home? (See "Asbestos" pages 82–84)

ENDNOTES

1. American Lung Association, "Indoor Air Quality." Available at www.lung.org/associations/charters/mid-atlantic/air-quality/indoor-air-quality.html (accessed June 20, 2014).

2. Environmental Protection Agency, "Questions about Your Community: Indoor Air." Available at www.epa.gov/region1/communities/indoorair.html (accessed June 23, 2014).

3. CDC *Vital Signs*, "Asthma in the US: Growing Every Year" (May 3, 2011). Available at www.cdc.gov/VitalSigns/Asthma (accessed June 23, 2014).

4. *National Cancer Institute Fact Sheet*, "Radon and Cancer." Available at www.cancer.gov/cancertopics/factsheet/Risk/radon (accessed June 24, 2014)

5. American Lung Association, "Indoor Air Quality."

6. Joseph Lstiburek, "Relative Humidity," Research Report 0203, Building Science Corporation, April 23, 2002. Available at www.buildingscience.com/documents/reports/rr-0203-relative-humidity/view?searchterm=Relative%20Humidity (accessed June 24, 2014).

7. Environmental Protection Agency, *AIRTrends 1995 Summary*, "Particulate Matter (PM-10)." Available at www.epa.gov/airtrends/aqtrnd95/pm10.html (accessed June 24, 2014).

8. Healthy Building Network, *Formaldehyde and Wood;* see under "Regulatory Efforts to Reduce Exposure." Available at www.healthybuilding.net/formaldehyde/ (accessed June 24, 2014).

9. US Environmental Protection Agency, *The Inside Story: A Guide to Indoor Air Quality*, see under "Three Basic Strategies." Available at www.epa.gov/iaq/pubs/insidestory.html#Intro (accessed June 24, 2014).

10. David H. Mudarri, "Building Codes and Indoor Air Quality," September 2010. Prepared for the U.S. Environmental Protection Agency, Office of Radiation and Indoor Air, Indoor Environments Division. www.eng.utoledo.edu/~akumar/IAQ/TEXT/buildingcodesand%20 IAQ.pdf.

11. Broan-NuTone LLC, *HRV or ERV, What's the Difference?* Available at www.broan.com/products/lifestyle/hrv-or-erv-whats-the-difference-bf711e80-2043-41a0-bf21-98542b29a2d0 (accessed June 24, 2014).

12. California Energy Commission, "Indoor Ventilation: Minimum Best Practices Guide," July 2010, www.energy.ca.gov/2010publications/CEC-400-2010-006/CEC-400-2010-006.PDF.

13. IRC R 303.3, IRC M 15077.2, IRC M 1507.3.

14. Environmental Protection Agency, *Indoor airPLUS Construction Specifications*, January 1, 2009. Available at http://apps1.eere.energy.gov/buildings/publications/pdfs/building_america/construction_specifications_iap.pdf, p. 5 (accessed June 24, 2014).

15. David Mudarri, "Building Codes and Indoor Air Quality." Available at www.healthy-houseinstitute.com/a-1325-How-Ventilation-Makes-Homeowners-Healthier-and-Wealthier (accessed June 24, 2014).

16. As quoted in Anthony C. Jellen, Brian M. Wolfgang, and Michael A. Turns, "Kitchen Ventilation Systems: Part 1: Evaluating the 2009 IRC Requirement for Makeup Air," Pennsylvania Housing Research Center Builder Brief, March 2012, www.engr.psu.edu/phrc/Publications/BB0312%20Kitchen%20Vent%20Systems%20FINAL%201-19-12%20USE.pdf, p. 7 (accessed June 24, 2014).

Materials, Appliances, and Fixtures

GETTING STARTED

Creating kitchens and baths that are functional and beautiful in addition to being sustainable is the responsibility of today's designer. Sustainably aware designers recognize their position as responsible stewards of our planet and its resources. Our planet is full. Past habits of continued economic growth, creating waste and overpopulation, have resulted in a planet that is overused. According to the *Living Planet Report 2010*, we currently need 1.5 earths to sustain our current economy and wasteful habits.[1] That means to sustain our current way of life, we need 50 percent more earth—which is not going to happen.

We need to make a change today!

This chapter focuses on material choices and other decisions you can help your client make that are not only feasible, functional for their lifestyle, and beautiful to look at, but most important are sustainable for our planet. Yes, you can have all of this, but it takes work.

Learning Objective 1: Apply green criteria to selecting materials.

Learning Objective 2: Research and specify appliances using sustainability criteria.

Learning Objective 3: Demonstrate best practices related to selection of material product.

A word of caution: We wish to preface this entire chapter with the caveat that "there is no perfect product." No matter how much we would love to be able to supply you with a list of perfectly sustainable products for your tool box, we cannot do so, for there are none.

We can, however, give you the tools to decipher information to help you and your clients make the best selections possible for them, for you, and for the environment.

Material Properties

Material selection begins on a project earlier than you might expect. There are a few reasons for this, but number one is clients' delight in choosing the surfaces they will interact with on a daily basis. In our experience, backsplash tile, cabinets, flooring, countertops, and more are often selected before the basic space planning is completed.

CABINET HARDWARE: Rocky Mountain Hardware
(Recycled Content)

YOLO Paint
(Lo-Voc)

CABINETS:
FSC – Certified Wood

TILE:
Pratt & Larson Tile
(Locally Sourced)

FLOORING:
Marmoleum
(Natural Product)

COUNTERTOPS: Eco by Cosentino
(Recycled Content)

FIGURE 5.1 Green materials palette created for a kitchen remodel: Wood for cabinets is Forest Stewardship Council–certified; countertops are Eco by Cosentino (recycled content); Marmoleum by Forbo (natural material) is chosen for flooring; Yolo Paint (zero VOC) and Pratt and Larson Tile (locally sourced) are used.
NKBA

Specifying materials can be overwhelming enough without the added criteria of sourcing green options. Without taking sustainability into account, here is snapshot of where material selection begins:

> Appearance
>
> Appropriate use (durability and maintenance)
>
> Cost (budget)
>
> Availability

Designers work with their clients to develop palettes of materials: groupings that represent the whole project (see Figure 5.1). As the palette is pulled together, research is conducted: price, durability, availability, material content, and installation methods.

This chapter focuses on understanding *which questions to ask* in regard to the sustainability of materials. The importance of third-party evaluators was discussed in Chapter 2. It is crucial to have access to ratings of materials so that you can make the best choices for your clients. Around the country, some companies specialize in offering only materials that are environmentally sound. Their showrooms are a valuable resource. Research into the sustainable nature of a material takes time, and a vetted company can offer time-saving advice. Learn how to decipher a product's material safety and data sheet (MSDS). This will tell you about which materials go into the fabrication of a finished product.

Material Safety and Data Sheets

The MSDS or product safety data sheet is a valuable component of product stewardship and occupational safety and health. Its intended use is to supply information for safe handling procedures of a product. It also aids emergency personal in case of any physical contamination created by accident or misuse. In both Canada and the United States, this information is required to be available for all products (adhesives, paints, grouts, etc.) installed on a project site (see Figure 5.2). Today MSDSs from most companies are downloadable from their Web sites.

Naturally Beautiful Walls™
U.S. PATENT 7485186

Material Safety Data Sheet

Date prepared: January 30, 2004   Date revised: April 25, 2013

Section I   General Information

Product Name: Color Pigments
Product Code: CP---
Product Description: Powder, naturally occurring mineral pigments
Product Use: Colorant for American Clay Plasters and Sealers
Chemical Family: Inorganic Pigment(s)

Manufacturer: American Clay, LLC
                      2418 2nd Street SW
                      Albuquerque, NM 87102
                      1-866-404-1634
                      Fax: 505.244.9332

Section II   Hazardous Ingredients

Ingredient: Crystalline Silica, Quartz   **CAS #:** 14808-60-7   **% by Wt.:** <2.3 – 2.8

OSHA PEL*:   0.10 mg/m³   (TWA)
ACGIH TLV*:   0.05 mg/m³   (TWA)
*Respirable limits for particles <10 um AD.

Ingredient: Iron Oxide (FUME) – FE2O3   **CAS #:** 1309-37-1   **% by Wt.:** <65 - 70

OSHA PEL**   (TWA)
ACGIH TLV**   (TWA)
**Under normal conditions, when this material is used as a pigment, no hazardous conditions exist. If this material is heated to produce an iron oxide fume or gas, ACGIH has issued a TLV of 5mg/m³ and OSHA has set a PEL of 10mg/m³.

Ingredient: Magnesite   **CAS #:** 546-93-0   **% by Wt.:** <0.0 – 0.2

OSHA PEL*   5 mg/m³   (TWA)
ACGIH TLV   10 mg/m³   (TWA)
*Respirable

Ingredient: Magnesium silicate   **CAS #:** 14807-96-6   **% by Wt.:** <10 - 12

OSHA PEL** 20 MPPCF   (TWA)
ACGIH TLV* 2.0 mg/m³   (TWA)

Non-Hazardous: **% by Wt.:** <15 - 20
OSHA PEL: N/A
ACGIH TLV: N/A

Nuisance Dust – This material is considered a nuisance dust. Please also observe the following exposure limits:
          OSHA PEL15mg/mg³ (Total Dust) 5 mg/m³ (Respirable Dust)

FIGURE 5.2 Material Safety and Data Sheet by American Clay for their pigments. Each product by American Clay has its own MSDS. Today, most companies have their MSDS available for download from their websites.
MSDS Courtesy of American Clay

(continued)

Material Safety Data Sheet

Date prepared: January 30, 2004   Date revised: April 25, 2013

- **WARNING:** This product contains a small amount of quartz that may cause delayed respiratory disease if inhaled over a prolonged period of time. Avoid breathing dust. Use NIOSH/MSHA approved respirator where TLV for quartz may be exceeded. IARC Monographs on the evaluation of the Carcinogenic Risk of Chemicals to humans (volume 68, 1997) concludes that quartz is carcinogenic to humans (IARC classification 1).
- **Note:** The Permissible Exposure Limits (PELs) reported above are the pre-1989 limits that were reinstated by OSHA June 30, 1993 following a decision by the United States Circuit Court of Appeals for the 11th Circuit. Federal OSHA is now enforcing these PELs. More restrictive exposure limits may be enforced by some other jurisdictions. National Institute for Occupational Safety and Health (NIOSH) has recommended that the permissible exposure limit be changed to 50 micrograms respirable free silica per cubic meter of air (0.05mg/m³) as determined by full shift sample up to a 10-hour working day, 40 hours per week. *See:* 1974 NIOSH criteria for a recommended Standard for Occupational Exposure to Crystalline Silica for more detailed information.

**Unless otherwise noted, all PEL and TLV values are reported as 8 hour time weighted average (TWA).

Section III Hazards Identification

Most important hazards: Eye & skin contact may cause irritation. Prolonged inhalation at excessive dust levels may cause damage to the lungs and respiratory tract. May irritate pre-existing respiratory diseases such as asthma.

Specific hazards: This product contains crystalline silica, an IARC probable carcinogen. Long-term repeated exposure to excessive levels of crystalline silica dust may cause silicosis, a progressive and sometimes fatal lung disease.

Incompatibility: Strong oxidizers, such as Chlorates, Bromates, and Nitrates.

Additional incompatibility: This material contains Synthetic Iron Oxide which is incompatible with Hydrazine, Calcium Hypochlorite, Performic Acid, and Bromine Pentafluoride.

Section IV First Aid Measures

Skin contact: Wash with mild soap and water. Remove severely contaminated clothing and clean before reuse. Seek medical attention in the event that irritation occurs.

Eye contact: Flush thoroughly with large amounts of water. Seek medical attention if irritation persists.

Ingestion: Rinse mouth with water, give subject water to drink and do not induce vomiting. Seek medical help.

Inhalation: Remove to fresh air and get medical help for any breathing difficulties.

Section V Fire Fighting Measures

Suitable extinguishing media: Dry chemical, foam, or CO2. A water mist, fog or spray can be used to control dusting and cool the material.

Special hazards in fire: This material is a very fine dust: Avoid the use of high-pressure water, which could spread burning material and create hazardous dust conditions.

Required special protective equipment for fire-fighters: Firefighters should wear full protective clothing and self-contained breathing apparatus.

(continued)

Material Safety Data Sheet

Date prepared: January 30, 2004   Date revised: April 25, 2013

Section VI Accidental Release & Disposal Measures

Personal precautions: NIOSH approved dust respirator suggested. Approved dust respirators are required when dust exceeds recommended TLV. Safety glasses with side shields or goggles are suggested. Cloth, leather, rubber, or plastic gloves are recommended.

Environmental precautions: Provide an adequate exhaust system that is filtered to avoid contaminating the environment, and that meets the TLV requirements in the work area.

Disposal: Vacuum or scoop up spilled material and dispose in an appropriate waste container. Misting with water or absorbent dust control products may help to keep airborne dust levels at a minimum. Provide proper ventilation and personal protection equipment for use during clean-up. Waste material can be buried in an approved landfill in accordance with Federal, State, and Local environmental regulations. According to 40 CFR, Part 261 of the Resource, Conservation, and Recovery Act (RCRA), this product is not classified as a hazardous material.

Section VII Handling and Storage

Handling: Provide adequate ventilation when handling this material. Material may become slippery   when wet. Avoid unnecessary contact; wash thoroughly after handling. Keep material away from food and beverages.

Storage: Store in a dry place at an ambient temperature and away from food and beverages. Keep material in closed container(s).

Section VIII Exposure Controls

Personal protection equipment: Protective clothing

Eye protection: Protective goggles

Hand protection: Gloves

Hygiene measures: Wash skin thoroughly with soap and water after contact with this material.

Inhalation measures: Approved dust respirators

Section IX Physical and Chemical Properties

Appearance: powder
pH: 5.8
Melting point: N/A
Explosive properties: N/A
Tap density: .7
Solubility: N/A

Odor: None
Boiling point: N/A
Flashpoint: None
Vapor pressure: N/A
Specific gravity: 3.6

(continued)

Material Safety Data Sheet

Date prepared: January 30, 2004   Date revised: April 25, 2013

Section X Stability and Reactivity

Stability: Stable under normal conditions

Materials to avoid: Strong oxidizers, such as chlorates, bromates, and nitrates. This material contains synthetic iron oxide which is incompatible with hydrazine, calcium hypochlorite, performic acid, and bromine pentafluoride.

Hazardous decomposition products: None

Section XI Toxicological Information

HAZARDOUS MATERIAL IDENTIFICATION SYSTYM (HMIS)
Hazard rating: Health: 1
4 = Severe   Flammability: 0
3 = Serious   Reactivity: 0
2 = Moderate   Personal Protection: (glasses, gloves, dust respirator)
1 = Slight
0 = Minimal

Section XII Ecological Information

Poses no threat to the environment if disposed of responsibly.

Section XIII Transport Information

D.O.T. Hazardous Classification: Non-regulated
D.O.T. Label required: None
D.O.T. Shipping name: None
Technical shipping name: Inorganic pigment
Label statement: CP---

Section XIV Regulatory Information

TSCA (Toxic Substance Control Act) United States   Listed on TSCA Inventory
DERCLA (Comprehensive Response Compensation and Liability Act)   No reportable quantity
DSL (Canada)   Listed
SARA Title III, Section 313: Not Listed
 EINECS (European Community)   Listed

Reasons for issue: Compliance with 29 CFR, Part 1910.1200.

(continued)

Material Safety Data Sheet

Date prepared: January 30, 2004   Date revised: April 25, 2013

Other Information

The data and recommendations made in this document are based on our own research and the research of others, and are believed to be accurate. American Clay makes no guarantee or warranty, either expressed or implied, as to the accuracy or completeness of the data and recommendations.

Green Product Declarations

While the MSDS does offer some information about a product, there are still holes in the available information. Globally, there is a movement towards more transparency of what goes in to each product. Creating a standard report or a "nutrition label" that includes environmental, social and health impacts would make choosing the appropriate materials for your project easier.

The goal is for full disclosure, but the vision is seen from two separate viewpoints. One camp is moving towards creating the Environmental Product Declaration (EPD). This report assesses the products environmental impact over its life cycle (LCA). The second camp, Health Product Declaration (HPD) assesses the product as it relates to the health impact on the human population.

Environmental Product Declaration

The goal of the EPD is to "provide a summary of the environmental characteristics of a product in a way that is accessible, consistent and ultimately comparable."[2] EPDs are used globally. It is a third-party verification report that helps to compare "apples to apples" of like products. "The goal of the global EPD system is to create a tool that helps purchasers understand product life-cycle impacts and therefore make smarter purchasing decisions," says Heather Gadonniex, EPD program manager at UL Environment. "To do that, you have to use the same LCA methodology, the same data quality, and report of the same additional criteria in the EPD."

The problem with an EPD is that the 20-page report includes the key points from the LCA only and it does not include social or human health impacts. The length of the report makes it too technical and long for most designers to assimilate the information. There is a movement to create an EPD label that is more user-friendly.

Health Product Declaration

Where EPD's evaluate a product based on its environmental impact, the HPD evaluates a product based on its human health impact. The creation of the HPD is backed by the HPD Open Standard Working Group, which includes members from the Healthy Building Network (HBN—the creators of the Pharos Index) and Building Green, Inc. (publisher of the *Environmental Building News*). The HPE Open Standard requires manufacturers to "provide the hazard profile for 100 percent of ingredients (that go into a product), even ingredients that are not identified."[3] Currently, the HPD is only used in North America, but the goal is to have it incorporated with the EPD.

Social Impacts

Neither the EPD nor the HPD include the company's social impact, downstream impacts of production or "includes the manufacturer's overall environmental footprint"[4] in their report.

The MSDS gives product information, such as:

- Physical data: melting point, boiling point, and flash point
- Toxicity
- Health effects
- First aid
- Storage
- Disposal
- Protective equipment required in its installation
- Spill handling procedures
- Instructions for safe handling
- Potential hazards
- Environmental risks

EMBODIED ENERGY

The biggest challenge the designer faces in materials selection is that each product is part of a bigger picture. Let's take flooring: You are not just purchasing flooring—for this example, cork flooring (a very sustainable option)—you are purchasing:

- Growing of the cork tree (including labor, fertilizer, watering)
- Labor and machinery to harvest the cork
- Transportation of the raw material to the processing plant
- Packaging (and all the energy and natural resources that go into the creation of the cardboard, plastic, labels, and more)
- Shipping
- Storing
- Shipping again
- Installation (including the glue, labor, setting materials)
- Final finishing

And this is not even a complete picture.

This entire process is referred to as embodied energy.

In Chapter 2 we began the discussion of embodied energy; here we complete the picture.

First we need to give you some parameters and definitions based on DuPont's "Glossary of Common Sustainability Terms":[5]

- **Cradle-to-gate.** An assessment of a partial product life cycle from the manufacture to the factory gate (before it is shipped to the warehouse, installer, or final end user). The term is used in the calculation of embodied energy.
- **Cradle-to-site.** An assessment of a product life cycle that continues on cradle-to-gate and includes all of the energy consumed until the product reaches its point of use (the client's home).
- **Cradle-to-grave.** An assessment that continues from cradle-to-site to include the life of the product in the client's home (including maintenance) to the end of its useful life and the disposing of the final product.
- **Cradle-to-cradle.** A design protocol that advocates the elimination of waste by recycling a material or product into a new or similar product at the end of its intended life rather than sending the product to a landfill. Embodied energy calculations start with the extraction of the raw materials (including the fuels needed in the extraction process), transportation of the raw materials to the manufacturing plant, the energy it takes to run the plant, and creating the packaging the finish product requires for shipping.

The decision to set the boundary for determining embodied energy from cradle-to-site to stopping at the gate was based on the assumption that "[i]n many cases, transport from factory gate to construction site would be negligible. Whilst this may be true for many materials, and normally true for high embodied energy and carbon materials, this is not exclusively the case. In the case of very low embodied energy and carbon materials, such as sand and aggregates, transportation is likely to be significant. For these reasons the ideal boundaries have been modified to *cradle to gate*.[6] Many of our materials travel long distances to get to the project site; as a designer, you should determine if this travel distance should be a factor in the final product decision.

Many clients consider transportation of a product to the project site in their buying decisions. It is commonly referred to as buying locally.

Embodied energy assessments do not consider the life of the product once it leaves the factory and arrives at the client's home. To accurately assess a product, one must include maintenance (materials and labor required to maintain the product and how the product is to be disposed of when it ends its usable life. We consider embodied energy assessments to be only half of the story.

LIFE CYCLE ASSESSMENT

A more complete way to look at material selections is through life cycle assessment (LCA) (see Figure 5.3). LCA is a comprehensive evaluation of the environmental impact a product has from the initial sourcing of raw materials to the product's eventual disposal.

According to the Athena Sustainable Materials Institute (ASMI), LCA includes:

- Resource extraction and product/materials transportation
- Material processing and product manufacturing
- On-site building construction requirements
- Occupancy and maintenance considerations
- Building decommissioning and demolition
- Materials disposal, reuse, and recycling[7]

Incorporating LCA in the decision-making process enables both governments and industry to determine the cradle-to-grave impact of a product. Government agencies are moving toward the incorporation of LCA in regulations. Businesses are voluntarily incorporating initiatives that contain LCA and product stewardship components. Finally, consumers are interested in knowing about a product's environmental qualities. LCA is a holistic approach to the selection of materials, fixtures, and appliances.

There are three aspects to consider when reviewing a product through LCA:

1. **Goal definition and scoping.** Identifying the purpose and what to include or exclude from your process. This is where you define your client's goals for sustainability. During your interview process, you can determine your client's focus. Consider these factors; are they important to your clients?
   - Indoor air quality (IAC)
   - Sourcing products locally
   - High recycled content
   - Water conservation
   - High energy efficiency
   - Low maintenance
2. **Life cycle inventory.** This phase determines the energy and raw material inputs and environmental outputs during each stage of production (the embodied energy used during manufacturing). What resources are used in the creation of the final product? What about transportation?
3. **Impact assessment.** This determines what waste produced during the production stage have an impact on the environment and human health. Does the processing release waste that contributes to global warming, acid rain, or fossil fuel depletion? This is where we assess the volatile organic compound (VOC) emissions and the product's impact on IAC, including the products needed for installation and continued mainte-nance. At this stage, we assess the end of life of the product. Can it be recycled or reused? Does it go into the landfill?

FIGURE 5.3 Applying the Life Cycle Assessment to the products you specify will help you and your client understand the product's green story. *NKBA*

Strengths to Using LCA Evaluation

The criteria for evaluating what is green change over time. What was once thought to be a green material can later be labeled something different. The reason for this is the increased breadth of the evaluation process. Ten years ago, everyone was concerned with renewable resources. Today products are subject to much more scrutiny, such as the LCA. Tomorrow there will be added criteria. This scrutiny can be overwhelming, but with third-party evaluators and some basic education on the part of the specifier, products with increased green value will be selected.

Systems Thinking

Recognizing that each product is only part of the big picture brings us to systems thinking.

Systems thinking (which is also discussed in Chapter 1) is the concept that to fully understand why a problem occurs and continues, we need to understand the parts in relation to the whole. We can apply this way of thinking to material selection.

Consider the process of choosing the appropriate flooring material for your client. Choosing a flooring option is not that easy. First you have to take into account the client's initial desires, (i.e., hand-scraped oak flooring), but mindful designers use that as a jumping-off point. Although you may want to begin the selection process, sustainability is only one factor; you must also consider:

Aesthetics. What is the overall look and feel to the room? What is the idea behind the idea or the design concept? Dark, warm, traditional or light, airy, and beachy?

Lifestyle. How many children and adults are there? What about pets? Do people wear shoes at home? If you take time to observe the details of your client's home, much will be revealed.

Maintenance. Do clients employ a housekeeper? Are they willing, for example, to have wood floors *resurfaced* every five to ten years or have stone sealed once a year? Or are they willing to live with a patina that develops as the material wears?

Body limitations. Do clients have back issues? Do they need a softer floor over a hard one? Should the floor absorb sound (noise reduction coefficiency)?

Environmental concerns. What are the clients' environmental goals for the project? IAC? Recycled content? Locally sourced? Minimal maintenance? How dedicated are they to sustainable choices?

Life expectancy in the home. Do clients intend to live in the home for more than five years? More than 20?

Specific LCA and Environmental Matters Items to Consider

- Does a third-party environmental evaluator certify the product?
- Does the product contain low or zero amounts of environmentally harmful substances?
- Does the supplier/manufacturer recycle preconsumer waste?
- Does the supplier/manufacturer have a mission statement that incorporates environmental stewardship?
- Is the distribution of the product efficient?
- Is the product packaged as simply as possible?
- Is the product designed for easier recycling at the end of its life (once un-installed)?

Consider cork flooring. Cork is an easily renewed material that is made from bark harvested from a type of oak tree. The tree is not cut down, and the cork tree's bark regrows, as seen in Figure 5.4. It takes 10 to 12 years for the bark to regenerate to the thickness needed before harvesting. Cork-producing oak tree plantations are credited with capturing 5 percent of the carbon dioxide (CO_2) in the local environment on their own.

"The cork industry does not destroy the ecosystem where the tree lives, but instead creates wealth while keeping nature as it is," says Paulo Nogueira, managing director of the cork producer and distributor Amorim Flooring in Hanover, Maryland. He adds that the cork industry represents $3 billion of Portugal's gross domestic product and employs over 150,000 people. "We can create jobs and economic activity in balance with the world in which we live."[8]

This might make cork an easy choice if it is *appropriate* for the application. Consider, however, the carbon footprint of cork. Cork bark comes from Portugal. It is then fabricated in the United States. Your project is in California and will require additional transportation. With these factors in mind, how does cork stack up against locally produced oak flooring?

Green Product Directories

Understanding what goes into the raw materials that create the finished product is the biggest step to choosing sustainable materials. But how do you gather all of this information to make the most informed decision? (See Table 5.1.)

FIGURE 5.4 Cork harvesting process

TABLE 5.1 Initial Product Assessment Guide

Basic Information	Best Practice (what to look for)	Where to Find Information
Raw material	Renewable sources	Manufacturer's specifications
Manufacturing	Embodied energy	Third-party evaluators: ENERGY STAR, Regreen, etc.
Transport	Embodied energy	Location of manufacturer

There are many avenues to help designers find the most sustainable products. These include building material stores that sell only green products, manufacturers' Web sites, third-party evaluators, and the Internet. Firms that are focused on sustainable practices use databases which evaluate the greenness of a product. Such databases can be found at these Web sites, among others: www.energystar.gov, www.buildinggreen.org, www.regreenprogram.org. Some databases, such as the Pharos Index (www.pharosproject.net), require a paid membership. Spend some time reviewing these sites and others to determine which will be most useful in your practice.

The Pharos Index was developed to help designers, architects, and builders make sustainable choices in material selection. The materials covered are specific manufactured products. You will not see simply "quartz countertop" in the Pharos Index but rather brand names. Note that the Pharos rating is a *system*. Since there is no such thing as a perfectly "green" product, users of the index can analyze each product to determine which is best for their client. The five rating components of the Pharos system are:

1. Presence of VOCs
2. Toxic content
3. Manufacturing toxins
4. Renewable materials
5. Renewable energy

When researching a product for your projects, ask these questions, among others:

Manufacturers
- What is their environmental policy?
- Do they comply with industry standards and voluntary testing programs?
- What is the company's social impact on their employees (do they offer health coverage, education benefits, retirement etc.) and the community (do they support community events, employee volunteering activities, etc.)?

Products
- Where are the raw materials extracted?
- Where is the product manufactured?
- What is the environmental impact of the manufacturing process?
- What is the composition of the final product? (Research the MSDS.)
- What products are needed for the installation and maintenance of the final product?
- How will the product impact the indoor air quality (IAQ) of the home?
- What is the life span of the product?
- What is the recycled content of the product?
- How much packaging is used in shipping the product?
- How can the product be disposed of at the end of its use?
- Does this product fit in the client's budget?

As you apply these questions to each product you specify, you will create your own list of sustainable products. Remember, though, as we have previously stated, the parameters for determining the greenness of a product change over time. Therefore, continuing education is a requirement for all highly successful designers. As you continue with your education, consider obtaining professional certifications, such as those offered through the National Kitchen & Bath Association (NKBA). Obtaining your AKBD, CKD, CBD, and eventually your CMKBD and others, will support your continuing education process and enhance your professional success.

Longevity and Universal Design

Sustainability involves much more than environmental issues. If we believe that sustainable design incorporates the following principles:

- Optimize site potential and protection of existing landscape
- Minimize the consumption of nonrenewable energy

- Conserve and protect water
- Maximize the indoor environmental quality
- Balance long-term economic, social, and environmental needs
- Provide cost-effective development solutions
- Enhance clients' quality of life

then the real definition of sustainable design is "Design created to meet the needs of the present without compromising the needs of the future." This is where the concept of universal design comes into play.

Universal design focuses on meeting the changing needs of inhabitants of a home. It really doesn't matter if the home you design today incorporates green materials if in 50 years the house has to undergo a major remodel that sends most of the green materials used to the landfill. Universal design is discussed in greater detail in the *Bath Planning* and *Kitchen Planning* volumes of the NKBA Professional Resource Library.

It is important to note that universal design is not only for older people. Children grow, and social patterns and the basic use of the home change over time. Today's designers must be able to incorporate these changes into their designs. The more flexible and ergonomic the design is, the more it can meet the needs of both homeowners and the planet. Incorporating high-tech energy-efficiency controls for heating may be wonderful, but if their use is not intuitive and easy, the efficiency factor will be compromised.

Incorporate and note blocking for grab bars on every bathroom design, whether clients specifically request them or note. Consider this story, for example, from certified designer Rhonda Knoche, CMKBD/CAPS. "We recently successfully completed a full bathroom remodel for a new client. Six months later we received a frantic call from the wife saying that we were going to need to tear out the newly tiled shower to add grab bar blocking. Her husband had had a stroke and needed support in the shower. Because we had incorporated the appropriate blocking in the shower and at the toilet, and properly noted the locations on the plans, by the time the husband came home from the hospital, we had grab bars installed."[7] Not only did the designer save the homeowner a costly remodel, the designer's thoughtful design created a client for life.

Incorporating the NKBA's accessible standards into your kitchen and bath designs gives you and your clients the opportunity to create homes that are durable, flexible, and environmentally supportive.

MATERIALS

As we have discussed, there are many aspects in determining the green factor of a product. In this section we break down product categories, their advantages, disadvantages, and applications. Remember, there is no perfect product.

Cement

Ordinary Portland cement (OPC) is a material seen everywhere. It is the main ingredient in all concrete, mortar, and grout. Cement is considered a hydraulic material because it absorbs and is activated by the addition of water. A relatively inert surface once installed, cement is a good example of how important it is to understand the carbon footprint of a material.

Manufacturing Process
Portland cement is mined from the earth and is the basic ingredient in concrete. It is made from calcium, silicon, aluminum, and iron. Other ingredients can include limestone, shells, chalk, shale, slag silica sand, and iron ore. At the final stages, gypsum is added to help in the setting-up time.

Once the raw materials are mined, they are transported to the processing plant, where the rocks are crushed, mixed with water, and fed into a kiln. The kiln is heated to 2700 degrees Fahrenheit (1482 Celsius). During this process, off-gassing occurs.

Contemporary manufacturing processes capture the heat from the cooling-off period and return that energy to the kiln, saving fuel and increasing burning efficiency. Some plants integrate the use of waste materials, such as sewer sludge and old tires, as fuel for the kilns. On one hand, this is good, as the plants are using waste materials to create new products, but, on the other hand, the off-gassing of some of these combustibles adds to poor air quality.

Environmental Impact

Although cement is durable and its ability to be formed into any shape makes it an attractive and affordable building material, cement has a very high embodied energy and releases large amounts of CO_2, nitrous oxides (NOx), sulfur oxides (SOx), and other pollutants. The largest environmental burden of cement occurs during the kiln phase, where the greatest amount of fossil fuel is used. Studies have determined that the creation 1 ton of cement produces over 1 ton of CO_2. The net result of the production of cement produces approximately 8 percent of the world's CO_2 emissions, which is a large percentage coming from one industry.[10]

Options Available

There are ways to reduce the environmental impact of cement-based materials. Consider specifying a custom concrete mix that incorporates the use of *fly ash*. Fly ash is a by-product of coal burning. While this may seem counterintuitive, fly ash can take the place of cement (up to 25 percent in many mixes), and it strengthens the concrete. Unfortunately, fly ash can contain a considerable amount of toxic metals, as this product survives the combustion process. While it is unlikely that these toxic metals will leach from the cured material, it brings into question the disposal of the concrete later.

Applications of Cement

As a designer, you will come across cement used in many ways. The two most common are:

Mortar. All mortars are an adhesive. They are used to bond one type of material to another. Mortars are made with cement for strength, sand as an aggregate, and lime for added bonding strength and for flexibility.

In tile installations, thinset (a type of mortar) will commonly be used. Thinset uses a cellulose-based product instead of lime to help it retain water and give the material flexibility. The aggregate in thinset is a very fine sand so that it is more flexible. A latex additive is sometimes added for more flexibility.

Most mortars and thinsets emit high levels of VOCs, however, with research, one can find products that are certified for IAQ standards for low VOCs.

Cement grout. Necessary for most tile installations, conventional grout is used to fill the joints between tiles to create a continuous, relatively impermeable surface. Its main ingredient is Portland cement and pigments. It is easy to install, has little to no VOC emissions, and cleans up with water. Its high alkaline content can be an irritant to skin so gloves are recommend for installation. Contact with the eyes can cause serious irritation, and eyewash should be used if the product comes in contact with an installer's eyes.

Cement grout does require the continued use of sealers to minimize the growth of mold and mildew and to create a waterproof surface. (See the section called "Sealers" for additional environmental considerations.)

Concrete

Concrete is the most widely used construction material in the world today. With its Portland cement content, the production of concrete is extremely energy and fossil fuel-intensive and is one of our largest emitters of carbon dioxide. The current method of production makes concrete one of the most environmentally destructive materials. Concrete is produced by mixing cement with fine aggregate (sand), coarse aggregate (gravel or crushed stone), water, and small amounts of various chemicals called admixtures that control such properties as setting time and plasticity. The mining of aggregates (gravel, stone and sand) further add to the environmental impact of concrete.

There are options available to minimize the environmental impact of concrete. Replacing Portland cement with recyclable materials and minerals helps to reduce the amount of CO_2 released into the atmosphere and diverts materials from landfills.

High-volume fly ash concrete is a promising alternative. Fly-ash is a by-product of coal-burning power plants. The mixture of fly-ash, lime and water forms a compound similar to Portland cement and is strong and durable. In the past, almost 75 percent of fly-ash went directly to the landfill; this product helps to divert approximately up to 50 percent from landfills.

Other concrete options include AshCrete, blast furnace slag, and carbon concrete. AshCrete is created from 97 percent recycled materials and is known for its strength, approximately twice as strong as Portland cement. Blast furnace slag uses byproducts from blast furnaces that are used to produce iron. Slag is easier to obtain than fly ash and when mixed with lime and water creates a very strong cement.

Carbon concrete, a byproduct of oil refineries, is new to the industry. As a thermoplastic it replaces the use of cement in the making of concrete. Due to its nature to settle, it is not used for tall buildings; it is primarily used as a flooring material and for road paving.

Applications of Concrete

Concrete flooring sits on the fence when it comes to its "sustainable" factor. The type of cement that goes into your concrete will greatly raise or lower its "sustainability" rating. If you do choose to incorporate concrete flooring into your project, it is helpful to know that it can be finished in a myriad of options: acid-stained, painted, textured, patterned, and more. Because of its ability to retain heat, incorporating concrete floors with radiant heat or installing in passive solar homes is environmentally beneficial.

Maintenance for concrete floors is relatively easy, making them a good option for homeowners with allergies.

Epoxy Grout

The development of an epoxy-based grout in recent years has given designers and homeowners reason to be excited. Epoxy grout is almost stain-proof, a welcome attribute for tile installations on the floor and in bathrooms where mildew can be a threat. The green reality, however, is that epoxy manufacturing and use is not good for the environment. Third-party evaluators are excellent sources for specific information on building products such as epoxy.

During the installation process, epoxy grout emits VOCs due to the presence of a chemical hardener. Once the product hardens, there is no additional release of harmful VOCs.

The cost of epoxy grout is higher than cement-based grout due to the product cost and additional labor required for installation. Cement-based grout goes on with a trowel or float and is wiped off with a sponge. Epoxy is much trickier. Uninitiated installers can ruin the tile if the epoxy is not applied properly. However, epoxy grout wears like iron, and its performance is far superior to cement-based grout.

Epoxy grout is easier to clean than cement grout and requires no sealing. If you do decide to research epoxy grout, check the product's MSDS for a good look at the contents of the product. Epoxy grout is an excellent example of the LCA conundrum. As we have stated throughout, the perfect green product does not exist.

WALL FINISHES

With the plethora of wall finish options available, it is good to have an idea of which finish you intend to use as it can affect the overall budget.

Wallboard (Sheetrock)

Most of our interior walls are created with a stud and sheathing system. Gypsum wallboard (Sheetrock) is the most popular interior sheathing material. Gypsum is affordable, and its installation is entrenched in our residential building culture.

The creation of gypsum is similar to that of concrete: The raw material is mined and delivered to a plant where the material is heated in kilns to very high temperatures to render the gypsum into a powder, also called plaster. The kilns do not need to go as hot as those for concrete, so less fuel is used to create the gypsum plaster, but this process gives gypsum a high embodied energy characteristic that is worth considering when designing an interior. Over 80 percent of the gypsum extracted is used in the manufacturing of drywall.[11]

In the United States, approximately 50 percent of all gypsum is flue-gas desulfurization (FGD) gypsum. FGD is the process of removing polluting gases from the stacks of fossil-fueled power plants and purifying them into a hard substance that is then manufactured into gypsum board.[12] This process minimizes the harmful emissions into the atmosphere.

For more than 50 years, the gypsum industry has used recycled newspaper and other post-consumer paper in the manufacturing of the wallboard face and back paper. Currently the industry diverts more than 40 million cubic yards of paper material from landfills.[13]

Gypsum wallboard can be readily recycled across North America, although according to the Construction and Demolition Recycling Organization, most ends up in the landfill. Determine if your local municipality offers this service, and have a conversation with your contractor to add this to the scope of the project.

Recycled drywall can be used in a number of ways; some examples are provided next.

- Content for new drywall
- Content for cement
- Added to soil and crops to improve drainage and plant growth
- Content for fertilizer
- Additive to composting

Moisture-Resistant Wallboards and Tile Backerboards

Moisture management is paramount to preventing mold growth in a home. (See Chapter 4 for a discussion on ventilation for the prevention of mold growth.) The selection of the most efficient backerboard for wet areas such as tubs and shower surrounds will aid in the prevention of mold and mildew. Options for tile backerboards are cementitious, coated glass mat, and fiber cement.

Whereas gypsum board can be recycled, these types of wallboards cannot. Both cementitious and fiber cement boards have a higher environmental impact due to the high embodied energy content of the cement. For a more sustainable product, specify backerboards with higher fly ash content.

In the case of tile backerboards, you and the client are making a choice between IAQ (health benefits) and high embodied energy.

Paint

Paint is the most economical and efficient way to make change in a room. Color can be incredibly uplifting, and a new, uniform finish can pull an entire room together. There are still many contractors and designers who consider an oil-based paint to be more durable than latex or water-based formulas. This may be the case, but bear in mind that oil-based paint will off-gas solvents for a much longer time period than water-based paint.

The Truth about Zero-VOC Paint

Conventional paints are manufactured from petrochemical-based solvents that off-gas (i.e., they are high-VOC). When specifying paint, instead of conventional paints, look for low-VOC and zero-VOC formulas. These paints both cover well and have the lowest amount of harmful emissions. The label "zero-VOC" is a misnomer. VOCs are present in all paints, although those labeled as zero VOC have not exceeded the applicable government limits. It is important to note that some paints of this type have lower emissions than others. This greenwashing is very prevalent in paints. Use a third-party evaluator rather than manufacturers' information to make your final choice of which brand to specify.

Natural Paints

"Natural paints" are made from renewable or naturally occurring materials and are available as water, oil, or milk based. Ingredients include citrus oil, lime, clay, linseed oil, casein, and chalk. They contain no petroleum products and emit few if any VOCs regulated by the US Environmental Protection Agency (EPA); however, they may emit VOCs from additives, such as citrus-based solvents.

The manufacturing process for natural paints is cleaner than that for traditional paints, but be sure to refer to a third-party rating system for more information on each specific brand's processes.

Typically, these products are healthier and environmentally safer than traditional paints, chemically sensitive clients may find some of the ingredients in natural products, such as citrus oil, hard to endure. Not all of the natural ingredients are safe; some, such as cadmium (a yellow pigment), are toxic. Refer to each product's MSDS ingredient list for compatibility for your client.

Milk-based paints (made from powdered casein) are the least toxic and environmentally impacting paint. They are not, however, recommended in high-moisture areas, such as kitchens or bathrooms, as moisture may damage the finish and encourage mold growth. If it is to be used in these locations, a sealer must be applied. The use of a low-VOC, water-based sealer will further support the health and environmental benefits.

Milk-based paints require the addition of a preservative to extend their shelf lives. Due to the paint's short shelf life after opening, touch-ups require a new batch and may not match the original finish.

Natural paints cost 20 to 80 percent more than traditional paints and take two or more days to dry. They may not always be compatible with existing latex or oil painted surfaces; therefore, they require extensive prep work as these paints are best used on clean-primed surfaces.

Clay Plasters

There are many alternatives to using paint as a covering of gypsum or plaster in an older home. Hand-applied clay-based mixes provide endless opportunities for custom, one-of-a-kind surfaces. The biggest hurdle you will experience with these surfaces is cost of installation. The application is in layers, which is time consuming (see Figures 5.5 and 5.6). The cost of the material is comparable to higher-end paint (in general), and the fact that it comes in powder form and is mixed with water on site means little waste of unused product.

Homeowners generally can make small repairs to walls with clay-based plaster, but large damage may require a professional.

FIGURE 5.5 American Clay installed in a bathroom

The advantage to using clay-based products in wet areas such as bathrooms is their ability to help control moisture. These products have can absorb moisture during high-humidity periods (e.g., after a shower) and release it during low-humidity times. This is referred to as humidity buffering (see Figure 5.7).

Painted surfaces do not absorb moisture. During a shower, the moisture level rises in a bathroom and condenses on the surface of the painted walls. This creates the perfect environment for the growth of mold and mildew.

Plastered surfaces absorb excess moisture, reducing the opportunities for mold and mildew to grow. As the room's humidity level drops, the plastered surfaces release the excess

FIGURE 5.6 American Clay installed in a kitchen

moisture, helping to maintain a constant humidity level. The release of moisture "continues until the plaster reaches about 10 to 12 percent moisture content."[14]

A waxed surface or Venetian plaster is similar to a clay-based wall surface. Natural pigments are mixed with plaster and troweled onto a wall. The next layer is mixed with paraffin and or beeswax. The result is a beautiful, custom surface that shines. There are no VOCs and little wasted product. The surface is amazingly durable but, of course, it is susceptible to damage as is any wall. Therefore, it is not recommended in high-traffic areas, such as entryways on walls that line paths of high circulation in a kitchen.

Ceramics

Tile made from clay is responsible for the surface durability of many kitchen and bath interiors. Ceramic tile can be an affordable and durable alternative to stone. However, it can also be one of the most unique and expensive materials in a project.

The installation of tile can cost more per square foot than the material cost itself. Clay tile needs to be installed on a dry and level surface. Most tile installation problems have to do with an uneven substrate. For most wall applications, a thinset installation is recommended. For floors, either a thinset method is specified or, if a slope is necessary, a thickset installation is recommended.

Clay tile is installed over a thinset mortar bed, which is a cement product. The embodied energy of cement is considerable, as previously discussed.

Any tile installation requires a sealant to the grout. Depending on the type of tile (low-fire ceramic or a softer stone such as marble), the sealant will also help to prevent staining. Again, look to the third-party evaluators to determine a sealant that has a relatively low VOC content.

Humidity Buffering

One of the key features of using American Clay plasters on your walls is its ability to help control water vapor in your living space. This is significant because of what it can alleviate from the rooms where you have used our earth plasters. This ability to absorb water vapor during periods of high humidity, and release this vapor during periods of low humidity is typically referred to as "humidity buffering."

HIGH HUMIDITY

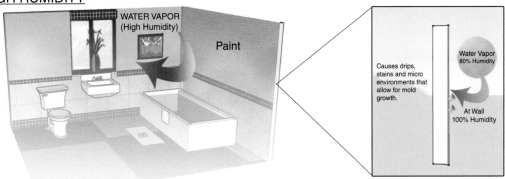

Painted walls allow for humidity levels to climb until moisture condenses on the surface. This allows moisture to collect on the surface of the finish and produce a micro-environment ideal for mold and mildew growth.

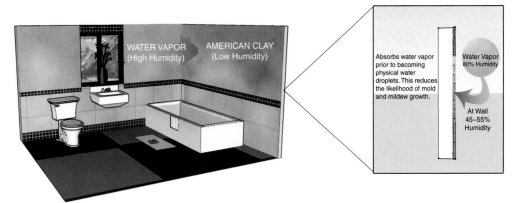

Walls with American Clay absorb the moisture before it can cause problems. This reduces the likelihood of mold and mildew growth.

LOW HUMIDITY

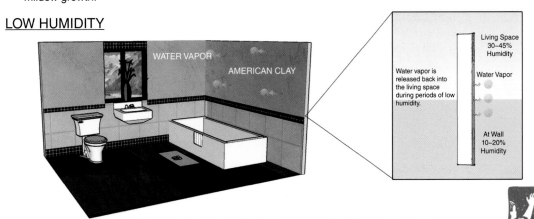

As the interior humidity drops, the American Clay plaster naturally releases the moisture back into the space, helping to maintain a more constant humidity. This continues until the plaster reaches about 10% to 12% moisture content, and the cycle stops.

**The more clay used in a space the greater capacity there is to capture moisture and the greater the humidity buttering.

FIGURE 5.7 Humidity buffering in a bathroom

There are locally made tile materials that can add an artistic touch to a project and will align your project with a local artisan community.

Sinks made of vitreous clay are popular for their high gloss and durability. Porcelain sinks can be both the drop-in and under-mount versions.

Countertops

Concrete

Artisans use concrete to create unique countertops that are very durable. Reinforcement in the form of glass fiber, rebar, or wire mesh is added to the fabrication. Labor is considerable in relationship to the raw materials, which results in a higher-end finished material.

Concrete countertops are unique, hand-crafted, and personalized. A designer has the ability to customize the color, finish, size, shape, and edge detail.

Concrete countertops are not for everyone. Staining is common, especially if used in a kitchen. Over time, minor hairline cracks may occur. These cracks usually are nonstructural, and are due to the shrinkage of the final product. Inform your client that scratches can and will occur with normal use. Acids (from vinegars, wine, mustard, citrus, and others) may etch the finished surface if they are not cleaned up immediately.

Due to the porous nature of concrete, it is recommended that a food-grade sealer or finishing wax is regularly applied to prevent staining and water absorption. See "Sealers" for more information. Concrete can withstand heat, but excessive heat can harm the integrity of the sealer, requiring a reapplication.

Some fabricators use glass-fiber-reinforced concrete (GFRC) instead of the conventional precast process. This option is considered more sustainable as it makes the final product lighter, uses less Portland cement, and incorporates more recycled materials. GFRC is stronger than conventional concrete and allows for a thinner application.

Concrete countertops can be repurposed at the end of their lives. They can be reused or cut for smaller applications. Old concrete can be crushed and used as aggregate for new concrete, saving energy through recycling.

To maintain a concrete countertop, clients should use a pH-neutral cleaner and avoid the use of abrasive cleaners and scrubbing pads. If a countertop gets stained, there may be options for removal. Contact your fabricator for removal methods they recommend.

Terrazzo-Type Products

Terrazzo by definition is a composite consisting of marble, quartz, granite, glass, and other materials in a cementitious, polymer, or epoxy base. It is typically poured in place or precast. Terrazzo flooring has been a building material for over 1,500 years and is one of the first recycled products. Terrazzo is manufactured from recycled product, has a long life, is durable (some original terrazzo floors have been in use for over 1000 years), and can be recycled at its end of life.

Terrazzo has been incorporated into slab material meant for countertop use. Examples of this application include Icestone, Vetrazzo, GEOS, and Fuez (see Figure 5.8). Icestone and Vetrazzo currently hold silver certifications with C2C. Their process for achieving this rating included discontinuing some products that did not comply with McDonough Braungart Design Chemistry's (MBDC) strict standards for material health; they also built a state-of-the-art water recycling system for their manufacturing process.[15]

Terrazzo is porous and should be sealed twice a year, unless your client is comfortable with some staining.

Paper Composite and Fiber Cement Countertops

Paper-fiber composite products typically use postconsumer recycled paper that has been soaked in phenolic resins. Phenolic resins are synthetic resins created through the reaction of

FIGURE 5.8 Recycled glass surface used for a kitchen island countertop
Courtesy of EOS Surfaces, LLC

phenol or a substituted phenol with formaldehyde. Paperstone® (see Figure 5.9) has created a proprietary PetroFree^tm phenolic resin. The formaldehyde and phenol become inert when combined and cured. Other products, such as Slatescape, incorporate Portland cement and ultra-fine silica as the binder for the recycled newsprint.

Originally created for use in industrial applications, composite countertops are water resistant and clean up easily. Most products are heat resistant to 350 degrees Fahrenheit (176 Celsius). Composite countertops will darken over time due to oxidation and sunlight exposure.

Colors for these products are earth based, ranging from browns to blues. The color goes all the way through. Maintenance includes daily cleaning with a soft cloth and warm water; nonabrasive

FIGURE 5.9 Kitchen counter made of Paperstone®
Courtesy of Paperstone®

cleaners are acceptable. Periodic sealing with mineral oil or wax is recommended. Cutting directly on these types of countertops is not recommended.

Stone

Stone has had a tough time staying popular with the focus on green materials. Treasured for its unique beauty (by nature, no piece of stone is exactly the same as another), stone presents a green dilemma. It is a natural material, quarried from the earth, and comes out of the ground ready to be shaped and installed. However, it is heavy. The transport of stone gives the material a considerable carbon footprint as does the energy required to fabricate the stone to usable "dimension-stone" sizes. Ethically, some stone quarries in some parts of the world exploit workers, making the installation of stone a conflicted decision. Do your homework and consider specifying stone that is not from across the globe but closer to your job site.

Choosing the correct stone for clients depends on uses and lifestyles. Granite is much harder than marble and is more forgiving. Some clients will appreciate the patina created over years of use on a marble countertop while others cannot live with stains. Limestone is a beautiful stone, but its use in a shower requires a much more diligent maintenance schedule.

Soapstone is expensive and available in limited colors (black and green) but needs no sealing and is virtually heatproof due to its excellent thermal qualities. It is stain resistant. Soapstone darkens as it ages. To speed up the darkening process, clients can apply food-grade mineral oil every few months.

Sealants are available to protect stone from staining, but the use of a volatile chemical sealant in a client's home is questionable. Slabs of stone that are impregnated with sealants at a factory prior to delivery to a stone yard are available but the question should be, for what purpose? Only cosmetic? If stains and wear are of considerable concern for your clients, you may want to steer them toward a quartz composite material.

Quartz Surfaces

Engineered quartz surfacing has become a very popular choice for homeowners as a countertop material due to its durability, stain resistance, and ease of maintenance. Many quartz countertops manufacturers are GREENGUARD and NSF certified (see Chapter 2) Some, such as Eco by Cosentino (see Figure 5.10) and Caesarstone, have been awarded C2C certifications.

FIGURE 5.10 This ECO countertop is made with recycled materials.
Courtesy of Cosentino

Quartz products are manufactured from preindustrial waste and many include recycled materials. Eco by Cosentino is 75 percent recycled content and holds both C2C Silver and GREENGUARD certifications.

Many of these companies, such as Cosentino (Eco and Silestone) and Caesarstone, have manufacturing processes that recycle as much as 94 percent of the water used.[16] Cambria quartz (also GreenGuard certified) offers a quartz product whose material is primarily mined and fabricated in North America, which gives designers in the United States and Canada a domestically produced option.

Engineered stone comes is many thicknesses and can be used for countertops, wall cladding, and even flooring in some cases.

Quartz does not need to be sealed, which makes it a popular choice for designers and consumers concerned about the environment and the impact sealants can have on the IAQ of their home.

Like other heavy materials, quartz has a considerable carbon footprint due to transport. For a more sustainable option, consider specifying domestically produced products.

Solid Surfacing

Polymer-based products (such as Corian) offer a continuous surface that is great for adding a seamless installation to kitchens and baths. Solid surfacing offers an antimicrobial, impervious surface with relatively low maintenance. Drawbacks include price and the susceptibility to damage with heat.

Solid surfaces offer designers the opportunity to create virtually seamless installations as sinks can be installed seamlessly. Major repairs can be done by professionals, and the product can be reused and refabricated years later.

Polymers are a synthetic material. If you and your client are concerned about the use of man-made materials, you may want to consider stone or wood countertops. Look to third-party evaluators for a complete rating of VOC emissions, toxicity, and a rating on regenerative content.

Wood Countertops

The most environmentally sustainable counter surface, wood countertops provoke the most passionate opinions. On one hand, this surface allows you to cut food directly on the surface; on the other hand, many clients cringe at the thought of cutting on a countertop.

> I have specified wood counters for my designs for over 20 years to divisive responses. For the clients who have chosen wood counters, they have found them to be easy to use and maintain. I tell my clients that they can cut anything on their counters from meat to vegetables as long as they use soap after cutting meat. Wood is naturally microbial, so bacteria does not live in the wood as long as you clean it regularly. Anti-bacterial soap is not a requirement in cleaning. Once every three months it is recommended to apply food-grade linseed oil on your wood counters—although I have personally had wood counters for 15 years and apply oil on them perhaps once a year. They hold up just beautifully!

—Robin Rigby Fisher, CMKBD

Choosing wood countertops that are certified as sustainably harvested by the Forest Stewardship Council (FSC) helps to protect wood as a natural resource. Specify hard, dense woods such as hard rock maple, madrone, cherry, bamboo (as end-grain butcher block), oak, or white ash (end-grain butcher block), which will best stand up to sharp knives.

Stains or burns on wood countertops can be easily repaired by lightly sanding and finishing with warm (food-grade) mineral oil. Rub it in, let it soak for 20 to 30 minutes, then wipe the excess with a clean cloth. Do not use cooking oils, which will turn rancid. For extra protection, apply 1 part beeswax or paraffin wax melted in 4 parts mineral oil, and rub it into the bare wood while the mix is still warm.

Laminates

Made from plastic-coated synthetics, originally all laminate countertops were manufactured with high-VOC papers and adhesives. Healthier versions are available today. Choose laminates that is certified by GREENGUARD, which are made from formaldehyde-free paper and low VOC or nontoxic glues.

Laminates are easy to clean and are inexpensive but are not repairable, have a short life span (15 to 20 years), and are not recyclable

If laminate is the best product for your client, specify a substrate made with non-urea-added formaldehyde (NUAF) and low-VOC, solvent-free or water-based adhesives.

Metals

Like wood, metals are used throughout a project. There are hidden sources of metal: nails, screws, reinforcement in concrete, drawer slides, and, in some projects, wall studs (just to name a few of the many locations). Metals are ubiquitous in a project. There are the exposed metals that every designer appreciates: hardware, light fixtures, tile finishes, appliances, and hoods for cooking surfaces—the list goes on. The coordination of metals is one of the first things a designer does to create a palette that is cohesive and makes sense.

The extraction of metal ore from the earth is done by mining, which causes extreme damage to the environment (see Figure 5.11). The creation of the mine requires energy and the use

FIGURE 5.11 Copper mining

By Peripitus (own work) [GFDL (www.gnu.org/copyleft/fdl.html) or CC-BY-SA-3.0-2.5-2.0-1.0 (http://creativecommons.org/licenses/by-sa/3.0)

of fossil fuels. Leaching from mining into nearby water sources such as rivers causes pollution from the mineral ore.

To minimize the use of new raw materials, look to companies that use some amount of recycled metal content in their hardware and sinks. Many metals, such as copper and cast iron, already contain recycled content. The Kohler Company creates cast iron tubs that are made with 80 percent recycled iron (see Figure 5.12). Cast iron lasts longer than fiberglass or composite.

Stainless Steel

Stainless steel is a combination of steel, chromium, and nickel. Although the mining of these materials does impact the environment, stainless steel contains a "minimum of 67 percent recycled scrap," according to North American Stainless, a metal manufacturer based in Kentucky.[17] Stainless steel is heat and stain resistant, durable, and easy to clean, and it can be recycled at the end of its life. Brushed or textured surfaces can minimize a myriad of scratches. It can, however, dent easily and is expensive.

Copper

Copper for kitchen countertops is a beautiful option. It is a naturally antimicrobial surface. Copper is easy to maintain, but clients need to understand that if it is not waxed on a regular basis, it will darken and achieve a rich patina. Copper dents and scratches easily and requires a substrate. (Substrates are discussed at the end of the "Countertops" section.)

FIGURE 5.12 Tub made with recycled iron
Courtesy of Kohler Company

FIGURE 5.13 A kitchen sink made of recycled copper
Courtesy of Native Trails

Sinks often are made from recycled copper. Native Trails, of San Luis Obispo, California, manufactures sinks (see Figure 5.13) from recycled copper.

Recycled Aluminum

Not recommended for kitchen countertops, recycled aluminum is a sustainable choice for sinks, hardware, light fixtures, and decorative tiles. Companies such as Eleek, located in Portland, Oregon, manufacture products made from cast aluminum (see Figure 5.14) from 100 percent recycled material, with postconsumer content between 85 to 100 percent, depending on the product line.[18]

Donate All Metal from the Project

Salvage and donate all fixtures that are removed from the job site and put that metal back into use rather than in a landfill. Hardware and fixtures are some of the most easily retrofitted building materials. In your specifications, incorporate a line item listing all materials that will be saved for donation or recycle.

FIGURE 5.14 A recycled aluminum custom hood

Design by Robin Rigby Fisher, CMKBD, CAPS, Robin Rigby Fisher Design, Portland, OR

Substrates

To minimize your environmental impact, specify a counter substrate made with NUAF and low-VOC, solvent-free, or water-based adhesives.

SEALERS

The use of sealers on finished surfaces depends on a few variables: the type of material used (concrete, granite, marble, soapstone, limestone, wood, etc.), where it is installed (showers, countertops, walls, floors), the client's commitment to reapplication, and the impact the sealer may have on the IAQ.

Why should a product be sealed? The purpose of a sealer is to protect a surface from staining and etching. Not all sealers are alike or are appropriate for all surfaces.

Types of Sealers

There are two types of sealers commonly used for stone, concrete, and tile. They are *penetrating* and *topical*:

Penetrating (or impregnators) **sealers** soak into the material (if the material is porous), minimizing absorption and staining. Penetrating sealers do not change the appearance of the finished surface.

In the case of concrete, a penetrating sealer is applied to bare concrete and allowed to soak in. These sealers are recommended for concrete surfaces with a polished or honed surface.

Tile with a crackle glaze should be sealed with a penetrating sealer if used in a shower in order to minimize the growth of mold and mildew.

Some types of stones, such as soapstone, only need mineral oil. Mineral oil is not a sealer; rather, it is a means to speed up the natural darkening process that the stone goes through over time.

Topical sealers include wax, acrylics, and epoxies.

Wax (carnauba and/or beeswax) is the most basic sealer and is recommended on concrete over a penetrating sealer. It leaves the surface with a low- to high-sheen finish that darkens or enhances the finish of the concrete. It is easy to apply and is very forgiving. Wax will not scratch, but anything left on the surface for a period of time will leave a mark. Hot temperatures can soften this finish, and acids like vinegar or lemon juice can remove the wax and etch the surface below.

Acrylic or solvent-based sealers are the most commonly used on concrete. They harden upon curing and provide fairly good stain protection but are easily scratched. The unprotected surface of the concrete is then susceptible to staining. These types of sealers contain high VOCs.

Although not very environmentally sustainable, epoxy sealers offer good stain resistance. Epoxy is an expensive sealer for concrete and must be applied by a professional.

Determining if Your Product Needs Sealer

Not all surfaces need to be sealed. Some, such as concrete, should be sealed regularly, but some stones, such as certain types of granite, do not need to be sealed. According to Rocky Mountain Bathrooms of Littleton, Colorado, "Less than 20 percent of polished granite actually requires being sealed. That means that upwards of 80 percent of polished granite installed in homes requires no sealer at all."[19] Sealing honed surfaces is strongly recommended.

How do you determine if the product you want to specify on a project should be sealed? There are a few tests you can do on a sample.

Using a sample, apply water on the surface for 10 to 15 minutes and then remove it. If the sample has not darkened, it will not absorb water-based products. To determine if your sample will absorb solvent-based products, apply mineral oil on your sample and wait 5 to10 minutes. If it hasn't darkened, your sample does not need to be sealed. If the mineral oil did darken the sample, wait a while, and the oil will evaporate, leaving your sample ready to be tested again.

In short, if neither water or oil darkens your sample, your choice does not need sealer, thus saving your client time and money and maintaining the health of the home.

Some finish materials, such as marble, may pass both of these tests but will etch from the chemical reaction between what is left on the surface and the minerals in the stone. These etches are not stains, and no sealer will protect the surface from these reactions. The etching can be removed only through resurfacing.

Industry Voices on Sealers

Amy Bright is a professional resource associate with many years of experience in stone and tile sales. She advocates for questioning the use of sealants and highly recommends getting to know your client and researching your material options: "What are your clients' wants and needs? How can a material best serve them? What is your client's approach to maintenance?" There are ways to guide your clients to create a green home with no added chemicals to add to poor IAQ.

Sandy Hayes is a Certified Master Kitchen and Bath Designer (CMKBD). She says: "We never sealed granite in Canada, and I often tell the story of my own countertops and how I do not seal them."

Helping clients choose the best material for their home that serves their lifestyle well and supports a healthy environment is not difficult; it does, however, require research and the support of your suppliers.

Flooring

Cork

Cork has been used as a flooring material for over 100 years. Naturally soft, cork is insulating (warm to the touch) and absorbs sound. Cork oak trees live for over 200 years; the cork is harvested every 10 to 12 years. Cork is self-healing; most dents will come out over time. Damaged areas can be removed, and the floor can be resealed. Cork is naturally water-resistant, and many types of cork flooring can be used in all rooms of the home including the bathroom.

Cork flooring comes in many options and at different price levels. Click, engineered, veneered, and glue-down options are available; different applications require different selections. Before finalizing your specifications, be sure to confirm with your supplier that the cork you chose is appropriate for your specific application. Some questions to ask:

- Is this product recommended for a bathroom installation?
- How often can this cork be refinished? (Some engineered corks are only a veneer and cannot be refinished.)
- If using a glue-down cork: What are the manufacturer's recommendations for substrate installation? What types of adhesives are required? The substrate of a glue-down cork must be installed properly, according to the manufacturer. If the substrate is not smooth, screws are not counter-sunk filled, the seams and screw holes will be seen on the finished floor.
- Does this product need to be finished after installation?
- How does this product need to be maintained after installation?

Linoleum

Made from renewable resources such as linseed oil, pine rosin, wood flour, limestone, and cork dust and natural pigments with a jute backing, linoleum was invented in the late 1800s by Frederick Walton.

Naturally nonallergenic and antistatic, linoleum is durable, lasting 30 to 40 years in high-traffic area. "From a resource standpoint, it's great," says *Environmental Building News* editor Alex Wilson. "It's made from natural, largely renewable, materials, and there are no environmental toxins involved in its manufacturing or disposal."[20]

Because linoleum is made from linseed oil, when it's first installed there will be a yellow cast to the flooring (called ambering). Linseed oil is a yellow liquid. As the floor gets exposed to the light, the linseed oil will evaporate, taking the yellow hue with it. This process cannot be rushed by washing the floor; only time and natural lighting will remove it. Be sure to inform clients that if they lay a rug on the floor, the yellowing will come back. Again, it will evaporate with time.

Linoleum requires specific underlayment and adhesives. Be sure to note in your specifications that "all installation must be done according to manufacturer's specifications."

Maintenance is easy with just sweeping and regular mopping required; waxing is not necessary. Repairs, including burns, scratches, and cuts, can easily be repaired by professionals.

Cabinetry

Making sure your clients are well informed about the environmental impact of their choice of cabinetry is an important part of your kitchen and design practice. Off-gassing from materials used to make cabinets can cause some of the worst IAQ. This is because of the presence of urea-based formaldehyde and other toxic adhesives used in much of the composite wood products that are used in cabinetry construction.

We spoke with Darrill Andries, CKD, a California-based NKBA designer and cabinetry installer who is dedicated to education regarding green cabinets. Darrill explained that the California Environmental Protection Agency (CalEPA) leads the way in emissions control. This includes toxic emissions and VOC emissions from composite wood products and cabinetry finishing. The state's environmental protection agency is behind the Air Resources Board (ARB), which determined an Airborne Toxic Control Measure (ATCM) in 2007 to reduce formaldehyde emissions from the use of composite wood products. This ATCM has changed the face of cabinetry manufacturing and installation in the state of California.

The ATCM established by CalEPA is also the inspiration in part for the green cabinetry certification from the Kitchen Cabinetry Manufacturers Association (KCMA). The KCMA represents the interests of over 300 cabinetry makers in North America. Darrill pointed out as an example the KCMA's Environmental Stewardship Program (ESP.) Here are just a few of the stringent standards that must be met to qualify in the voluntary ESP program:

- 100 percent of the particleboard, medium-density fiberboard (MDF), and plywood used in the cabinets must meet the formaldehyde emission level of the California Air Resources Compwood ATCM and must be third-party certified to meet low formaldehyde emission standards.
- 75 percent of cabinets must be finished in the United States or Canada. Finishes emit no greater hazardous air pollutants than allowed by local plant operating permits.
- 80 percent of the particleboard and medium-density fiberboard used in cabinets must contain 100 percent recycled or recovered fiber content
- Manufacturers utilize an annual, written training plan to educate their hardwood suppliers of their preference for purchasing certified lumber.
- Manufacturer has a comprehensive recycling program for process waste.
- Manufacturer is required to have a written policy stating a firm commitment to environmental quality.[21]

Best Practices for Specifying Sustainably Constructed Cabinets

Two of the largest expenses of a kitchen remodel are the cabinets and appliances. Many times clients who start the design process with sustainability as their end goal wind up deviating from their original path due to budgetary restrictions. More often than not, cabinet quality ends up on the budget chopping-block. As a designer, it is your responsibility to assist your clients in understanding the value of investing in higher-quality and more sustainable cabinet options, and to explain how these choices will benefit them for many years into the future.

Drawer boxes. Quality cabinetry is constructed of solid wood drawer boxes rather than particle board. Ask about FSC-certified wood. Also, easily renewable and strong options such as poplar and alder are good choices for drawer boxes.

Hardware. Look for domestically manufactured hardware. Hardware is a great example of an LCA application. Poorly made hardware is more likely to bend and break, thus creating the need for replacement. Drawer runners and closures aren't seen but their quality is felt each time the drawer is used.

Doors and drawer fronts. Look for wood and veneers that are FSC certified. If you are working with painted surfaces, speak to the fabricator about the use of low- and no-VOC paint.

Finishing. If you are working with a cabinet maker, make sure to specify paints, stains, and all finishes with low to no VOC emissions. There are advantages and disadvantages to the use of low-VOC finishes. Conventional finishes *in general* cure to a harder surface and protect the cabinetry better. Do your homework and learn about what types of finishes your cabinet supplier or fabricator is using.

Source locally. The use of wood that is locally produced will mean less fossil fuel is used in the transport of the wood. This adds to local economy and gives your project a strong sense of local character (see Figure 5.15).

If you are going to install cabinets on a smaller budget, most likely the drawer boxes and the bodies of the cabinets will be made of MDF. Ask your manufacturer or local fabricator about its use of products that are aligned with California's ATCM standards.

FIGURE 5.15 Locally sourced cabinets built by L & Z Specialties, Portland, Oregon. NUAF plywood case construction.

Courtesy of L & Z Specialties. Photo by Dale Lang

Appliances

There is a certain point in the design process when everything comes to a halt and there is only so far you can proceed until appliances are chosen. Assisting clients in assessing which appliances best fit their needs is partly the designer's responsibility and mostly the appliance specialist's responsibility. We recommend creating a strong relationship with an appliance specialist; this person will be instrumental in aiding in the success of the project and the ultimate happiness of the client.

On using the services of a professional resource associate, author Robin Rigby-Fisher writes:

> I have been working with Michael for over 12 years. During my initial meetings with my clients, I determine their cooking needs, aesthetic style and budget. I then send this information along with preliminary designs to Michael and schedule a meeting for my clients with him to discuss their appliance needs. Because of my relationship with Michael, he knows my design style, what products I recommend and trusts my suggestions. The client does not need me to be a part of this process. I trust Michael to serve my client well and they love him!

The technology in appliances changes so rapidly it would take full-time work just to keep up. Designers need to know enough about appliances to help direct clients in the right direction. While a designer needs a general knowledge of appliances, a strong relationship with an appliance specialist only adds to your professionalism. A designer should do the homework, researching appliances endorsed by ENERGY STAR, the EPA's WaterSense program, *Consumer Reports*, and Good Guide (www.goodguide.com) to evaluate the green characteristics of various appliance choices.

Source domestically made appliances. Sourcing appliances that are made domestically means your client will have access to a warranty that is much easier to work with. The carbon footprint of the transport of the appliance is much less than if it was created overseas or in another country. You are also helping the domestic economy.

Cooking Appliances

The cooktop is the workhorse of kitchen. For years, gas has been the cooking fuel of choice in high-end kitchens. But recently, induction cooktops have gained the interest of the industry and of consumers. Induction cooking has been around for many years. It holds a large market share in Europe but accounts for only 5 percent of the market in the United States.

Induction cooking works through the use of magnets. A magnetic field is created between the cooking element and the pan. The cooking appliance does not get hot, which results in less energy being used and wasted. Pots and pans that contain ferrous material are required for induction cooking. This type of electric cooking performs at the level of gas (instant on and off.)

Induction has three advantages over gas (see Figure 5.16):

1. Safety: The unit itself does not get hot, which eliminates residual heat. Once the pan has been removed from the cooking surface, there is less heat to affect the ambient air. This type of cooking appliance is well suited for a home with small children or a family member with developmental disabilities or dementia. Even after bringing a pot of water to a full boil, within 1 to 2 minutes it is safe to touch the cooking surface. Many of these units incorporate a lock-out option to further enhance the safety feature.
2. Energy efficiency: Induction cooktops require a 220-volt electrical source. The unit transfers energy directly to the food more efficiently than any other cooking surface, and the residual heat is minimal resulting in energy savings of approximately 20 percent over coil electric and almost twice the savings over gas.
3. Indoor air quality: Induction cooktops do not release any impurities into the air the way natural-gas-fueled cooktops do. Their use will not require additional venting, as commercial-grade gas-fueled cooktops require. Therefore, induction cooktops are highly recommended for any client who has an environmental sensitivity or diminished immune system.

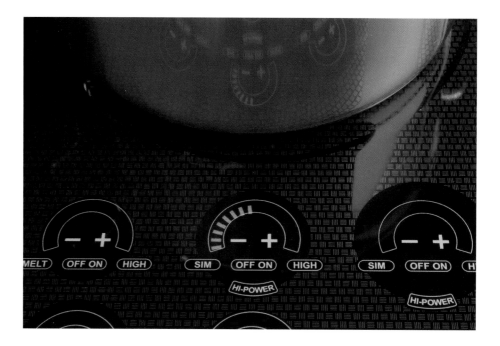

FIGURE 5.16 An induction cooktop
Courtesy of Wolf

Gas will be the most popular choice for your clients. Although natural gas is an affordable fuel, its use deteriorates the quality of the air in the home. See Chapter 4 for specifics on IAQ and the use of gas cooking surfaces.

Electric cooktops are affordable. New products work very efficiently. Similar to induction cooking surfaces, they do not release impurities into the air as gas-fueled cooking surfaces do.

Dishwashers

In regard to efficiency, many ENERGY STAR–rated dishwashers use 41 percent less energy than those that meet the government's minimum efficiency standards.[22]

In regard to water conservation, ENERGY STAR–rated versions use about a third less water (approximately 4 gallons per load rather than the standard 6 gallons used in a conventional dishwasher).

Additional Appliances

Determining the additional appliances in the kitchen is based on your client's needs, wants, desires, and budget. For energy efficiency, consider the ENERGY STAR label if available or look to the Good Guide for information on energy efficiency. The smaller the ENERGY STAR label number is, the less energy the appliance will use.

Warming Drawers

At first glance, a warming drawer seems more of a frivolity than a sustainable choice. This could not be further from the truth. Consider the costs of eating out or worst of all, the garbage involved with take-out. Warming drawers allow a busy family to cook a healthy meal early in the day, and keep it at a safe temperature (160 degrees Fahrenheit, 71 Celsius) and in a moisture-controlled environment until they are ready to eat.

The ENERGY STAR program rates and recommends warming drawers, those wonderful add-ons to a custom kitchen that make serving dinner so much easier. Look to the Good Guide for a sense of how energy efficient some choices are. Opt for domestically manufactured drawers.

Wine Storage

Currently, wine coolers are not listed under the ENERGY STAR program. According to *Consumer Reports*, some of the models that were tested used as much energy as an 18-cubic-foot refrigerator and some models required twice the energy as similar models in the same category. Do your homework and check about the energy use. Wine coolers are on constantly, which makes energy conservation important. The Good Guide rates wine coolers for energy use on their website.

FIXTURES AND FITTINGS

After the refrigerator, the sink and faucet are the most used items in the kitchen. Since many of these items have a high embodied energy content, the designer may have to consider other options and sustainability factors such as recycled content, water flow, and where the product is manufactured. Luckily, we have many manufacturers who produce their products in North America and even incorporate recycled or pre-industrial waste in the fabrication process.

Sinks

Kitchen sinks are specified by how they look first and then how they perform. How noisy are they? Do dishes break more easily in some models rather than in others? How do they react to heat and very hot pans just off the cooktop? Which version is the most sustainable choice?

Do your research and look for models to choose from that are created domestically. Many sinks, particularly stainless steel versions, are created overseas, adding to the sinks' carbon footprint. Planning for longevity is very important as well. If a sink is susceptible to scorching and burning, its likelihood of needing to be replaced is higher than another choice may be. Consider the embodied energy conversation in the beginning of the chapter on metal versus ceramic. This may help tip the scale as you help your client make choices.

Consider a repurposed sink from the local Habitat for Humanity ReStore or a local building salvage shop (see Figure 5.17). You may find something totally unique and interesting. Check carefully. Repurposed sinks often have no warranty, and it is the responsibility of the client and/or designer to coordinate the installation.

FIGURE 5.17 With careful and diligent searching, a sink may be sourced from building salvage stores, such as the Habitat for Humanity ReStore.

Photo courtesy of ReStore. Photo by Harvey Thomas

FIGURE 5.18 Faucet with low-flow aerator option
Courtesy of Kohler Company

Faucets

A WaterSense faucet can cut water flow by 30 percent of a regular faucet. This is done in various ways, but the main technique is through aeration of the water by the faucet (see Figure 5.18). A WaterSense-labeled faucet has a maximum flow of 1.5 gallons per minute (gpm).

As previously discussed, the use metals and metal finishes has a considerable impact on the environment. It is best to specify the most durable faucet that the budget can afford so it will not need to be replaced soon. You can also donate the used faucets from your project to your local building salvage shop or a Habitat for Humanity ReStore. Don't simply throw usable fixtures in the trash.

Composting and Garbage Disposals

I hate taking out the compost. Oranges, cauliflower, rotten stuff. It is so far away, it stinks. It's disgusting. I wish there was no such thing as compost.

—*Kenneth Fisher, age 10*

Conversations regarding the best practice of composting versus disposals have been raging for years. Unfortunately, the two studies (Wisconsin and Australia) most quoted most often were sponsored by In-sink-Erator, a disposal manufacturer. Details on these studies may be found in Appendix A.

There are many arguments for and against the use of food waste processors (garbage disposals or gaburators) versus composting. As long as grease and fats are not sent down the food disposal (as they cause blockages and ultimately overflows), most of our water treatment facilities can handle the waste that goes down the disposal.

There are still environmental costs. Evidence shows that processed food waste has an effect on our local waterways and aquatic life. The waste that enters the waterways can affect the nitrogen and phosphate levels, which are linked to eutrophication.

The term "eutrophication" refers to the addition of artificial or natural substances, such as nitrates and phosphates, to the ecosystem. Nitrates and phosphates enter the water system

Agriculture - use of fertilizers high in N & P
Manure runoffs from Feedlots - Nitrogen

Industrial & Power Plants - combustion of
fossil fuels emit N & P into the atmosphere
which enter our waterways during rainfall.

Wastewater treatment plants -
releases nitrogen (N) & phosphorous (P)
along with raw sewage into waterways

Algae bloom created by excess N & P- uses up available
oxygen & blocking sunlight, resulting in aquatic plants
and animals death, creating an unhealthy balance in the
bio-diversity

Nitrogen compounds
produced by cars

FIGURE 5.19 Runoffs from agriculture, city roads, home pesticides, fertilizers, and industry all find their way into the water supply, creating havoc on the organisms that live there.
NKBA

from runoffs from agriculture and development and from pollution created by septic systems and sewer systems (see Figure 5.19).

Depending on the efficiency of the wastewater treatment plans, excessive amounts of nitrogen and phosphorus from sewers can enter our water system. Phosphorus is linked to algae blooms in lakes, which result in the depletion of oxygen in the water, resulting in decreased biodiversity, changes in species composition and dominance, and raised toxicity levels of the water for aquatic life. A disposal also requires the use of potable water and energy to run. With our increasing population, there is a larger impact on our water treatment facilities. Composting offers another solution.

FIGURE 5.20 Single counter-mount stainless steel waste container installed flush to countertop. All parts are easily removed for cleaning.
Courtesy of Rev-A-Shelf LLC

If your client composts at home or lives in an area where there is a municipal composting system in place, you need to plan for the food waste. Options include closed containers that sit on the counter or built-in options, such as the one designed by Rev-A-Shelf seen in Figure 5.20. Whichever you and your client choose, ensure that it is easy to clean.

Water Filters

By means of water, we give life to everything.

—Koran 21:30

According to the EPA, there are more than 2,100 toxic chemicals in our public water supplies, including arsenic, sodium, chloride, copper, chromium, lead, cadmium, and many organic chemicals and bacteria.

If your clients are more vulnerable than most to water impurities, you may suggest having their water tested. Clients who are more sensitive to contaminants might include:

• Persons undergoing chemotherapy
• Living with HIV/AIDS

- Transplant patients
- Children and infants
- Frail elderly
- Pregnant women

Municipal water suppliers must sent out annual reports to their customers. Clients who suspect contaminants in their water can request additional testing of the water in their home. Depending on the amount of contaminants you are testing for, the test will cost from $15 and up. This information will be helpful for you when determining the correct water filter cartridge.

Water filters help remove most of these impurities and more. Installing a water filter offers a number of benefits, including:

- Taste—removal of chlorine
- Health benefits—removal of bacteria and toxins
- Cost—less expensive than bottled water
- Environment benefits—reduction in use of single-use plastic bottles

There are many types of filters, each with its own advantage and disadvantage.

Types of filters for the home

- **Carafes.** Inexpensive but slow to refill. These are not a good choice for a client who wants to use filtered water in cooking.
- **Faucet mounted.** Inexpensive. Does not require a professional plumber to install. Does not fit on all styles of faucets and can be unsightly.
- **Under sink.** Must be installed by a professional plumber. May require electrical (if adding a chiller or hot water dispenser). There are many choices of styles and finishes to match the faucet. There are multiple filter options to remove impurities and contaminants specifically to meet your clients' needs. Many companies that sell filter systems are aware of the types of contaminants in specific areas. Supply them with the project zip code, and they will recommend the correct filter.
- **Reverse osmosis.** Uses the household's water pressure to move water through a semipermeable membrane. It is the only type of filter certified to remove arsenic. It is not recommended for a whole-house filter as it takes 3 to 5 gallons of water to create 1 gallon of filtered water.
- **Whole-house filters.** The most expensive system. Two filters are usually installed on the main line before to the hot water tank. (For larger homes, more filters may be required.) This filters all the water in the house, including the water to the toilets and outdoor spigots. This system is best for homes that have high sediment issues.
- **Shower filters.** In Chapter 4 we discussed radon and how it enters the house. If your client's home has a radon problem, the gas can enter the home through the water system and be breathed in during bathing. Medical research has determined that while showering, chlorine becomes a vapor, which can be inhaled, causing adverse reactions in some people. There are two types of filtering systems to install at the shower; one is attached directly to the shower head (a more unsightly option), or a point-of-use system is used in the supply to the entire bathroom.

Take the time to determine your client's needs before specifying a filter system. Investigation into the quality of their water and their water requirements will result in a filter system that best meets their health and budgetary needs.

WATER HEATING AND DISTRIBUTION

When remodeling a bathroom or kitchen, one of the first questions a designer should ask is: "Do you have to run the water for a time to get hot water?" In many older homes or homes with copper pipes, getting hot water to the kitchen sink or shower can take time. Running water without using it is a waste. Consider installing a point-of-use tankless hot water heater or a hot water recirculating system (see Chapter 3).

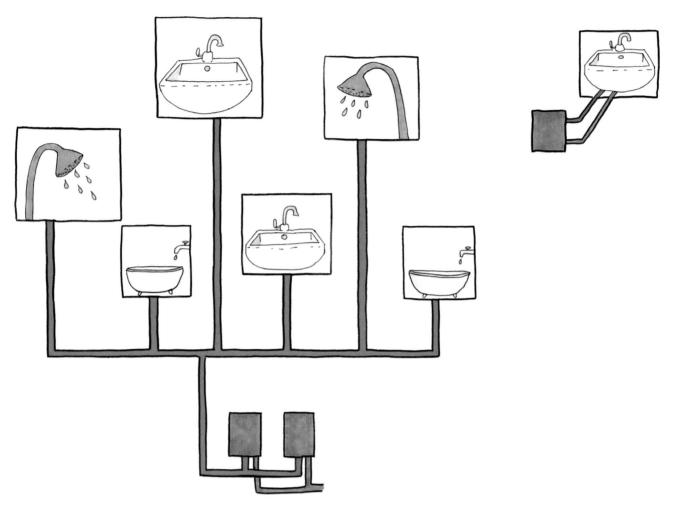

FIGURE 5.21 Hot water on-demand tankless system
NKBA

Point-of-Use Tankless Hot Water Heaters

A point-of-use hot water heater is a small, tankless heater that is placed either under the kitchen sink or very close to a bathroom. When clients turn on the hot water, they do not have to wait. Hot water is provided instantly.

In kitchens, an electric tankless heater is better than a gas-fired system as a point-of-use system. These appliances are not used for long, and a gas-fired system does not reach full efficiency before shutting off.

In bathrooms, gas-fueled tankless water heaters are better to use than electric ones (assuming that the home has gas as an option). Gas is more efficient than electric, but you do need to plan for proper gas line sizing, combustion air requirements, and venting of the combustion gas.

There are two ways to install on-demand tankless system: as a support to an existing hot water supply and as a stand-alone unit (see Figure 5.21).

Serving as a support to an existing hot water supply has a disadvantage. The hot water from the main source is restricted when flowing through the auxiliary source. This may result in a reduction in water pressure.

Another option is to bypass the main hot water tank and run cold water directly to the new tankless system. This will require a larger unit and a larger electrical circuit or gas line, but water pressure in the shower will not be sacrificed (see Figure 5.22).

FIGURE 5.22 Point-of-use hot water heaters are small and can be installed in a cabinet in bathrooms or kitchens where they are farthest from the main hot water heater. No more waiting for hot water!

Courtesy of Rheem

Bathrooms: Showers, Baths, and Steam

The design interview for a bathroom remodel includes some personal conversations, such as "What are your bathing rituals?" Understanding how your client bathes will aid in the environmental and budgetary impact of the finished project.

Naturally, the bathroom is where your choices can save clients money on their water bills and add to the need for water conservation. For reference, Figures 5.23 and 5.24 show water use by fixture in a bathroom.

Showers and Bathtubs

Low-flow shower heads that are part of the EPA's WaterSense program are recommended. These require 2.0 gpm. A 4-minute shower with a conventional shower head uses 20 gallons of water while a low-flow shower head requires only 10.

According to the WaterSense program, if every household in the United States would install a low-flow shower head, the country would reduce water consumption by 250 billion gallons.

Many clients believe that every master bath must have a bathtub. This cannot be further from the truth. It is important for resale to have at least one tub in the home, but if clients do not use a tub on a regular basis (even once a month may be considered "regular"), why would they spend the money on installing a new one? Casual studies in our classes over the past nine years show that 25 percent of the students use a tub on a monthly basis; typically only 1 in 15 uses a tub every week. Having a conversation with clients will show exactly what their needs are.

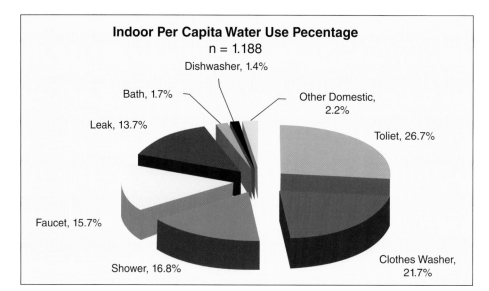

FIGURE 5.23 The 1999 study shows a snapshot of how water is used in a single-family household in twelve North American locations.
Courtesy of Alliance for Water Efficiency

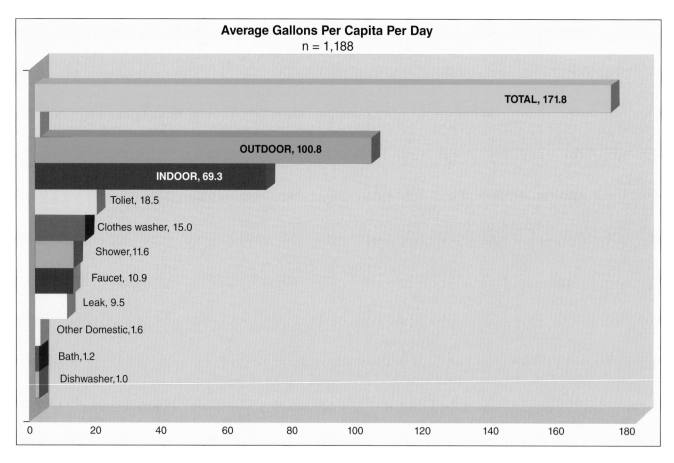

FIGURE 5.24 Average water use per household was found to be approximately 69 gallons.
Courtesy of Alliance for Water Efficiency

Tub Choices

A typical tub uses between 30 to 50 gallons of water.

As discussed, consider the recycled content of a cast iron tub. This choice has a lower embodied energy level than a fiberglass or composite tub. Seek other options, of course, and speak to clients about their desires and needs.

If clients decide that a tub is not necessary in their renovation project, you have more opportunities to create a larger shower. Again, the conversation becomes personal: "Do you need a shower big enough for two to take a shower in or is a two-person shower more for relaxing?" The overall size of a shower for the former will be bigger than the latter option. In either case, consider having one shower head fixed and the other a hand-held option with a hose long enough to aid in the cleaning of the shower.

Designing the Shower for Long Term

Make it a habit to *always* specify the installation of grab bars in the shower, and be sure to note it on the plans. (Some designers tape a set of plans placed in a plastic bag to the underside of a cabinet drawer for future homeowners.) Consider installing a small seat in the shower for comfort. (Be sure to maintain the 30- by 30-inch minimum size without the seat for code requirements—the NKBA recommends a 36- by 36-inch space.)

Steam Showers

For the client who would like a relaxing option for bathing but doesn't require a tub, consider the option of a steam shower. For water efficiency, a steam shower is an option. A 20-minute shower uses 50 gallons of water with a water-saving shower head. In contrast, a steam shower for the same amount of time uses 1 to 2 gallons of water. The estimated costs for the installation of a steam shower (2013) are between $2,500 and $11,000, depending on size and material selection.

There are also many health benefits of a steam shower:

- Increased metabolism
- Improved circulation
- Aids in the recovery from exercise
- Pain relief
- Skin care
- Stress management

Toilet Fixtures

A green home is outfitted with water-efficient toilets that use only 1.6 to 1.28 gallons per flush (see Figure 5.25). As discussed in Chapter 2, look around for local and state incentive programs that will give your client rebates for the replacement of conventional toilets. A great place to begin your search is to look to the EPA's WaterSense program, which will tell you what toilets are approved by the program and great choices for your project.

All things being equal—aesthetics, WaterSense endorsed, and a comfortable seat—for your most green option, consider the next step and specify a domestically manufactured toilet.

Laundry

According to a study conducted by Tufts University, 90 percent of European households have front-loading washing machines versus only 5 percent in the United States. It is estimated that high-efficiency washing machines use 50 percent less water (www.epa.gov/watersense), yet still many choose top loaders out of convenience (easier to reach), price (tend to be less expensive than front-loading ones), and habit. Consider speaking with your client and consult *Consumer Reports* for ratings. The energy savings from less water being heated and from reduced water use can help mitigate the higher price of a front-loading machine. Front-loading washing machines spin the clothes at a higher speed and extract more water than top loaders. This cuts down on drying time and the electricity necessary to run the dryer.

FIGURE 5.25 One-piece 1.28-gallon-per-flush toilet
Courtesy of Kohler Company

Like toilets, dryers need to be updated. New advancements in technology and energy efficiency make new dryers much more efficient than older ones.

Look to the ENERGY STAR program to help you and your client select the best washer and dryer for the project. ENERGY STAR washers all use 30 percent less water than low-efficiency models. The WaterSense program currently does not rate washers; this could change as more consumers look to the program to advise them on how to select and purchase appliances. *Consumer Reports* also takes water and electricity use into account in their recommendations.

LIVING ROOM APPLIANCES

New energy codes state the need for makeup air, as discussed in Chapter 4. When specifying a fireplace, take the CalGreen lead, which states that any gas fireplace must be a direct-vent-sealed-combustion type. (See Figure 5.26.) High-efficiency gas fireplaces can be a great source of heat in a project. Ventilation is key to maintaining healthy IAQ.

FIGURE 5.26 Direct vent fireplace installation details
Courtesy of Heat & Glo Fireplaces

ENERGY STAR has rating for televisions on its website. There are also some rebate programsavailable there. Remember to check their website and help your client navigate the application process for rebates.

SUMMARY

Research into the best possible materials, appliances, and fixtures for your client should begin early in a project. The theme of this chapter is to consider research to be a process. The process results in an equation. The equation is to help you with a balanced formula. The presence of a material that is more impacting on the environment, such as mortar made from Portland cement or stone that is quarried thousands of miles away, can be part of an equation. Can the use of locally produced tile help to mitigate the use of mortar? Can the installation of domestically produced appliances reduce the impacting nature that a self-leveling epoxy has on the environment? Only you and your client are able to answer those questions. The authors of this book offer the questions, not the answers. When we refer back to the concept of best practices, this approach fits. Decide what is best for your client, the project, and the environment.

REVIEW QUESTIONS

1. What is LCA? Why is it important? (See "Life Cycle Assessment" page 115)
2. Discuss the environmental benefits of incorporating longevity and universal design in the specification of materials for projects. (See "Longevity and Universal Design" pages 119–120)
3. How would you apply systems thinking to the selection of a material? How would you apply it to the selection of a refrigerator? (See "Life Cycle Assessment" page 115, and "Systems Thinking" pages 116–117)
4. Explain the concept of humidity buffering and why this would be advantageous to a home? (See "Clay Plasters" pages 124–126)

ENDNOTES

1. WWF International, *Living Planet Report 2010: Biodiversity, Biocapaciy, and Development*. Chapter 2, "The State of the Planet," p. 34. Produced in cooperation with the Zoological Society of London (ZSL) and the Global Footprint Network. Available at http://issuu.com/globalfootprintnetwork/docs/lpr2010#/signin
2. Jennifer Atlee and Paula Melton "The Product Transparency Movement: Peeking behind the Corporate Veil" Environmental Building News 21(1) (Jan 2012), 10.
3. Ibid., p. 12.
4. Ibid.
5. "A Glossary of Common Sustainability Terms," http://www2.dupont.com/Tyvek_Graphics/en_US/newsletters/jan09_nwsl_glossary.html. Accessed June 24, 2014.
6. Geoff Hammond and Craig Jones, "Inventory of Carbon and Energy (ICE)," Version 1.6a, Sustainable Energy Research Team (SERT), Department of Mechanical Engineering University of Bath, UK, 2008; http://perigordvacance.typepad.com/files/inventoryofcarbonandenergy.pdf, p. 6.
7. Lifecycle Assessment Software, "Definitions and Assumptions: Global Assumptions." Available at http://calculatelca.com/software/ecocalculator/definitions-and-assumptions/ (accessed June 24, 2014).
8. Quoted in C. C. Sullivan, "Standing on Green Principles: Sustainable Flooring Choices and Life Cycle Assessment." *Architectural Record* (April 2008).
9. Personal communication with the author, November 9, 2013.
10. V. M. Malhotra, "Role of Supplementary Cementing Materials in Reducing Greenhouse Gas Emissions." In Odd E. Gjorv and Koji Sakai (eds.), *Concrete Technology for a Sustainable Development in the 21st Century* (London: E&FN Spon, 2000).

11. Construction and Demolition Recycling Association, "Drywall Recycling," www.cdrecycling.org/drywall-recycling. Accessed June 24, 2014.

12. Gypsum Association, "What Is Gypsum? Two Types of Gypsum: Natural and FGD." Available at www.gypsum.org/stewardship/minimizingenvironmentalimpact/.

13. Gypsum Association, "Minimizing Environmental Impacts: Industry Efforts." Available at www.gypsum.org/stewardship/minimizingenvironmentalimpact/ (accessed June 24, 2014).

14. American Clay, "Humidity Buffering," available at http://media.wix.com/ugd/9fd6d9_e1ea838d8d7047e99f6b72fd4398a835.pdf.

15. www.c2ccertified.org/products/scorecard/icestone_durable_surface. Retrieved November 2013

16. Ibid.

17. www.northamericanstainless.com/wp-content/uploads/2010/10/Leeds_Letter.pdf (accessed June 24, 2014).

18. www.eleekinc.com/sustainability/. Retrieved November 2013

19. Rocky Mountain Bathrooms, "Sealing Granite Slabs—Seal or Not to Seal?" www.Rockymountainbathrooms.Com/Sealing.Granite.htm.

20. Cynthia Sanz, "Working with Linoleum Flooring." *This Old House* magazine, available at www.thisoldhouse.com/toh/article/0,,202857,00.html (accessed June 24, 2014).

21. *KCMA Environmental Stewardship Program*, KCMA ESP 05-12 (January 1, 2012). Available at www.kcma.org/uploads/file/esp%2005-12%20standard.pdf (accessed June 24, 2014).

22. ENERGY STAR Qualified Appliances, p. 2. Available at www.energystar.gov/ia/new_homes/features/appliances_062906.pdf (accessed June 24, 2014).

Creating an Environmentally Sustainable Design Practice

You never learn by doing something right 'cause you already know how to do it. You only learn from making mistakes and correcting them.

—*Russell Ackoff*

WHY CREATE AN ENVIRONMENTALLY SUSTAINABLE DESIGN PRACTICE?

You may have already heard the quote "If you fail to plan, you plan to fail." Nowhere is planning more important than in running a business. Many businesses are started by creative people with no experience in successful business management practices.

This chapter outlines the opportunities available when you incorporate sustainable business practices into a successful kitchen and bath business. In the *Kitchen & Bath Business and Project Management* volume of the NKBA Professional Resource Library, you will learn the details of creating a business plan. The focus of this chapter is to help future kitchen and bath designers to create successful environmentally sustainable business practices.

> *Learning Objective 1: Define the 4 Ps of a sustainable design business and incorporate them into your business plan*
>
> *Learning Objective 2: Apply your knowledge of the 5 marketing segments as defined by the Natural Marketing Institute to creating a marketing plan.*
>
> *Learning Objective 3: Summarize the legalities of an email conversation.*

Why would kitchen and bath designers want to incorporate an environmental business practices into their businesses?

That's where the money is. According to the U.S. Green Building Council (USGBC) Report *Green Jobs Study*[1] the economic impact of the total green construction market through 2013 will be:

- Contribution to the U.S. gross domestic product (GDP)
  - 2000–2008: **$**173 billion
  - 2009–2013 forecast: $554 billion
- Jobs created or saved (includes direct, indirect, and induced jobs)
  - 2000–2008: 2.4 million
  - 2009–2013 forecast: 7.9 million
- Wages
  - 2000–2008: $123 billion
  - 2009–2013 forecast: $396 billion
- Energy savings
  - 2000–2008: $1.3 billion saved
  - 2009–2013 forecast: $6 billion saved

There has never been a better time to launch a green business. High demand is driving an expansion of the market for environmentally friendly products and services. A number of tax incentives and public policies support green businesses, and the sector is experiencing a high rate of capital investment.[2]

The 2009 study by Boston Consulting Group (BCG), *Capturing the Green Advantage for Consumer Companies*, found that consumers find value in the benefits offered by green products and services, including superior freshness and taste, health and safety benefits, and savings on energy and life cycle costs.[3] The study further found that consumers surveyed were willing pay more for green products and services if they offered added value.[4]

The Four Ps for Creating a Sustainable Business

The most successful designers understand that incorporating environmentally aware practices is just good business. Many large consumer-driven companies have made major efforts to convince the buying public that they are on the environment's side. It is important to note that companies do not simply change their business practices without a proven strategy. Like creating a set of drawings and clear set of specifications for a kitchen remodel, a business must design a step-by-step plan in order to successfully integrate new business practices.

Business owners and their employees must be at least as versed in sustainable practices as their clients are; the goal should be becoming an authority in the green arena. Just jumping into the green movement without a detailed plan is a recipe for disaster. Everyone within the company from the bottom up must fully embrace the goal for full success.

Creating a green agenda for your company gives your business "competitive advantage in product (or services) differentiation and cost savings."[5] The more detailed the agenda, the more you will separate yourself from the rest of the crowd. This includes creating a top-down vision and must include what BCG calls the "four Ps of green advantage":[6]

1. **Green planning.** Incorporating green targets and resources into your corporate strategy
2. **Green processes.** Allows companies to practice what they preach
3. **Green product.** Your product and services
4. **Green promotion.** Marketing your message

Begin by compiling a list of ways your business currently impacts the environment and how it could lower its impact and contribute to the green economy.

Green Planning

Details on creating a business plan are covered in the NKBA's *Kitchen & Bath Business and Project Management* book. In this section we will be focusing on the green planning aspect of your business.

Creating a green business agenda is no different from creating a design for your clients. It serves as a road map, keeps your business focused on your goals, and aids in the financial success of your business. The most important part of planning is to share your goals with your staff and customers. If everyone knows where your business is heading, you will be certain to have success in the implementation and process.

Successful planning includes the three steps discussed next, according to the Boston Study Group[7]:

Step 1. Factor sustainability into strategy, future resources, and budgets. Incorporating sustainability into your company's strategy is a formula for success.

Step 2. Make the rules, don't just follow them. Specify materials that have been certified by third-party evaluators, such as Cradle to Cradle (C2C), Green Guard, ENERGY STAR, and Earth Advantage. Incorporate into your designs certifications such as airPlus, LEEDs for Homes, Living Building Challenge, and others. Encourage staff (including yourself if you are the owner) to obtain certifications.

Step 3. Make a clear business case for sustainability initiatives.

The World Resource Institute's working paper *Aligning Profit and Environmental Sustainability: Stories from Industry* recommends four areas that will drive a company to fulfilling its environmental goals:

1. Set goals that add environmental concerns into core business decisions.
2. Incorporate internal practices that support environmental sustainability.
3. Incorporate your sustainable goals into your yearly budget planning.
4. Be aware of risks and opportunities for your business and those of your suppliers and collaborators.[8]

Certain parts of our project are nonnegotiable items. Our clients come to us for a certain baseline of business practices, for example: We only use FSC [Forest Stewardship Council] wood on our projects—we will deviate from this only when engineered lumber is the best option. We specify locally sourced lumber, ENERGY STAR appliances and light fixtures, we incorporate water conservation plumbing techniques on all of our projects, and our insulation is set for sound and a higher R-value than code requires.[9]

—Alex Boetzel, Chief Innovation Officer
Green Hammer Design Build, Portland, OR

Take the time to list your company's strengths, weaknesses, opportunities, and threats (SWOT) both internally (your employees, business practices, finances) and externally (your trade contractors, subcontractors, competition) in relation to how you and they work in a sustainable manner. The World Resources Institute created a new level of the SWOT—the sustainability SWOT (sSwot)—as a tool to "help drive action and collaboration on environmental challenges creating real business risks and opportunities."[10]

We incorporate advanced framing on all new construction and where applicable on remodeling with the goal to save on lumber. Deconstruction is our mantra. On every project, our goal is to divert as much from the landfill as possible.[11]

Alex Boetzel

A green business plan takes into account the environmental and social aspect of the business. It incorporates the triple-bottom-line approach to measure the success of your business in terms of its impact on people, planet, and profit.

Supporting the Triple Bottom Line

Native Trails of San Luis Obispo, California, produces high-quality, artisan-crafted kitchen and bath sinks, tubs, countertops, ventilation hoods, cabinetry from reclaimed wood, and home décor. Founder and CEO Naomi Neilson Howard started her company while traveling during a vacation break from her college studies. Her stepfather is from Mexico, and she spent a lot of time there. During her travels, she admired the work of the local artisans and founded her company with the goal of bringing their work to the global marketplace. The company offers no-interest or low-interest loans to the artisans of Central Mexico for business improvements. As Neilson Howard explains, "I founded Native Trails with a dream of bridging cultures, of combining artisan heritage with innovative design and sustainable materials. This is a passion I gratefully live out every day" (www.nativetrails.net/our-story/).

Among the company values is care of the environment: "We influence the health of our planet through our actions, words and deeds; we infuse sustainability into the products we create" (www.nativetrails.net/our-mission/).

Through Native Trails, Naomi also established Community Trails, which donates $20,000 yearly to nonprofits through a dollar-for-dollar match with their employees. Community Trails also encourages volunteerism within the company by offering employees two days per year of paid volunteer time to charities of their choice. It also organizes group volunteer days to local charities. If employees donate 30 or more volunteer hours, Native Trails will donate an additional $200 to that organization (see Figure 6.1).

Location of Your Business
Choosing the location for your business can impact your green plan. Is your business located near mass transit, bike paths, and the services you need to run your business?

FIGURE 6.1 Native Trails incorporates the full triple bottom line—People, Planet, and Profit—into its daily business practices as well as its business plan.

One of the authors of this book, Robin Rigby Fisher, CMKBD/CAPS, principal designer for RRF Design, an independent design firm, recently relocated her business from her home to a remodeled office building in southeast Portland, Oregon:

> I chose the Ford Building specifically for its location. A new MAX transit station is nearing completion directly behind our building. It is located on one of Portland's many bike paths. The majority of the businesses we work with are within walking or biking distance. In addition, my commute by car is only 13 minutes from my home, and my bike commute (which I try to do two to three days per week) is just under 10 miles each way. Our building has showers for our use. My favorite days are my bike commuting days—I usually come up with design or business ideas during my 35-minute commute, and I am much more relaxed at work!

Options to consider when choosing a location for your business
- Is the building certified green by a third party?
- Is the property management company knowledgeable about green practices?
  - Are nontoxic products used in cleaning?
  - Is recycling easy to access?
  - Is bike storage and/or electric car plug-ins provided?
- Are the green features of the building accessible to the tenants?
  - Are carbon dioxide (CO_2) monitors installed in offices and shared spaces?
  - Has the heating, ventilating, and air-conditioning (HVAC) been updated and are they regularly monitored?
  - Does the building get some or all of its energy from renewable resources?
  - Does the building allow for individual control of heating and cooling?
  - Is natural daylighting present in all offices?
  - Does each office have the option for fresh air and proper ventilation?

Robin says: "Our lease requires that each tenant use only zero-VOC paints in our offices."

Green Processes

Green processes are about practicing what you preach. Creating your green processes are both internal (your office) and external (your projects). First, we explore the internal operations of your business.

- Set up a waste management system.

  > We encourage office recycling by not letting people have trash cans at their desks. Make it inconvenient for them and they won't create (as much) garbage, plus all those little garbage bags holding a couple items is a huge waste. Office waste goes into one common collection center. Recycling is provided at each station and throughout the office.
  >
  > **—Richard DeWolf, owner of Arciform, a design/build firm in Portland, Oregon**

- Consider your office's energy efficiency.

  > [We] switched to efficient lighting when the older, less efficient items were at the end of their life cycle. I don't believe in removing perfectly good things for more efficient ones. This is a concept that is exploited and wastes more than it saves. Same with toilets, urinals, etc. Our monitors are turned off when not in use. Lights in our office are on sensors that shut off when the sun shines in the office. Thermostats are set appropriately, and we have operable windows that allow for fresh air. (I am amazed at how uncommon this is!) The carpeting used in our office was purchased as seconds from projects that had extra materials.
  >
  > **—Richard DeWolf**

- Discourage the use of plastic bottles both in the office and on the project site.

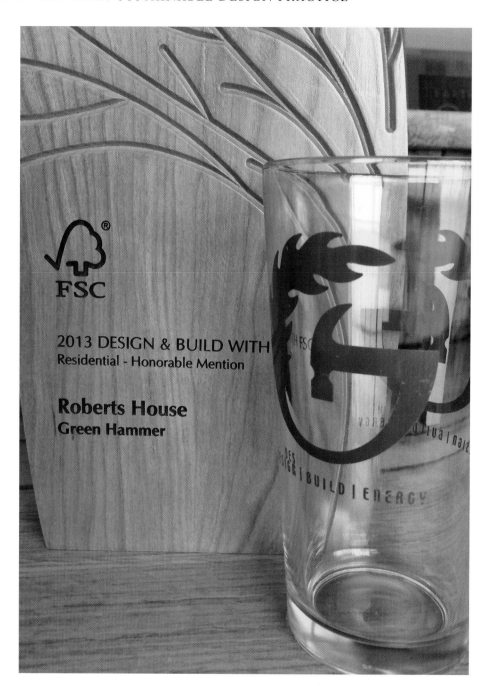

FIGURE 6.2 Green Hammer follows through with its goal to build for the environment. It does not offer clients bottled water (those bottles have to be recycled); rather, clients are offered fresh water in glasses with the company logo.

See Chapter 5 for the environmental costs of plastic water bottles. Serve clients who visit your office water in reusable water glasses (see Figure 6.2). It may seem like a little thing, but every plastic water bottle you don't use does impact the environment for good.

• Consider optional transportation.

Coauthor Robin Rigby Fisher added a shared company bicycle to her company's transportation options, explaining: "We recently purchased a commuter bike. Since we are so close to many of our suppliers and parking spots are scarce, we had our bike outfitted with baskets so that my staff and I can pick up samples without having to use our cars" (see Figure 6.3).

• Minimize your company's reliance on paper.

In the United States alone, paper accounts for more than half of all the recyclables collected. In 2011, approximately 46 million tons of paper and paperboard were recycled. The American Forest and Paper Association estimates that this amounts to 334 pounds for each person living in the United States.[12]

FIGURE 6.3 Portland, Oregon, is an easy bike commuting city. For nearby projects or shopping for samples, it is easier for designer Robin Rigby Fisher to use the bike than trying to find a parking spot.

Going paperless (or close to it) is not just good for the environment, it makes good business sense. Consider this: How many hours have you spent looking for a specific piece of paper? Today's technology is an opportunity to make your business run more efficiently; it can also reduce the amount of paper your company is using. Corey Klassen, CKD, CBD, owner of Corey Klassen Interior Design in Vancouver, BC, runs a nearly paperless business:

> My business is mostly paperless; I still have to print final sets of specifications and drawings. During the design process, I save pdfs of my drawings to Dropbox and by using Penultimate; I am able to mark up my drawings with the client. I then make the changes when I am back in my office. We organize all notes in Evernote and Dropbox by client's name and by using Cloud storage, my entire staff has access to changes, drawings, specifications and emails with clients and subs. The most important part of this is to be *organized* and establish *one system* so that all members of our staff can find everything![13]

Steps toward a paperless office

- **Use your printer's scanner.** Purchase orders, invoices, and drawing revisions can be saved as PDFs and filed in your client's file.
- **Utilize cloud storage.** There are many options available to the business owner. The advantage is secure backup and access to all your files wherever you or your staff members are.
- The key to document retrieval in the digital age is to set up your filing system in an organized fashion. An example of a client file:

- Client name
- Drawings (CAD file, PDFs, sketches [if you save current versions by date, unless you are willing to delete previous renditions])
  Specifications (contract specs) (Save these as separate files so that it is easier to forward the correct specs to specific trade contractors.)

  > Appliances
  > Plumbing
  > Lighting
  > Windows
  > Others
  Purchase orders
  Photos
  > Before
  > During construction
  > After

  Contest entries (or Media Information)
  > Design statement
  > Articles/media

- **Name each file consistently.** This cannot be stressed enough. Consider naming a file: [client name, drawings, date]. However it is done, just be sure that your entire staff embraces this system.
- **Utilize paperless statements and bill paying.** There are many options available, just be aware of monthly and transaction fees. These services usually take a few days for the funds to transfer into your account.

Legalities of an E-mail Contract
By Peter J. Lamont, Esq.

There was a time when a contract was not legally binding unless all the parties involved sat down, reviewed the agreement, then signed and dated it in front of witnesses. In today's digital age, formal contract signings such as the one just described have become passé. Companies of all sizes, from successful Fortune 500 corporations to the kitchen and bath designer, now use e-mail as their primary means of communication. Consequently, people receive and review documents e-mailed to them on their smartphones, tablets, and other mobile devices. Some even sign documents with a digital signature. Although most businesses enjoy the ease of digital communication and negotiation, many have questions as to whether their e-mail communications or digital signatures are actually legally binding. This article explains the legal ramifications of using e-mail and digital signatures to conduct business and to negotiate and sign business documents.

There are two primary federal laws that must be discussed in order to have a full understanding of the legality of electronic communications. The first law is referred to as the Uniform Electronic Transactions Act of 1999 (UETA). This act makes it legal for contracts to be negotiated and agreed to via e-mail. UETA specifically states that e-mail and fax contracts are legally binding. This means that any agreement made through an electronic medium, such as e-mail, will, assuming all other required contractual conditions are met, hold up in court. The second law is known as the Electronic Records and Signatures in Commerce Act (also known as the Electronic Signatures in Global and National Commerce Act [ESIGN]). This law, which was signed by President Clinton in June 2000, gives electronic signatures (e-signatures) on contracts the same weight as those executed on paper. Some specific exemptions from this act, such as contracts concerning student loans, still must be signed by hand.

Enforceability of E-mail

Although the use of e-mail in business is nothing new, questions remain as to what binding effect e-mail may have. The law has developed rapidly over the past 20 years since UETA was passed. Both clarifications of the original law and developing case law have made it reasonably clear that an e-mail can be considered a legally binding contract. Therefore, it is important for designers and design firms to be mindful of what they write in e-mails in order to avoid inadvertently creating a contractual obligation.

Unlike formal negotiations and signings, e-mail communications can be very casual and often fail to reflect the level of thought or care that goes into the preparation of hard-copy contract documents.

Over the past few years, there have been a number of federal and state cases involving the creation of contractual obligations through e-mail that the writer later sought to revoke. For example, a kitchen designer had been negotiating a contract with a client that had gone back and forth via e-mail for several days. Tired with the way the process was dragging on, the designer sent back an e-mail to the client indicating that "the current terms of the contract are acceptable." Five days after sending the e-mail, the designer reviewed the terms and realized that he had agreed to the contract out of frustration, not because the terms were favorable to him. He immediately contacted the client and sought to revoke the agreement. The client refused, arguing that they had already turned down a number of other designers and that they wanted to use him. The designer filed a lawsuit seeking the court's permission to void the contract on the grounds that it was not formally entered into but rather informally agreed to via e-mail. The court determined that the e-mail clearly showed the designer's intent to enter into a contract with the client and refused to let him void the agreement simply because he later determined that many of the terms were not in his favor. The court compared his request to the request of an individual who had signed a formal, hard-copy contract and then later sought to avoid his obligations simply because he had not fully read through the document.

Despite the fact that e-mail communications can create a binding contract, the courts still require that all of the elements of a contract be met. In general, a contract is an agreement with specific terms between two or more persons or entities in which there is a promise to do something in return for a valuable benefit. The courts have been applying standard contract law requirements to e-mails and other electronic communications since the late 1990s.

(continued)

It is important for kitchen and bath designers to understand the potential power of an informal e-mail and to recognize the steps to take to protect themselves against unintended contractual obligations. The best way to limit the power of the electronic communication is to include a disclaimer.

For example, let's assume that you are negotiating a contract with a client. You have sent more than ten e-mails back and forth trying to hammer out various clauses in the document. You do not want any of your negotiations to be considered acceptance of a formal agreement. For that reason, you should include a disclaimer at the bottom of your e-mail correspondence that states that e-mail does not legally bind either party and serves only for the purpose of negotiating a final agreement. You can also state that the electronic correspondence may provide the basis for the preparation of a legally enforceable agreement but that e-mail does not address all issues contemplated by the transaction, and as such will be the subject of further negotiations. You should also include a sentence that states: "In the event that the parties are unable to agree upon and execute for any reason whatsoever a mutually acceptable formal agreement, the parties understand that each party reserves the right to cancel all negotiations and consider other offers thereafter. Finally, you should include a sentence that states something to the effect of "In the event an agreement is executed and delivered by both parties, the terms of that document shall supersede all prior discussions and negotiations, and such documents such constitute the entire agreement between the parties."

Electronic and Digital Signatures

Hundreds of Web sites offer digital and e-signature solutions. Furthermore, many sites make a distinction between electronic and digital signatures; it can be quite confusing.

Although most people use the term "digital signature" to mean either a digital or an e-signature, it is becoming standard to reserve the term "digital signature" for cryptographic signature methods. (Cryptography is the science of securing information and is generally associated with signatures on encrypted documents.) "Electronic signature" is used for other paperless signature methods (see Figure 6.4).

A number of online and mobile applications utilize cryptography, including DocuSign (docusign.com) and SignNow (signnow.com). It is a sophisticated process; an algorithm is used to encrypt online documents (MS Word or PDF) to protect them from unauthorized signatures. With encrypted documents, a key is generated that allows only the proper parties to sign the documents.

An e-signature can be a secured digital signature, it can also be a typed name or a digitized image of a handwritten signature. These e-signatures can be problematic with regard to maintaining integrity and security, since there is nothing to prevent a person from typing someone else's name. Although an e-signature may be legally enforceable in a number of circumstances, it is generally considered to be less secure than an encrypted digital signature.

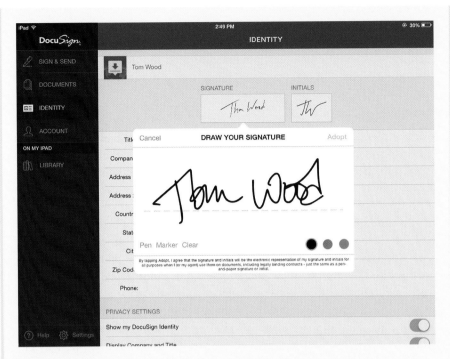

FIGURE 6.4 Mobile applications such as DocuSign help keep paper to a minimum and contracts can be filed electronically. Applications like these are invaluable to businesses that offer services to clients in distant geographic locations.
©DocuSign Inc.

Generally, digital signatures are fully enforceable. Both UETA and ESIGN state that electronic records and signatures carry the same weight and legal effect as traditional paper documents and handwritten signatures.

Many documents cannot be signed by a digital or electronic signature. They include wills, leases, deeds, adoption papers, divorce papers, court orders, notices of termination of leases, notice of repossessions, and notices of foreclosure.

It is important to note that when a kitchen and bath designer wants to use a digital signature on a client contract, federal law permits consumers to opt out of electronic agreements. Thus, prior to using an electronic contract and signature, the designer must provide the consumer with a notice concerning the use of electronic documents and signatures and an explanation as to the designer's digital security. The law does not have the same requirements for business-to-business agreements.

Electronic documents and digital signatures are becoming widely accepted as a legally enforceable means of conducting business. Using digital means of conducting business can often be quicker and more cost effective than traditional methods of signing and negotiating contracts and other business arrangements; nonetheless, it is important for kitchen and bath designers to follow the developing areas of law relating to digital signatures and electronic documents so that they, and their clients, are best served when entering working agreements.

Green Product

The construction/remodeling industry creates a large percentage of what goes into the landfill, and the items we specify for the kitchen and bath are high on embodied energy once they are produced. How can your materials and fixtures choices have a lower environmental impact?

Make sure the client understands how effectively you steward environmental resources. As Richard DeWolf of Arciform says:

> We have our own cabinet shop. [Our clients tour our] shop, see how each station has four waste receptacles: general recycling, wood recycling, wood that can be used in fireplaces, and general trash. They see the stacks of reclaimed wood, see the wind-fallen trees being salvaged, and they just get it. We let them know that we use formaldehyde-free plywood and products. I explain how we originally made the switch to low-VOC materials for the health and safety of our staff many years ago. Now it's being touted as a sustainable thing for the end user.[14]

Get the pricing right. DeWolf explains:

> Part of having a sustainable business means not wasting time, money, or energy. With that in mind, our goal is to build everything we design. We have created a process that ensures confidence and trust with our clients.
>
> After our designers have their initial design consultation with a new client and it is determined that there will be a fair amount of construction involved, we schedule our next appointment with one of our construction team members. By having our designer work side by side with our construction staff, we create a project that fits both the client's budget and the way they live in their home.
>
> Talking budget with a client can be challenging because clients don't always want to share that information. By incorporating our design and construction teams early in the design process, we gain our client's trust. They know we have their best interest as our goal.[15]

Green Promotion

You can walk the walk, but if no one knows it, how is that going to help your business? You have to tell the world about your green practices. Successful businesses let clients know of their sustainability practices. Incorporate your green practices into your website and in your advertising (see Figure 6.5). Join associations where sustainability is the focus and position yourself as an expert resource. Write about what you know through a blog or other social media outlet. Showcase your projects that have sustainable features. Put together a seminar on some aspect of green design and share your lessons with others.

Create Your Company's Sustainability Mission Statement

You must remember to "be consistent in order to be credible." Your business's "goals, actions and messages must have a common underlying vision."[16]

Tracey Stephens, CID, principal designer of Tracey Stephens Interior Design in Montclair, New Jersey, was among the first designers in the state to be certified as a ReGREEN Trained Professional through the U.S. Green Building Council and the American Society of Interior Designers[17] (see traceystephens.com). She has incorporated sustainable design tenets in her practice for as long as she has been practicing design.

> My sustainable mission comes from *Our Responsibility to the Seventh Generation*, published by the International Institute for Sustainable Development in 1992. The basic tenet is that our time on this earth is limited, but our choices today last way beyond our demise. For real sustainability to take place, we must think about how our decisions today will affect our seventh generation into the future, this is true sustainable design. This philosophy is how the indigenous people of this world have practiced.

🔲 973-202-8130
✉ tracey@traceystephens.com

🏠 Home | Projects ⌄ | Green Design | About Us ⌄ | Newsletter | Reviews | FAQs | Contact

"It isn't often that you hear an interior designer say her mantra is 'reduce, reuse, recycle' but Tracey Stephens isn't your usual designer."
Bergen Record ~ Homescapes

GREEN DESIGN ~ ECO-FRIENDLY DESIGN ~ SUSTAINABILITY ENVIRONMENTAL STEWARDSHIP

FIGURE 6.5 Interior designer Tracey Stephens has made a mark in her industry by becoming an expert in sustainable design. Being clear about her environmental standing has enhanced her business's success.

Although I have been incorporating these concepts into my designs for years, it wasn't until I posted my sustainable mission statement on my website that I became known for green design—it has impacted my business noticeably.

I am committed to creating comfortable, inviting spaces for my clients that are healthy, efficient, and safe for people and the environment. In all my design projects, I offer sustainable options that replace wasteful or toxic materials and practices. Reusing or repurposing my clients existing furnishings or materials is a great place to start. [18]

Creating an environmental mission statement supports your business goals. It should consist of these three parts: the "why," the goal, and a measurement of success.

1. Why is environmental sustainability important to us and our company?
2. What is our end goal?
3. How will we know if we obtained our goal?

1. The "why." Take time to define why your business is taking this step. Create a list of action words or phrases that reflect your commitment to the triple bottom line (people, planet and profit):

- Promote energy efficiency.
- Improve indoor air quality.
- Provide a better quality of life for our clients.
- Create an environment of collaboration with our trades.

- Reduce our company's carbon footprint.
- Provide products that reflect global concern.

2. The goal. Look at the "ways in which your business negatively impacts the Earth and defining all the area in which you need to change will help bring your road map into focus. Keep in mind, your environmental mission statement should evolve as your company and our world move ahead. Consider it progress when you have to edit your statement because you have accomplished your goals."[19]

3. Measuring success. How do you define your environmental success? Where will your company be in one, five, or ten years? What about your relationship with your trades, employees, customers?

The purpose of a mission statement is to motivate. The clearer you are in defining your direction, goals, and measurement of success, the more likely you are to achieving your environmental objective.

TODAY'S GREEN CLIENT

In *The New Rules of Green Marketing*, author Jacquelyn Ottman suggests that businesses review the next checklist to more deeply understand the buying influences of today's mainstream green consumers and how your business needs to respond:

- Be aware of your client's environmental awareness and concern.
- What are your clients' top environmental concerns? What about your employees? Suppliers? Retailers? Community?
- What products do you currently specify that contain high environmental risks (i.e., polyvinyl chloride, formaldehyde, and other potentially hazardous chemicals)?
- For products that you specify, what are the long-term projections for the natural resources to create those products?
- Who is your client by generation, and how do those clients express their environmental and social concerns? Political motivation? Purchasing influence?
- Who is your competition? What is their environmental statement and practices?
- How does your client get environmental information?
- Which legislators and policy makers may impact your environmental business practices?
- What are the opportunities you could gain through green marketing? [20]

Understanding Your Client

Today's client is increasingly informed about building and the environment. In many cases, you will not be selling the concept of sustainable design; rather you be educating the client on specific details of the project. According to a 2009 survey by the Natural Marketing Institute (NMI), 83 percent of the US population classify themselves as having some level of green influence in their values, activities, and consumerism. The remaining 17 percent remain unconcerned about the environment and purchase "green" only as a result of legislation.[21]

Who exactly are green consumers, and what are their buying habits?

According to the International Institute for Sustainable Development, green consumers are:

- Sincere in their intentions, with a growing commitment to greener lifestyles
- Likely to perceive their own current environmental practices as inadequate
- Willing to seek out companies who are taking qualitative actions toward sustainability and have made a commitment toward improvement

In addition, they:

- Tend to overstate their green behavior, including the amount of green products they consume and incorporate into their lifestyle
- Want environmental protection to be easy with little or no sacrifice on their part

- Distrust corporate environmental claims, unless they are independently verified
- Lack knowledge about environmental issues but are willing to learn[22]

This means that consumer education is one of the most effective strategies that you as a designer should implement in your business practices.

In the United States, it is the children who influence the family's buying decisions, whereas in Canada, adults, children and the more mature generations have "strong environmental concerns" and are more active green consumers.[23]

A 2011 survey conducted by Insightrix Research, Inc. for IPAC-CO2 Research Inc. found that 57 percent of Canadians believe that our environment's problem is a result of human impact and "partially due to natural climate variation" with an additional 31 percent believing that human activity is the cause of climate change."[24]

> In Canada, we grew up watching David Suzuki.* I watched his show, *The Nature of Things*, every week. His message on how we live and how we can live better has shaped my life, my designs and business practices. Canadians have been watching him weekly since the 1960s. I don't advertise my business as environmentally sustainable; we should all be using these practices.[25]
>
> **—Corey Klassen, CKD, CBD, Corey Klassen Interior Design, Vancouver, British Columbia**

If the designer takes on the role of educator, demonstrating the environmental benefits of each product in terms of air quality, recycled content, and water or energy conservation, the project's environmental goal will be greatly enhanced. It is important to also address with your client the "traditional values" of price, quality, convenience, and availability for each product you specify.

Companies that are interested in incorporating sustainability into their marketing plan should look at consumers not only in the traditional groups by generation (Baby Boomers, Gen X, Gen Y, etc.) but should incorporate information based on the five segments of population created by the NMI. It has been determined that these segments are found equally across the traditional generational consumer groups.

The five segments as defined by their eco-consciousness are:[26]

LOHAS

Naturalites

Drifters

Conventionals

Unconcerned

LOHAS. "As their name suggests, the LOHAS (Lifestyles of Health and Sustainability) segment represents the most environmentally conscious, holistically oriented and active of all consumers."[27] This group represents 19 percent of all US adults. They believe in a "connection between health and global preservation" and purchase products that maintain that connection. A LOHAS is typically a "married, educated, middle-aged" woman and has the second highest income of the five segments. Buying decisions of LOHAS are influenced by environmental issues. LOHAS consumers do their own research into businesses and are loyal to their decisions. They are very environmentally savvy, are leaders in energy and water conservation, and are politically aware.

---

* David Suzuki is the cofounder of the David Suzuki Foundation. He received his doctorate in zoology from the University of Chicago in 1961. His long-running, award-winning radio and TV shows in Canada have influenced the way Canadians look at and impact the environment. For more information on his foundation and additional information on environmental news and green living tips, visit his website at www.davidsuzuki.org.

Naturalites. One in six US consumers is defined as a "Naturalite." Naturalites take a personal approach to the environment, concerning themselves with the harmful effects of paint, cosmetics, and food. They look for safer alternatives and are receptive to education where there is a personal connection to health.

Drifters. This group is driven more by trends than by beliefs. With 57 million consumers, they are the largest segment and are most attractive to marketers. Drifters want to belong; they typically choose "green" options based on how they look to others. Typical drifters are young, live in coastal states, have moderate incomes, and have larger households with children under 18. They are avid recyclers and energy conscious; however, they are less apt to engage in the more nuanced eco-conscious behaviors.

Conventionals. This segment will more than likely lower the heat in the home and put on a sweater. With over 53 million consumers, this is the second largest segment. They are proponents of the "reduce, repurpose, reuse, recycle" attitude. They are fiscally conservative but will invest in items if they know it will reduce energy costs. They research and are open to learning. Conventionals are more than likely to be males in their mid- to late 40s with a high income. Twenty-five percent of this segment is retired, and more than 45 percent pay off their credit card balances monthly.

Unconcerned. Over 61 percent of the unconcerneds say that they care about the environment, but only 24 percent of the total unconcerneds actually recycle.

The NMI estimates that these five segments are a $290 billion–a–year market. [28]

Marketing a "Life" versus a "Lifestyle"

Our way of marketing has changed. In the past, marketers sold a "lifestyle." Green marketers sell the consumer a "life."

To sell a lifestyle, a company is selling how the consumer chooses to be at a particular moment in time. A lifestyle is external; it can include people, material things, and how you spend your time, money, and energy. Example of lifestyle marketers are Abercrombie & Fitch, BMW, Apple, and Louis Vuitton.

"Lifestyle" is a term coined by Austrian psychologist Alfred Adler. It came into mainstream use in the 1950s and is characterized by the following:

- Lifestyle is a group phenomenon influenced by social group or relationships.
- Lifestyle permeates various aspects of life and gives marketers the ability to predict behaviors.
- Lifestyle implies a central life interest: activities, family, work, politics.
- Lifestyles vary according to social groups, such as age, sex, religion, ethnicity, and social class.

Selling or marketing to a "life" is more internal; it includes our beliefs, values, preferences, and outlooks. Selling a "life" will support your client's lifestyle. Products are marketed as "locally sourced" and have a regional flavor. Marketing your business this way is holistic: You are your marketing beliefs, values, and community.

Companies that are successful in green marketing are proactive, interdependent, and incorporate this belief throughout their business. They are focused on the triple bottom line (people, planet, and profit).

INCORPORATING SYSTEMS THINKING IN YOUR BUSINESS

We discussed systems thinking in Chapter 1. Successful businesses recognize that the way their business is run affects the success of the client's project. It is a holistic approach.

Let's look at another way.

Take an iceberg, for example. The tip of the iceberg is visible to the world (consider this your clients), but the driver of the iceberg, what is affected by the ocean currents, is way below the surface (your business practices). For example, your competitors do not take away business; they take advantage of an opportunity that poses itself based in part on your business practices.[29]

Incorporating this type of thinking is very similar to the story of the blind men and the elephant. Each man touches one part of the elephant and draws his own conclusion:

The man who touches the trunk believes it is a rope.

The man who touches the ear believes it is a tent.

The man who touches the leg believes it is a tree, and so on.

No one man sees the big picture. Taking all these parts and understanding that the elephant is made up of all these pieces is the way system thinking works. Your parts and pieces of your company, clients, employees, subs, office management, advertising, marketing, and so on are is all part of a finely tuned system where one piece affects the other.

Taking this concept one step further, your business is part of a community, which is part of the environment. This is the base of the iceberg, the driving force of all successful and sustainable businesses.

It really boils down to this: That all life is interrelated. We are all caught in an inescapable network of mutuality, tied into a single garment of destiny. Whatever affects one destiny, affects all indirectly.

—Martin Luther King Jr.

SUMMARY

Making the decision to be a steward for the environment is admirable. Any change, no matter how small, will be a positive one.

You have the opportunity to effect change in both our industry and our environment. As we have stated, as a designer, you are not only the creative entity of a successful project; you are also the educator and the driver. By effectively communicating your clients' needs, wants, and desires, you can steer the project toward environmental stewardship and not sacrifice design.

Part of being a designer is being open to new ideas. Most successful designers are curious. Create alliances with your trades, bring them in early in the design process, and use their expertise to discover the best solution for your clients. Ask questions; do not be afraid to challenge your suppliers and trades. Remember, you are the link between clients and the success of the project.

The environment requires the same level of curiosity. Read trade publications, attend seminars, join your local NKBA chapter and attend the meetings, and get involved with the USGBC. Never stop learning.

Scientists now believe that our environment is in dire crisis. The time for contemplation is over. Now is the time to act!

Make a habit of two things: to help or at least to do no harm.

—Hippocrates

REVIEW QUESTIONS

1. Explain the value of a sustainability mission statement. How could a company use such a statement to its advantage? (See "Green Promotion" page 166)
2. Review the SWOT User Guide at: http://pdf.wri.org/sustainability_swot_user_guide.pdf. What is a SWOT? Why should a business owner create one, and what information could

be gleaned from this information? (See "The Four Ps for Creating a Sustainable Business" page 156.)

3. Explain the difference between marketing to a lifestyle versus to a life. How would the difference apply to marketing your company as green? (See "Today's Green Client" page 168.)

ENDNOTES

1. *US Green Building Council Green Jobs Study* (McLean, VA: Booz Allen Hamilton, undated), p. i; available at www.usgbc.org/Docs/Archive/General/Docs6435.pdf.

2. *The Green Business Plan Guide* (Oakland, CA: Green for All, n.d.), p. 3; available at http://greenforall.org/wordpress/wp-content/uploads/2012/06/Green-Business-Plan-Guide.pdf (accessed June 3, 2014), citing "Pew Finds Clean Energy Economy Generates Significant Job Growth" (Philadelphia, PA: Pew Charitable Trusts, June 10, 2009), available at www.pewtrusts.org/news_room_detail.aspx?id=53254, accessed June 3, 2014.

3. Joe Manget, Catherine Roche, and Felix Münnich, *Capturing the Green Advantage for Consumer Companies* (Boston: The Boston Consulting Group, 2009), p. 17 Exhibit 10 Available at www.bcg.com/documents/file15407.pdf; accessed June 3, 2014.

4. Ibid.

5. Ibid., p. 20.

6. Ibid., p. 8.

7. Ibid., p. 20.

8. Alexander Perera, Samantha Putt del Pino, Barbara Oliveira, *Aligning Profit and Environmental Sustainability: Stories from Industry* (Washington, DC: World Resource Institute, 2013), 20; available at www.wri.org/sites/default/files/pdf/aligning_profit_and_environmental_sustainability_stories_from_industry.pdf.

9. Personal communication with the author, August 15, 2013.

10. Eliot Metzger, Samantha Putt del Pino, Sally Prowitt, Jenna Goodward, and Alexander Perera, *sSwot: A Sustainability SWOT* (Washington, DC: World Resources Institute, December 2012), 1; available at http://pdf.wri.org/sustainability_swot_user_guide.pdf; accessed June 3, 2014.

11. Conversation with the author, August 15, 2013.

12. See www.epa.gov/osw/honhaz/muncipal/msw99.htm and www.paperrecycles.org.

13. Telephone conversation with the author, September 16, 2013.

14. Email interview with the author, November 2, 2013.

15. Ibid.

16. Manget, Roche, and Münnich, *Capturing the Green Advantage for Consumer Companies,* p. 22.

17. http://traceystephens.com/about/tracey-stephens-design-philosophy.php.

18. Telephone interview with the author, September 15, 2013.

19. Matt Courtland, "Environmental Mission Statements: How to Develop Your Own." *Environmental Leader*, April 23, 2010. Available at www.environmentalleader.com/2010/04/23/environmental-mission-statements-how-to-develop-your-own (accessed June 5, 2014).

20. Jacquelyn A. Ottman, *The New Rules of Green Marketing*: *Strategies, Tools, and Inspiration for Sustainable Branding* (San Francisco: Berrett-Koehler Publishers, Inc., 2011), pp. 43-44.

21. Ibid, p. 45, citing the National Marketing Institute.

22. International Institute for Sustainable Development, www.iisd.org/business/markets/green_who.aspx (accessed June 5, 2014).

23. Ibid.

24. IPAC CO2 Research Inc., Public Awareness and Acceptance of Carbon Capture and Storate in Canada (Executive Summary) (Saskatoon, SK: Insightrix Research, Inc, November 2011); available at www.cmc-nce.ca/wp-content/uploads/2014/01/IPAC-CO2-National_Report-Executive-Sum.pdf.

25. Telephone conversation with the author, August 9, 2013.

26. Natural Marketing Institute, *The LOHAS Report: Consumers and Sustainability*, as quoted in Ottman, *The New Rules of Green Marketing*, pp. 23–28.

27. Ottman, *The New Rules of Green Marketing*," p. 25.

28. See www.lohas.com/about (accessed June 11, 2014).

29. *The Green Business Plan Guide* (Oakland, CA: Green for All, n.d.), p. 3; available at http://greenforall.org/wordpress/wp-content/uploads/2012/06/Green-Business-Plan-Guide.pdf (accessed June 3, 2014), citing "Pew Finds Clean Energy Economy Generates Significant Job Growth" (Philadelphia, PA: Pew Charitable Trusts, June 10, 2009), available at www.pewtrusts.org/news_room_detail.aspx?id=53254, accessed June 3, 2014.

APPENDIX

Composting versus Garbage Disposals

The battle between using food waste processors (FWPs; garbage disposals or garburators) and composting continues to rage. The most comprehensive study done to date on this topic was funded by InSinkErator and was conducted in Australia. (Australia is the smallest continent and faces a severe water shortage.) This study concluded that home composting (aerobically) was best for the environment but that using a garbage disposal has less of an impact on our ecosystem than disposing of food waste in a landfill. It is this study that we will be citing most in this conversation.[1]

The study compared home composting (both aerobic and anaerobic), codisposal (municipal waste management systems [MWMS], the mixing of waste and food waste), central composting (CC; municipal organic composting), and disposals (FWPs).

Aerobic composting. Composting that occurs that provides air circulation. For most efficient composting, turn compost occasionally and keep moist.

Anaerobic composting. Composting that occurs underground or in a tightly enclosed area. This type of composting occurs in landfills and creates methane gas (a greenhouse gas).

Codisposal. Mixing of organic matter (yard debris and food waste) with inorganic matter in municipality landfill.

Centralized composting. Municipality composting.

Eutrophication. Refers to the addition of artificial or natural substances, such as nitrates and phosphates, to the ecosystem. Nitrates and phosphates enter the water system from runoffs from agriculture and development and from pollution created from septic systems and sewers. (See Chapter 5.)

Depending on the efficiency of wastewater treatment plants, excessive amounts of nitrogen and phosphorus from sewers can enter our water system. Phosphorus is linked to algae blooms in lakes, which result in the depletion of oxygen in the water and lead to decreased biodiversity, changes in species' composition and dominance, and toxicity effects.

The study was based on the production of 182 kilograms (wet) of food waste per year for a household of 2.1 persons and incorporated the embodied energy of each item involved (garbage disposal, composting unit, and equipment used in each of the municipal systems: trucks, fossil fuels, wastewater treatment plant). The study also included the life cycle assessment (LCA) of the containers, vehicles, processing facilities, and wastewater treatment plants.

Embodied Energy

To fully define the impact each type of food disposal system has on the environment, the study included the embodied energy of the "container" which aids in the composting of the food waste.

- Garbage disposals (garburators) (FWPs)
  - Require potable water, energy in the kitchen, and processing in the wastewater treatment plant.
  - The treated water is linked eutrophication in our waterways.
  - Life span of a FWP is approximately 12 years.
  - Life span of a wastewater treatment plant is estimated at 35 years.
- Home composting unit
  - Life span of plastic unit is 12 years.
- Codisposal landfill
  - Food waste in the landfill releases methane (which contributes to global warming). According to the US Environmental Protection Agency (EPA), the release of methane from landfills accounts for 34 percent of all methane emissions in the United States.[2] The EPA estimates that approximately 34 million tons of food is added to our landfills yearly.[3] This waste accounts for one-quarter of all the fresh water consumption and consumes approximately 300 million barrels of oil yearly.[4]
  - Highest-level embodied energy: The study included vehicles that used fossil fuels, although some composting companies are updating their fleets to compressed natural gas (CNG; a fossil fuel that is considered a more environmentally clean alternative to conventional fuels).
  - Process
    - Municipal street collection occurs weekly.
    - Waste is transported to a landfill via a transfer station.
    - Waste is deposited and compacted at the landfill.
    - Degradation of organic waste takes place under anaerobic conditions.
- Centralized composting
  - Medium-level embodied energy: The study incorporated vehicles that used fossil fuels, although some composting companies are updating their fleets to CNG.
  - Process:
    - Municipal street collection occurs weekly.
    - Organic waste is transported to a landfill.
    - In some municipalities, organic waste is then transported by a private carrier to a composting facility,

The study concluded that the best option for the disposal of organic waste is under aerobic home composting systems. Using FWPs was the next most efficient method.

This study does not take into effect the current state of the US infrastructure. According to the 2013 Report Card for America's Infrastructure published by the American Society of Civil Engineers, the wastewater treatment plants in the United States currently get a D+ (between a poor and mediocre rating). Many of the nation's 700,000 to 800,000 miles of public sewer mains were installed after World War II and are nearing the end of their useful life. Many of our wastewater treatment facilities are in poor condition and have inadequate capacity. This results in an estimated 900 billion gallons of untreated sewage being dumped into our waterways yearly.[5]

The untreated sewage also includes food waste. It is important to note that waste from the use of FWPs has been found to aid in the progression of algae blooms and the eutrophic process.

In Canada, many cities, including Toronto and Ottawa, have banned FWPs. This leads us to the question: What do they know that we don't?

ENDNOTES

1. Lundie S. Peters, GM (Feb. 2005) "Life Cycle Assessment of Food Waste," *Journal of Cleaner Productions*, 13(3): pp 275–286.
2. EPA, (2013), "Inventory of US Greenhouse Gas Emissions and Sinks: April 12, 2013, p. ES-13.
3. http://www.epa.gov/waste/conserve/foodwaste/index.htm, Retrieved June 14, 2014.
4. K. D. Hall, J. Guo, M. Dore, C. C. Chow, "The Progressive Increase of Food Waste in America and Its Environmental Impact." *PLoS ONE* 4(11): e7940. doi:10.1371/journal.pone.0007940.
5. American Society of Civil Engineers (ASCE), "2013 Report Card for America's Infrastructure," pp. 29–32.

APPENDIX

Water Bottles versus Water Filters

The plastic one-time use water bottle is cause for concern.

Studies show that only one in five single-use water bottles is recycled every year. In 2005, for the 30 billion water bottles used in the United States, only 12 percent were recycled. Another way of thinking about this number is that for every second, 100 water bottles are recycled but *877 are put into the landfill.*[1] Astonishing numbers, but consider that from 2001 to 2007, bottled water sales increased by 70 percent—far surpassing sales of beer and milk— and the use only continues to grow.[2]

In 1997, Charles Moore, a competitive sailor, was returning home to southern California after finishing the Los Angeles to Hawaii Transpac sailing race and discovered trash floating in the North Pacific Gyre, a remote area of the ocean.

> "As I gazed from the deck at the surface of what ought to have been a pristine ocean," Moore later wrote in an essay for *Natural History*, "I was confronted, as far as the eye could see, with the sight of plastic. It seemed unbelievable, but I never found a clear spot. In the week it took to cross the subtropical high, no matter what time of day I looked, plastic debris was floating everywhere: bottles, bottle caps, wrappers, fragments."[3] An oceanographic colleague of Moore's dubbed this floating junkyard "the Great Pacific Garbage Patch," and despite Moore's efforts to suggest different metaphors—"a swirling sewer," "a superhighway of trash" connecting two "trash cemeteries"—"garbage patch" appears to have stuck.

> This discovery led to his 1999 study, which found that there were "six times more plastic in this part of the ocean than the zooplankton that feeds ocean life. This number was increased in a 2002 study which showed that off the coast of California, "plastic outweighed zooplankton by a factor of 5:2, numbers that were much higher than most scientists expected."[4]

It takes over 1,000 years for plastic bottles to biodegrade.

A great deal of embodied energy is used during the life cycle of a bottle of water that you purchase at the store. Research shows that the entire chain from the manufacturing of the bottle, processing the water, filling and labeling the bottle, transporting the filled bottles to your store, and chilling it so that you have cold water to drink uses an estimated 32 to 54 million

TABLE B.1 Some Key Differences between EPA Tap Water and FDA Bottled Water Rules

Water Type	Disinfection Required?	Confirmed *E. coli* and Fecal Coliform Banned?	Testing Frequency for Bacteria	Must Filter to Remove Pathogens or Have Strictly Protected Source?	Must Test for *Cryptosporidium, Giardia*, Viruses?	Testing Frequency for Most Synthetic Organic Chemicals
Bottled water	No	No	1/week	No	No	1/year
Carbonated or seltzer water	No	No	None	No	No	None
Big-city tap water (using surface water)	Yes	Yes	Hundreds/month	Yes	Yes	1/quarter (limited waivers available if clean source)

Used with permission from the Natural Resources Defense Council, www. NRDC.org

barrels of oil per year, and these are only US statistics. To meet the worlds bottled water demands, 96 to 162 million barrels of oil are required yearly![5]

So, we have a bottle that is contributing to the world's oil use and is difficult to get rid of. What about the water: It's healthier than tap water, right?

Well, actually, no.

Tests conducted by the National Research Defense Council of more than 1000 bottles of 103 brands of bottled water found that 25 percent contained some levels of contamination, including synthetic chemicals, bacteria, and arsenic. In at least one sample, contaminants exceeding limits allowed by industry guidelines or standards were found.[6]

Although the Food and Drug Administration (FDA) regulates bottled water safety, its rules do not apply to the 60 to 70 percent of all water that is bottled and sold within the same state. Approximately one in five states has no regulation for bottled water. To date, there is no regulation for carbonated water and seltzer.

But the water is tested, right?—Well again, no, at least not on a regular basis. Bottled water is not required to be tested as often as city tap water for bacteria and chemical contaminants. Whereas *E. coli* or fecal coliform is prohibited in tap water, bottled water regulation allows for some of these contaminants. In addition, bottled water has no requirements for the testing and decontamination of parasites such as *Cryptosporidium* or *Giardia*.

Table B.1 presents key differences between Environmental Protection Agency (EPA) rules for tap water and FDA rules for bottled water.

Finances are a huge factor in consumers' buying decisions. Complaints ensue when gas goes over $4.00 a gallon, but no one complains when buying a 16-ounce bottle of water that they can get for free. Why? If you do the math and multiply it out, that comes to almost $8.00 a gallon. Just consider the expense.

As a designer, you have the opportunity to make a change in this pattern. Suggest to clients that they add a water filter to their kitchen project. Explain the health benefits and cost savings and the fact that, as an added bonus, they will be helping the environment.

ENDNOTES

1. www.Container-Recycling.org/indes.php/issues/bottled-water; video, *Animating Water Bottle Recycling Rates* (Doug James, Cornell University).
2. Ibid.
3. Charles Moore, "Trashed: Across the Pacific Ocean, Plastics, Plastics, Everywhere." *Natural History* 112(9): 43; as quoted in http://en.wikipedia.org/wiki/Charles_J._Moore.

4. *Wikipedia*, s.v. "Charles J. Moore," accessed May 19, 2014, http://en.wikipedia.org/wiki/Charles_J._Moore.

5. P. H. Gleick and H. S. Cooley, "Energy Implications of Bottled Water." *Environmental Research Letters* 4(1), available at http://iopscience.iop.org/1748-9326/4/1/014009/fulltext/.

6. Bottled Water Contamination: An Overview of NRDC's and Others' Surveys. Study by NRDC: Bottled Water – Pure Drink or Pure Hype? July 2013. Available at www.nrdc.org/water/drinking/bw/chap3.asp.

APPENDIX

Case Studies

CASE STUDY 1: MORGAN RESIDENCE, PORTLAND, OREGON

Designer: Robin Rigby Fisher, CMKBD/CAPS

Square footage: 300 square feet

Creating a new kitchen for an energy consultation expert can put designers on their toes. The goal for this project was to focus on the view and incorporate materials and products that are energy efficient and as locally sourced as possible. Storage was a major concern, as was making the space accessible for the client's elderly parents and the clients themselves as they age in their home.

The initial kitchen had an eating bar and a breakfast table in addition to the formal dining table. The original island had the cook facing an interior wall with the view behind them. This needed to be fixed!

An island was created that incorporated storage, cooking, and a custom table with built-in seating. The new design allows the chef, while cooking, to face guests sitting at the banquette (see Figure C.1).

The new design incorporated LED lamps in the recessed cans, induction cooking, Forest Stewardship Council (FSC) cherry cabinets with no-added-urea formaldehyde (NUAF) plywood, and a water-based finish low in volatile organic compounds (VOCs) from Neil Kelly Signature Cabinets (see Figure C.2).

Construction techniques included the use of low-VOC adhesives, refinishing of the existing oak floors, high-efficiency windows, and low-VOC paint. All existing materials, including appliances, cabinets, lighting, and plumbing, were donated to the ReBuild It Center for repurposing.

The custom-built table and chairs were designed and built by The Joinery, a Portland, Oregon, company that uses sustainably harvested FSC wood (see Figure C.3).

One area of compromise was the granite countertops. The original goal was to use Cambria Quartz (manufactured in the United States), but after a visit to a local stone supplier, a granite from Brazil was chosen. The choice to use a leathered finish allowed the client to forgo the use of sealers.

Environmental goals
- Energy efficiency
- Locally sourced, sustainably harvested woods
- Low-VOC adhesives, finishes, and paints

FIGURE C.1 Neil Kelly Signature Cabinets made with NUAF FSC plywood and hardwood, and low VOC water-based finish.

Photo by Russ Widstrand

FIGURE C.2 The working side of the island features an induction cooktop.

Photo by Russ Widstrand

FIGURE C.3 Island features custom storage and built-in seating. Table by The Joinery.
Photo by Russ Widstrand

NKBA Access Standards were incorporated in the design of this kitchen.

Materials used
- Devine Paint
- Neil Kelly Signature Cabinets (FSC cherry and NUAF plywood)
- Décor Induction Cooktop
- Custom-built, locally sourced table and chairs
- Water-based finish for both cabinets and floors
- LED lamps

CASE STUDY 2: MACCABBEE RESIDENCE, PORTLAND, OREGON

Designer: Robin Rigby Fisher, CMKBD/CAPS

Square footage: 145 square feet

"Fun and sustainable with good energy flow" were the requirements set by the client at the first meeting with the designers. As a feng shui consultant, the client requested that her new kitchen encourage good *chi*. Since the original kitchen was shut off from the entire home and was dark all year long, it was decided that opening the kitchen to the public space was the first order of business. This incorporated more natural daylighting, minimizing the amount of artificial light used during the day. The door to the dining room was relocated and part of

FIGURE C.4 FSC cherry cabinets made with NUAF plywood, Oceanside tile blend was chosen from the colors with the highest recycled content. *NKBA*

the adjoining wall was removed. Due to financial restrictions (to keep the kitchen remodel below $75,000), it was decided to retain a post at the intersection of the removed walls. Eventually, a custom buffet cabinet will be installed in the opening.

To achieve the sustainable goal of the client, the following materials were selected.

Health and wellness
- Low-VOC paint: Rodda Horizon paint
- Cabinets: Neil Kelly Signature cabinets (low VOC finish, MIAF agri-board construction)
- Flooring: Marmoleum (a natural product, and the continuous oxidation of the linseed oil from which it is made creates an antimicrobial surface)
- Feng shui: During construction, prior to installation of Sheetrock, the client added elements for each of the *bagua* to create harmony and unity within the home
- All construction adhesives Green Seal Certified
- Water purifier at sink for hot and cold water

Energy conservation
- Recessed cans: Compact fluorescent lamps (CFLs) with Alzak Trims
- Dimmers: Installed to control the amount of lighting to control energy usage
- Hot water dispenser: Minimizes energy use in heating water for hot beverages

Material conservation
- Laminate countertops: Laminart (incorporates 40 percent postconsumer waste and banana leaves to create a texture on the surface)

- FSC-certified maple countertops on island and to right of range
- Oceanside Glasstile (40 percent recycled content)

Water conservation
- Kitchenaid ENERGY STAR–rated dishwasher

Among the client's requests were an island, a message center, and a pantry. Although the kitchen is small (only 145 square feet), this space packs a real punch. Included in the island are areas for recycling/composting, cookbook storage, and a "perching" place for guests to hang out in the kitchen.

The message center/pantry houses a microwave, a push pin board, and a regenerating station for small personal electronics (see Figures C.4, C.5, and C.6).

CASE STUDY 3: REPURPOSING MATERIALS, PORTLAND, OREGON

Designer: Anna De Wolf, Arciform Design Build, LLC, Portland, Oregon

Square Footage: 2500 square feet (whole house remodel)

Not every project requires a full gutting. More often than not, some elements of the existing home can or should be maintained, either in its original form or used for an entirely different purpose. Anna De Wolf is no stranger to reusing and repurposing. "I'm German. We don't like to throw out things that still have use. Besides, not only is it environmentally sound and saves the client money, it is more creative to work with these elements."

FIGURE C.5 All appliances were chosen for their high Energy Star rating for efficiency.
NKBA

FIGURE C.6 Message center is tucked between pantry storage. Island top is FSC maple butcherblock finished with food-safe linseed oil.

NKBA

On a recent whole-house remodel on a 1960s daylight ranch, Anna and her firm, Arciform Design Build, had the opportunity to renovate the living room.

"The existing space surrounding the fireplace had built-ins, which were inefficient and made the room feel short, but the fireplace with its beautiful stonework had merit. We reworked the cabinetry, adding painted open shelves and mirrors above the fireplace. The results are beautiful. The reflection of the existing beams makes the room seem so much bigger and brighter!

On this same project, the utility room was remodeled, which still had its original teal linoleum. After a good cleaning and restoring process, the floor looks brand new. The client was dubious at the thought of retaining the existing floor but loves it now!

Not only did we retain the original charm and midcentury elements, we saved them money!"

Anna De Wolf

Mudroom Magic

Mudrooms are the unsung hero of the home. Not so when you add a playful element. According to De Wolf, "While doing some research for another project, I visited a local renovation hardware store and saw that they had used leftover doors on the ceiling. I suggested this idea to the client, along with using mismatched doors as lockers. They loved it!" (see Figures C.7, C.8, C.9, and C.10).

FIGURE C.7 Designed by Anne De Wolf, owner/designer at Arciform
Photo by Photo Art Portraits

FIGURE C.8 Designed by Anne De Wolf, owner/designer at Arciform
Photo by Photo Art Portraits

FIGURE C.9 Designed by Anne De Wolf, owner/designer at Arciform
Photo by Photo Art Portraits

FIGURE C.10 Designed by Anne De Wolf, owner/designer at Arciform
Photo by Photo Art Portraits

Reusing the doors for lockers and the ceiling kept materials out of the landfill, did not require the purchase of new doors along with all of the embodied energy that goes with the creation of new products, saved the client money, and created a fun space.

CASE STUDY 4: BATHROOM RENOVATION, MONTCLAIR, NEW JERSEY

Designer: Tracey Stephens, CID, ReGreen Certified, Principal at Tracey Stephens Interior Design

Square footage: 88 square feet

The existing bathroom was dated, falling apart, and not very functional. The fixtures leaked and the cabinets were hard to access.

The solution for updating this main bath began with the vanity. Using reclaimed wood from an Amish barn from Pennsylvania, a six-drawer vanity was created that steps back at the sides (see Figure C.11). This allowed for more room as the family members entered the small bath. The same reclaimed wood was used to build floating shelves for towel storage (see Figure C.12).

The Caesarstone quartz counters, seen in Figure C.13, with 24 percent recycled content, require no additional maintenance or sealers, which supports the health of the home. Rather than send the existing vintage medicine cabinet to the landfill, it was given a fresh coat of paint.

General contracting for this project was by European Craftsman, LLC.

FIGURE C.11 Vanity made from reclaimed wood
Photo by Wing Wong/Memories TTL

FIGURE C.12 Floating shelves made from reclaimed wood
Photo by Wing Wong/Memories TTL

FIGURE C.13 This quartz countertop does not require sealers.

CASE STUDY 4: KITCHEN RENOVATION, MONTCLAIR, NEW JERSEY

Designer: Tracey Stephens, CID, ReGreen Certified, Principal at Tracey Stephens Interior Design

Square footage: 294 square feet

This remodel won the 2012 American Society of Interior Designers (ASID) NJ Award for Design Excellence—Sustainable Design Recognition.

The cramped kitchen no longer worked for the homeowner, an enthusiastic cook and baker. The dark kitchen had a few issues: In addition to inadequate storage and work spaces, the corner sink was inconvenient and the powder room, which didn't work properly, took up valuable real estate.

By relocating the powder room and door and adding a large bay window, the kitchen was brightened and much-needed space was added. (See the before plan in Figure C.14 and the after plan in Figure C.15.) The red Bertazzoni range was the inspiration for the colors of the kitchen. The base cabinets were colored to match the range using water-based paint (see Figures C.16 and C.17).

These clients were committed to sustainable design from the beginning. All of the existing cabinets, appliances, fixtures, and fittings were donated to Habitat for Humanity. To update the home's energy efficiency, new recycled denim insulation was added to the exterior walls. New energy-efficient windows and doors were installed in the kitchen. LED lighting was

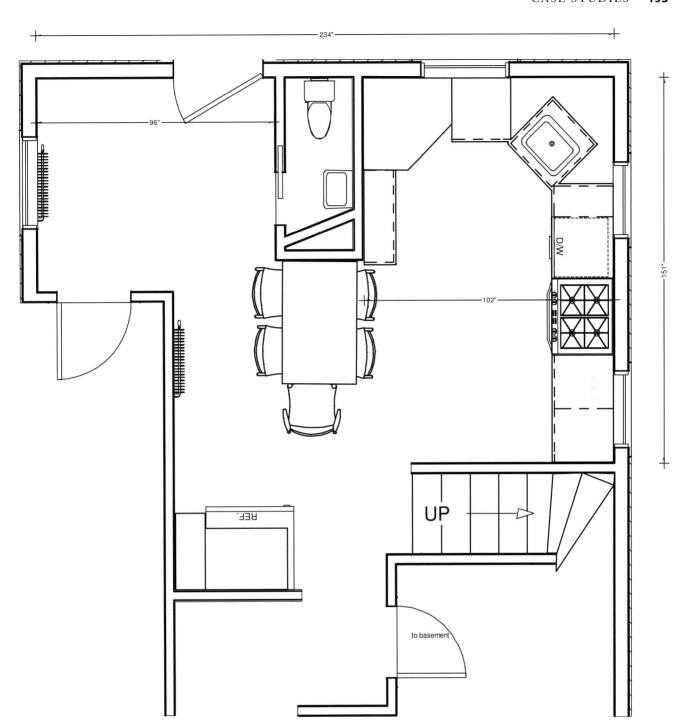

SCALE: 1/4" = 1'-0"

"BEFORE" KITCHEN PLAN

FIGURE C.14 Before plan
Tracey Stephens Interior Design

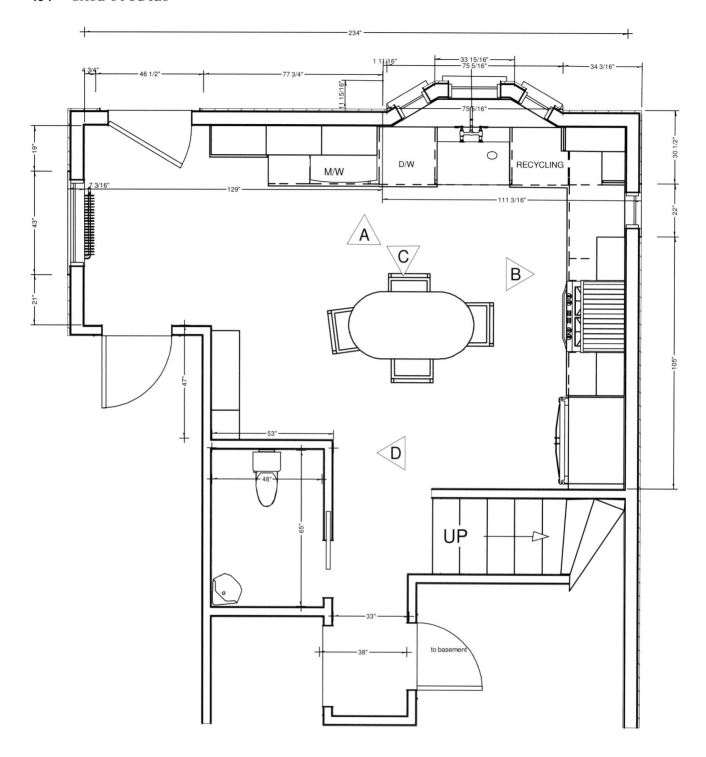

MEDIUM KITCHEN PLAN
SCALE: 1/4" = 1'-0"

FIGURE C.15 After plan

Tracey Stephens Interior Design

FIGURE C.16 Cabinets made with FSC-certified wood and NUAF plywood were painted with water-based low-VOC paint.
Photo by Wing Wong/Memories TTL

installed as under-cabinet lighting, and Lutron dimmers and switches were installed. The Bosch dishwasher and JennAir refrigerator are ENERGY STAR rated.

The new cabinets from Modern Cabinet Company were fabricated using NUAF plywood and FSC-certified lumber. The walls, ceiling, and trim were painted with Benjamin Moore Aura low-VOC paint.

General contracting for this project was by European Craftsman, LLC.

FIGURE C.17 The red Bertazzoni range was the inspiration for the kitchen.
Photo by Wing Wong/Memories TTL

APPENDIX

Summary of Product Standards for Green Specifications

This list is used with permission from "Building Materials: What Makes a Product Green?" *Environmental Building News* 9(1) (January 2000), by Alex Wilson, E Build, Inc. Brattleboro, VT, and Dorothy Payton, environmental designer and consultant, Portland, OR.

1. Products made from environmentally attractive materials
   Products that reduce material use
   Salvaged products
   Products with post-consumer recycled content
   Products with post-industrial recycled content
   Certified wood products
   Products made from agricultural waste material
   Natural or minimally processes products
2. Products that are green because of what is not there
   Alternatives to ozone-depleting substances
   Alternatives to products made with PVC and polycarbonate
   Alternatives to conventional preservative treated wood
   Alternatives to other components considered hazardous (asbestos, mercury, chromium, lead, radiation)
3. Products that reduce environmental impacts during construction, renovation, or demolition
   Products that reduce the impacts of new construction
   Products that reduce the impacts of renovation
   Products that reduce the impacts of demolition
4. Products that reduce environmental impacts of building operation
   Building components that reduce heating and cooling loads
   Equipment that conserves energy
   Renewable energy (fuel cell, solar, wind, small turbine) equipment
   Fixtures and equipment that conserve water
   Products with exceptional durability or low maintenance requirements
   Products that prevent pollution or reduce waste
   Products that reduce or eliminate pesticide treatments

5. Products that contribute to safe, healthy indoor air environment

Products that don't release significant pollutants into the building

Products that block development and spread of indoor contaminant

Products that remove indoor pollutants

Products that warn occupants of health hazards in the building

Products that improve light quality

6. Products that promote social equity and justice, and teach/remind/connect us to one another, the planet, spirit, life force

Products manufactured employing fair labor

Products attentive to and mitigating of environmental justice issues

Products that develop sustainable economics/local green wealth

Products that address health and safety concerns during manufacturing, installation, and operation

Products that are modeled, mentored, and measured by nature

SUSTAINABILITY CRITERIA

Key questions should include:

What makes it "green"? What are the criteria generally used?

Which attribute has the most significant negative impact?

For any given product (structure, system, strategy), what is its most earth-friendly attribute?

What is its least earth-friendly attribute?

Products made from environmentally attractive materials are

Sized or made to reduce use and waste

Salvaged

Made from recycled content (post-industrial, post-consumer, post-agricultural)

Sustainably gathered or harvested (e.g., FSC certified)

Rapidly renewable (bio-based)

Mindful of life cycle assessment issues (ecological footprint, species and habitat preservation and restoration)

Locally harvested/manufactured/assembled

Products that are green because of what is not there are

Ozone-friendly

PVC/polycarbonate-free

Pesticide free

Heavy metal free

Other bio-accumulative toxins free

Low in embodied energy

Free of unnecessary finishes or layers

Practices and strategies that reduce environmental impacts during construction, renovation, demolition, or manufacturing

Soil horizon protection: compaction, excavation

Erosion and sedimentation prevention

Efficient and effective use of raw materials

Existing materials can be saved for reuse or donation

Solid waste management separable

Storm water management: use of permeable surfaces

Products that reduce the environmental impacts of building operation are

Energy conserving/energy efficient

Renewable sources of energy

Water conserving/water efficient

Multipurpose

Life cycle cost issues (durability, maintenance and repair considerations)

Products that contribute to a safe, healthy indoor air environment

Are non-polluting

Consider indoor air quality and are low in VOC, allergens, particulates, combustion, byproducts, and fragrances

Determining Your Client's Commitment to Green Design

Use the following matrices to judge your client's desire for and interest in green remodeling measures *prior* to your design programming phase. Having your client complete this questionnaire will help you to better understand their feelings about and commitment to sustainable design.

DESIGNING FOR GREEN LIVING

The support of green activities in a kitchen will make integrating environmentally healthy habits into your life easier.

Please rate your interest in green design:	Very likely	Likely	Likely	Not likely
	Would even consider spending more for this design measure.	But only if costs were comparable.	But only if costs and performance were exactly comparable to others.	Prefer to work with the designer to choose these items based on other factors.
Design a recycling center based on your municipality's recycling program.				
Design a recycling center that goes beyond your municipality's recycling program.				
Design for composting while doing food prep.				
Use materials that require little or no maintenance with sealants (potential VOC contamination).				
Design for shoe storage at entry (removing shoes is one way to enhance clean indoor air in your home).				

CONSTRUCTION

The use of a builder who is knowledgeable in green building can be a wonderful way to be confident that your project's site, construction, and finish work will be aligned with sustainable building practices. Look for contractors who have completed the National Association of Homebuilders Green Building education: NAHB Green, or LEED-AP, or other sustainable building certifications.

Please rate your interest in "green" construction practices:	Very likely	Likely	Likely	Not likely
	Would even consider spending more for the services or measures.	But only if costs were comparable.	But only if costs and performance were exactly comparable to others.	Prefer to work with the designer to choose these items based on other factors.
Using the services of a "green" general contractor				
Using the services of a "green" subcontractors				
Deconstruction over demolition				
Donation of useable salvaged fixtures to nonprofit organization				
Donation of useable salvaged materials to nonprofit organization				
Use of alternative framing methods				
Use of alternative construction methods: low-cement concrete mix				

MATERIALS

The specification and installation of materials that are considered "green" can greatly reduce the impact your project has on the environment.

Please rate your interest in using "green" materials:	Very likely	Likely	Likely	Not likely
	Would even consider spending more for this aspect of a green material.	But only if costs were comparable.	But only if costs and performance were exactly comparable to others.	Prefer to work with the designer to choose these items based on other factors.
Product is C2C or Green Spec rated				
Recycled content				
Low embodied energy				
Salvage material				
Locally produced materials				
Domestically produced materials				

WATER CONSERVATION

The specification of appliances and fixtures approved by the Watersense program can greatly lessen your impact on the environment. There are also measures you can take to lessen your water use in your home.

Please rate your interest in Watersense-approved appliances:	Very likely	Likely	Likely	Not likely
	Would even consider spending more for water-saving appliances and fixtures.	But only if costs were comparable.	But only if costs were comparable.	Prefer to work with the designer to choose these items based on other factors.
Dishwasher				
Refrigerator				
Washing machine				
Toilet				
Shower heads				
Bathroom sink faucets				
Kitchen faucet				
Point-of-use water heater				
Consider changes to current irrigation system in the surrounding yard/site				
Install a cistern to collect rainwater for irrigation				

ENERGY CONSERVATION: ENERGY USE

The Energy Star program endorses appliances that are very efficient with their energy use and can lessen your impact on the environment. There are also design measures that create energy (solar) and appliances that conserve energy by means of their efficiency.

Please rate your interest in Energy Star-endorsed appliances and alternate energy sources:	Very likely	Likely	Likely	Not likely
	Would even consider spending more for energy appliances and fixtures.	But only if costs were comparable.	But only if costs and performance were exactly comparable to others.	Prefer to work with the designer to choose these items based on other factors.
Solar power—create electricity with solar source				
Solar hot water—heat water using solar source				
Dishwasher				
Refrigerator				
Washing machine				
Dryer				
Electric or induction cooktop or range				
Oven(s)				
Tankless water heater				
Energy-saving lighting, preferable LED source throughout				
Pre-set dimming systems on light sources				
Domestically manufactured appliances (lower embodied energy)				

ENERGY CONSERVATION: HEATING AND COOLING

There are energy-saving systems you can install to heat and cool your home or your new addition/ remodel. Some of these alternative heating and cooling measures can be somewhat expensive at the onset but over the life of the system, the efficiency in managing thermal comfort, increasing indoor air quality, and conserving energy use can greatly offset the initial cost of the system.

Please rate your interest in energy-saving measures.	Very likely	Likely	Likely	Not likely
	Would even consider spending more for energy-saving system or measure.	But only if costs were comparable.	But only if costs and performance were exactly comparable to traditional system.	I prefer to use a system I am familiar with and/or do not want to spend money to upgrade to an alternative system.
Radiant heat—floor				
Radiant heat—radiators, closed water				
Heat pump				
Programmable thermostat				
Use *zonal* heating and cooling.				
Heat recovery ventilator				
Energy recovery ventilator				
Passive solar heat				
Replacing windows with a low SHGC (solar heat gain coefficient) to cut down on solar heat gain in your home				

ENERGY CONSERVATION: PREVENTING ENERGY LOSS

There are energy-saving measures you can choose to increase the efficiency of your home or your new addition/remodel. This is done from the perspective of designing to decrease energy loss in a home. Many of these measures are simple (insulation) while others are more costly (energy-efficient windows).

Please rate your interest in energy conservation measures.	Very likely	Likely	Likely	Not likely
	Would even consider spending more for energy saving system.	But only if costs were comparable.	But only if costs and performance were exactly comparable to traditional system.	I prefer to use a system I am familiar with and/or do not want to spend money to upgrade to an alternative system.
Replace windows with a low U value to prevent against heat transfer				
Increase insulation to create walls that have a higher R (heat loss) value than the levels recommended for my zone by the Department of Energy				
Insulate air ducts				
Insulate hot water pipes in the interior.				
Insulate wall outlets in exterior walls				
Add insulation to attic spaces or roof (if applicable to project)				
Install drain heat recovery in showers, sinks, and bath tubs				
Use alternative wall types such as Insulated Concrete panels (ICP) or structural insulated panels (SIP)				

INDOOR AIR QUALITY

The specification and installation of measures to enhance the purity of the air of your home can decrease chances of respiratory illnesses and improve your quality of life.

Please rate your interest in:	Very likely	Likely	Likely	Not likely
	Would even consider spending more.	But only if costs were comparable.	But only if costs and performance were exactly comparable to others.	Prefer to work with the designer to choose these items based on other factors.
Installing a hood with a CFM (amount of air removal) that is above the recommended (minimum) levels for my range or cooktop				
Considering induction cooking over gas				
Installing direct vent fireplaces only				
Giving careful attention to the quality of plywood and other composite wood products in the project				
Considering a ductless heating and cooling system				
Installing ventilation that may be beyond code in bathrooms (mold prevention)				
Installing operable windows for passive ventilation				
Introducing additional air or "make-up air" to provide safer, cleaner air				
Using paints with low-zero VOC characteristics				
Using stains with low-zero VOC characteristics				
Using finishes with low-zero VOC characteristics				

DESIGNING FOR LONGEVITY

The integration of Universal Design principles into your project will ensure that your remodel will serve the needs of more users than conventional design methods, and for the needs of the client over a lifetime. Universal Design also increases the value of your kitchen and/or bath remodel.

Please rate your interest in Universal Design.	Very likely	Likely	Likely	Not likely
	Would even consider spending more for this design measure.	But only if costs were comparable.	But only if costs and performance were exactly comparable to others.	Prefer to work with the designer to choose these items based on other factors.
Varied counter heights in kitchen: plan for a lower counter height so that a user can sit while preparing food				
Base cabinets with drawer storage over door storage				
Cabinets designed with articulating corner storage to provide ease of access in hard-to-reach places				
Minimize upper cabinet storage if possible				
Use of cabinet drawer and door pulls instead of knobs				
Installation of levers instead of door knobs on all doors				
Installation of a wall oven at an accessible height rather than a range (low access)				
Resilient flooring in kitchen (dropped objects are less likely to break)				
Stainless steel sink in kitchen (prevents breaking)				
Induction cook top rather than gas or electric (for safety)				
Slip-resistant flooring in kitchen and bath				
Installation of grab bars in bathrooms or the installation of "blocking" for future installation of this safety measure				
Design shower with thermostatic controls for safety (prevents scalding)				
Installation of seat in shower if possible				
Installation of easy-to-reach storage in shower				
Installation of hand-held shower fixture in shower and tub if applicable				
Tub (if applicable) installed with surround for easy in and out access				
Lighting for tasks				
High illumination (light levels) without glare				
Flexible lighting (dimming)				

Glossary

Advanced framing
Method of wall construction that improves the energy efficiency (R-value) of a wall and also reduces material waste.

Affordable Comfort Incorporated (ACI)
Independent nonprofit organization educational resource for the home performance industry. Based in North Carolina, the ACI sponsors local conferences throughout the United States.

American Society of Heating, Refrigeration and Air Conditioning Engineers (ASHRAE)
Founded in 1894, ASHRAE's mission is "to advance the arts and sciences of heating, ventilating, air conditioning and refrigerating to serve humanity and promote a sustainable world" (www.ashrae.org/about-ashrae).

Anaerobic decay
Any number of processes where biodegradable materials are broken down by microorganisms without the presence of oxygen.

Appraisal Institute (AI)
Global membership organization representing professional real estate appraisers.

Asbestos
Silicate compound that was developed as an additive for various building materials. When particles become airborne from materials breaking, they cause severe damage to the lungs if inhaled. Asbestos abatements are an important part of remodeling projects on older homes.

Best practices
Methods of creating a collection of proven approaches to problem solving that serve as a benchmark for solving similar problems.

Black water
Wastewater that contains or has been exposed to human waste, such as wastewater from a toilet or bidet.

Blower door test
Test conducted to determine the airtightness of a home. Part of a home energy audit.

British thermal unit (Btu)
Unit of measurement for energy. Refers to the amount of energy needed to heat or cool 1 pound of water. Used to describe the amount of energy released by cooktop, range, or oven in a home.

Building science
Practice of using scientific data to understand the effects of physical forces (heat, cold, wind, and inhabitation) in building practices.

CalGreen
First statewide green energy code in the United States. The code covers energy conservation, air quality, and energy efficiency of building.

California Air Resources Board
Advisory board to the state environmental law making processes in the state of California. Duties of the board include research into protecting air quality and minimizing pollution.

Carbon dioxide (CO$_2$)
Molecule comprised of two oxygen atoms and one carbon atom. Found in the natural world. In gas form, it is the major greenhouse gas.

Carbon footprint
Total sum of all greenhouse gases created and/or emitted from the production of a material or of an activity.

Carbon monoxide (CO)
Molecule comprised of one oxygen atom and one carbon atom. As a gas, it is toxic to humans and animals in high concentration. It is produced by combustion of fossil fuels.

Combustible pollutants
Term used to define a class of gases and toxins produced from the burning of fuel. Most commonly the building industry is concerned with combustible pollutants created from the burning of natural gas.

Compact fluorescent lamp (CFL)
Source of electric illumination that uses fluorescent technology to make light and is self-ballasted. Developed to replace incandescent "light bulbs," the efficacy of CFL ranges from 50 to 70 lumens per watt.

Cradle to Cradle (C2C)
Approach to design developed by William McDonough that calls for regenerative design, design that mimics the ability of the natural world to utilize all waste so that energy is saved and reused.

Cubic feet per minute (CFM)
Unit used to measure the amount of cubic feet of air that is moved over the time of 1 minute. Used to describe the efficiency of ventilation processes or exhaust systems.

Daylighting
The sustainable building design practice of locating openings in a building to achieve high-quality natural light in the interior.

Deconstruction
The manual removal of building materials that mimics the construction process in reverse. Developed to save and recycle materials that would otherwise be disposed of in landfills.

Depressurization
State of pressure loss in the indoor air of home when air is mechanically exhausted out of a home. Can lead to dangerous backdrafting if the depressurization is too severe.

Direct vent
A type of fireplace that has an enclosed burning chamber that requires a chimney. The burning chamber can vent horizontally to a sidewall or vertically to the roof.

Drain heat recovery (DHR)
A system installed in homes to capture heat from wastewater of showers, bathtubs, and sinks.

Earth Advantage
Nonprofit organization dedicated to green building education.

Efficient Window Collaborative
Nonprofit organization whose mission is to provide resources and education for the installation of windows, doors, and skylights that will save energy.

Electronic Signatures and Records Commerce Act (ESRA)
Implemented in 2000, this act awards electronic signatures the same legal stature as physical signatures.

Embodied energy
The gross aggregate of energy necessary to create goods and services.

Energy and Environmental Alliance (EEBA)
Nonprofit organization created to advocate for the green building sector. Stands behind various definitions of green buildings.

Energy factor (EF)
A measurement label that provides information on the energy efficiency of residential appliances. The EF applies to dishwashers, water heaters, clothes washers, and clothes dryers.

ENERGY STAR
Voluntary program that promotes appliances and fixtures that have low energy use. *(Chapter 1,3,5)*

Engineered openings
Openings made to the outside of home for the introduction of fresh or makeup air.

Energy recovery ventilator (ERV)
A mechanical air-to-air exchanger that improves indoor air quality by bringing fresh air into the interior. An ERV also saves energy in the home by transferring the heat or cold from treated indoor air to outside untreated air. An ERV also humidifies incoming, untreated air.

Environmental Protection Agency (EPA)
Agency of the US government founded to protect human health from the effects of environmental destruction.

Eutrophication
The pollution of the natural environment through the introduction of nitrates and phosphates. Exacerbated by the use of food waste disposals (garburators), and poor municipal wastewater treatment infrastructure which send nitrogen-rich waste into the earth's water systems.

Forest Stewardship Council (FSC)
An international not-for-profit organization established in 1993. The FSC encourages responsible management of the world's forests.

Formaldehyde
A chemical additive for binders and adhesives used throughout an interior. Urea-based formaldehyde is a toxic volatile organic compound that can cause respiratory and ophthalmic irritation when experienced in the air.

Fossil fuels
Forms of combustible energy formed in the earth's crust primarily out of carbon. Includes petroleum (oil), coal, and natural gas.

Four Rs of sustainable design
Reduce, reuse, recycle, recover.

Friable
A trait or condition where a material can break apart and release particulate matter into the air. A term commonly related to a poor-state of asbestos materials found in the home.

Glazing
Building industry term for the use of glass. Most commonly used to describe windows and doors with windows.

Graywater
Wastewater from hand-washing sinks, showers, and baths that can be reused in some capacity, such as for toilet flushing and irrigation. Laundry wastewater is excluded from graywater as is dishwasher wastewater due to its high nutrient level from food residue.

GREENGUARD
Division of the Underwriters Laboratory (UL) formed to help consumers choose materials that have low chemical emissions. Provides certification for materials.

Greenhouse effect
Process by which infrared radiation is re-released by greenhouse gases toward the earth, thus warming the earth's surface.

Greenhouse gas (GHG)
Name given to the gases present in the earth's atmosphere that absorb and then emit radiation, thus creating the *greenhouse effect*. Greenhouse gases include carbon dioxide, nitrous oxide, and methane.

Greenwashing
A practice of deceiving consumers about the level of sustainable character of a product or service.

Gypsum wallboard
The most popular material to finish interior walls in the United States, Canada, and Europe. It made of two layers of paper over a layer of gypsum plaster that has cured to form a sheet.

Heat recovery ventilator (HRV)
A mechanical air-to-air exchanger that improves the indoor air quality of a home by bringing in fresh air. An HRV also saves energy in the home by transferring the heat or cold from treated indoor air to outside untreated air.

Heating, ventilation, and air-conditioning (HVAC)

Technology dedicated to the comfort of the indoor environment.

HOGs

An acronym used to describe the four major pollutants in a kitchen: heat, odors, grease, and smoke.

Home Energy Rating System (HERS)

A means of determining the energy efficiency of a home. Administered by RESNET, the Residential Energy Services Network.

Home Ventilating Institute (HVI)

A nonprofit organization that certifies ventilation products sold in North America but manufactured worldwide.

Indoor airPLUS Program

A voluntary certification program administered by the US Environmental Protection Agency for builders. airPLUS certification means that the building conforms with best indoor air quality guidelines as set forth by the EPA.

Indoor air quality (IAQ)

The characteristics or properties of the indoor atmosphere in regard to its impact on human respiratory health.

Insulated concrete panel (ICP)

A type of prefabricated wall made of two sheets of concrete with a layer of expanded polystyrene foam in between.

International Council for Local Environmental Initiatives (ICLEI)

Global organization dedicated to environmental causes conducted at local levels.

International Energy Conservation Code (IECC)

Code that encourages energy conservation through efficiency in envelope design, mechanical systems, lighting systems, and the use of new materials and techniques.

International Residential Code (IRC)

Stand-alone residential code that prescribes minimum regulations for one- and two-family dwellings of three stories or less. Concerns plumbing, mechanical, fuel gas, energy, and electrical provisions.

Lead

A common metal popular because of its malleability. Lead was a popular additive to paint prior to 1978, when it was banned from use in the United States. Ingestion of lead causes lead poisoning and harm to brain tissue.

LEED

Leadership in Environmental and Energy Design. A series of ratings developed by the US Green Building Council to encourage the design, construction, and operation of green buildings.

Life cycle assessment (LCA)

Method to evaluate a product's impact on the environment. Beyond calculating the raw materials, LCA also considers fabrication, transport, and durability or likelihood of needed replacement.

Lifestyles of Health and Sustainability (LOHAS)

Segment of consumers as identified (and named) by the Natural Marketing Institute. LOHAS are considered the most concerned consumers when it comes to making sustainable choices.

Light-emitting diode (LED)

A solid state light source. Also called a semiconductor light source. Developed to save energy, LED lamps have an estimate life of 35,000 to 50,000 hours and an efficacy of 60 to 80 lumens per watt.

Makeup air

Required for today's tighter-built, heavily insulated homes with mechanical ventilation to remove polluted air. Makeup air "makes up" the new air necessary in home to prevent too much pull of air out of the home.

Manometer

Instrument to measure the inside pressure of a home.

Material safety and data sheet (MSDS)

A document that provides builders and handlers information on how to handle and install a material safely. Also provides information on a material's hazardous nature.

Megajoule

A unit of expended heat. The measureable unit is part of the International System of Units.

Methane

A molecule composed of one atom carbon and four atoms of hydrogen. It occurs in the earth's crust and is a main component of natural gas. It is also created by decomposing waste in landfills and contributes to global warming as a greenhouse gas.

Mold

A superficial growth in the fungus family, responsible for the degradation of natural materials, such as wood and wood-based products and food in the homes. Some molds produce mycotoxins that cause health effects when inhaled.

Municipal solid waste landfill (MSWLF)

Site dedicated to the management of disposed materials.

National Association of Home Builders (NAHB)

Established in 1942, the NAHB's goal is to promote policies that support the housing industry

National Fenestration Rating Council (NFRC)

A nonprofit organization that publishes performance ratings of windows, doors, and skylights. The NFRC oversees specific ratings and certifications.

Natural Marketing Institute (NMI)

Organization that seeks to inform businesses on consumer approaches to sustainability.

Net metering

A program for businesses and homeowners who create their own electricity (i.e., from solar array panels) to help them sell unused energy to the public grid. The meter will run backwards when excess energy is being created. Customers are only billed for their "net" energy consumption.

Net zero

Term used to describe a building that creates as much or more total energy than it consumes.

Neutral pressure plane (NPP)

The point where pressure between outgoing air and incoming air is balanced. What an indoor air quality ventilation system strives for.

Nitrogen dioxide
A colorless gas with a sharp odor produced from combustion in a home. Known to cause respiratory irritation and damage.

Off-gassing
Process of volatile organic compounds moving into the indoor air (evaporation) at room temperatures.

On-demand water heater
An appliance that heats water for use in showers, sinks, and other areas only when the need is presented. An alternative to traditional water heater that maintains hot water continually in a large tank.

Pacific Northwest National Laboratory (PNNL)
One of many US Department of Energy laboratories.

Particulate matter
Liquid or solid particles found in the air.

Passive House
Residential building method that produces a very well-insulated, virtually airtight building that relies primarily passive solar gain and by internal gains from people, electrical equipment, and the like for heat.

Payback period
The time needed to recover the costs of an investment.

PEX tubing
A type of polyethylene-based plastic tubing that is excellent in radiant heat systems and indoor plumbing systems. An alternative to copper piping.

Phenolic resin
A synthetic resin comprised of phenol and formaldehyde. Most phenol is a petroleum-based product. Once cured, the formaldehyde is inert. It is used in plastic laminates and paper resin countertops.

Point-of-use water heater
A small tankless water heater that serves as a secondary water heating method; it curbs water waste caused by waiting for the water to be warmed by the primary water heating method.

Polymers
Large molecules made up of large monomers. Component in plastics and synthetic-based building materials.

Power venting
Ventilation system that uses a blower to facilitate movement of air.

Radon
Naturally occurring radioactive gas identified as a cause of lung cancer.

Relative humidity (RH)
A measurement of the amount of water in the air.

Renewable energy
A continually replenished supply of energy, such as energy from the sun (solar energy) or wind (wind power, turbine energy).

Renewable resource
A natural material that can be replenished over time. Examples are wood, grasses, wool, and bamboo.

Residential Green and Energy Efficient Addendum
Evaluation form created by the Appraisal Institute to aid real estate appraisers with the evaluation of the green character of a property.

Rio Charter on Universal Design and Sustainability
Declaration that the practice of universal design became part of the sustainability movement. Drafted at the 2004 International Conference on Universal Design.

R-value
Measure of thermal resistance. Used in the building construction industry.

Salvage, Building
Reclaimed or recycled materials, appliances, fixtures, hardware, and other building components

Sensible Accounting to Value Energy Act (SAVE)
Proposed legislation to outline and promote accuracy in evaluating the energy efficiency of a home for mortgage underwriting.

Sheetrock
A brand name; see *gypsum wallboard*.

Sick building syndrome
The experience of poor health and discomfort due to poor air quality and toxic materials in a built environment. Term was first used by the World Health Organization in 1984 to describe symptoms of poor health experienced by individuals but without any specific cause.

Solar energy
Energy source created by the capturing of the radiant energy from the sun.

Solar heat gain coefficient (SHGC)
A measurement used in the United States to demonstrate the rise in temperature in a building's interior caused by solar radiation.

Sone
A unit for measuring the loudness of sound; used to measure noise from sources of ventilation.

Strengths, weaknesses, opportunities, and threats (SWOT)
A planning strategy to evaluate the potential success of a venture.

Structural insulated panel (SIP)
A type of prefabricated wall made of two sheets of oriented strand board with a layer of expanded polystyrene foam in between.

Sustainability mission statement
A declaration of one's dedication to sustainable practices. Usually used by a business or organization in conjunction with a more general mission statement.

Systems thinking
An approach to decision making that takes into account a wide variety of variables. It leads to a solution that considers the interconnectivity of making choices.

Triple bottom line (TBL)
A concept developed by economist John Elkington to serve as a model for sustainability practices. The triple bottom line includes people, planet, and profit.

Uniform Electronic Transactions Act
Passed in 1999, this act makes electronically transferred contracts legal documents with the same legal standing as paper-based transactions.

United States Energy Information Administration (EIA)
Agency of the US government that oversees and publishes analysis and statistics of energy use on both global and national levels.

United Nations Environment Programme (UNEP)
Conducts the UN's efforts to assist countries in implementing environmentally responsible practices and policies. UNEP cofounded the Intergovernmental Panel on Climate Change with the World Meteorological Organization.

United States Green Building Council (USGBC)
A nonprofit, membership-based organization founded to promote the development of green building practices. The USGBC administers the LEED award system to commercial buildings, residences, and commercial interiors.

Universal design
Approach to the design of the built environment attributed to architect Ronald Mace. Comprised of seven principles to create environments that serve users of all abilities and capabilities.

U-value
Measure of heat loss through a material. Used in the building construction industry.

Ventilation, Active
Introduction of clean air into areas of polluted air and removal of polluted air by mechanical methods such as fans, heat recovery ventilators, and exhaust systems

Ventilation, Passive
Introduction of clean air into areas of polluted air and removal of polluted air by natural methods of dissipation

Volatile organic compound (VOC)
Any one of the organic gases emitted from solids at room temperature due to a low boiling point. Many VOCs have serious effects on human health and are found at higher concentrations indoors.

WaterSense
Water-saving program sponsored by the US Environmental Protection Agency to guide consumers on water-saving choices. WaterSense rates toilets, urinals, shower heads, faucets, and irrigation supplies for low water compliance.

White water
Clean, unused potable water.

World Health Organization (WHO)
An agency within the United Nations that is dedicated to protecting the health of all citizens on a global level. The WHO is also part of the United Nations Development Group and is based in Geneva, Switzerland.

World Resource Institute
Nonprofit organization whose purpose is to study and collect data on the relationship between environmental stewardship and socioeconomic development.

Resources

CHAPTER 1

"Buildings and Their Impact on the Environment: A Statistical Summary"
www.epa.gov/greenbuilding/pubs/gbstats.pdf

CHAPTER 3

Arizona Department of Environmental Quality, www.azdeq.gov
CalGreen Web site, www.bsc.ca.gov/Home.aspx
David Johnson, *Green From the Ground Up* (Taunton Press, 2008)
Metro (Portland, OR) Web site www.oregonmetro.gov
Sustainable Sources, http://sustainablesources.com/
US Environmental Protection Agency Lead Safe program, http://www2.epa.gov/lead

CHAPTER 4

US Environmental Protection Agency, "Particulate Matter,"
www.epa.gov/ncer/science/pm/
Princeton University, "Asbestos Fact Sheet"
http://web.princeton.edu/sites/ehs/workplacesafety/asbestosfactsheet.htm
Wisconsin Department of Health Services, www.dhs.wisconsin.gov/eh/chemfs/fs/pah.htm
World Health Organization, "WHO Guidelines for Indoor Air Quality: Dampness and Mould"
www.euro.who.int/__data/assets/pdf_file/0017/43325/E92645.pdf?ua=1

CHAPTER 5

Build It GREEN, "Countertops," www.builditgreen.org/attachments/wysiwyg/22/Countertops.pdf
Cradle to Cradle Products Innovation Institute, "Cradle to Cradle Certified SILVER,"
Cradle to Cradle Products Innovation Institute, www.c2ccertified.org
National Terrazzo and Mosaic Association, "The Environmental Impact of the Use of Cement and Epoxy Terrazzo"
www.naterrazzo.com/documents/Green_Terrazzo_Information_Guide.pdf
Sierra Club GreenHome, http://www.scgh.com/
Tufts University, "Front-Loading Washing Machines," http://sustainability.tufts.edu/frontloading-washing-machines/
United States Environmental Protection Agency "WaterSense," www.epa.gov/watersense/

CHAPTER 6

Natural Marketing Institute (NMI) Consumer Sustainability Trends Database, www
.nmisolutions.com/index.php/syndicated-data/nmis-proprietary-databases/lohas-
consumer-trends-database

S. Sathish and A. Rajamohan, "Consumer Behaviour and Lifestyle Marketing," *International Journal of Marketing, Financial Services and Management Research,* http://
indianresearchjournals.com/pdf/IJMFSMR/2012/October/13.pdf

"Successful Green Transformation: The Four Ps," *MIT Sloan Management Review,* http://
sloanreview.mit.edu/reports/capturing-the-green-advantage/successful-green-
transformation-the-four-ps/

Index

If you enjoyed this book, you may also like these:

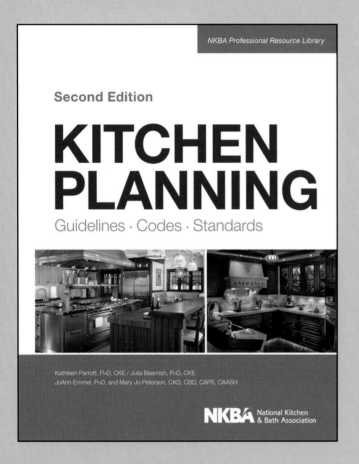

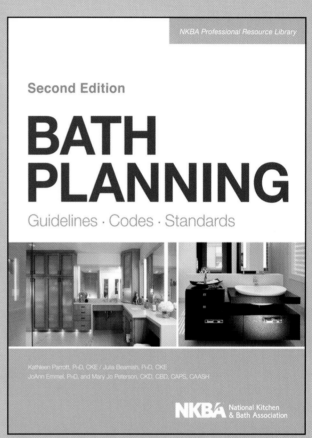

Kitchen Planning 2e
by Kathleen Parrott, Julia Beamish, JoAnn Emmel,
and Mary Jo Peterson
ISBN: 9781118367629

Bath Planning 2e
by Kathleen Parrott, Julia Beamish, JoAnn Emmel,
and Mary Jo Peterson
ISBN: 9781118362488

To see all of the titles in NKBA's Professional Resource Library, visit www.wiley.com/go/nkba